Edexcel International GCSE
Business Studies

Student Book

Rob Jones

D1612733

000000988782

PEARSON

Published by Pearson Education Limited, a company incorporated in England and Wales, having its registered office at Edinburgh Gate, Harlow, Essex, CM20 2JE. Registered company number: 872828.

www.pearsonglobalschools.com

Edexcel is a registered trademark of Edexcel Limited

Text © Pearson Education Ltd 2011

First published 2011

20 19 18 17 16 15 14

IMP 10 9 8 7 6

ISBN 978 0 435046 74 3

Typeset by Gantec Publishing Solutions, LLC

Original illustrations © Pearson Education Ltd 2011

Illustrated by Tech-Set Ltd, Gateshead and Gantec Publishing Solutions, LLC

Cover design by Creative Monkey

Cover photo © Getty Images: Jacobs Stock Library

Printed in China (GCC/06)

Acknowledgements
The author and publisher would like to thank the following individuals and organisations for permission to reproduce photographs:

Fotolia.com: Aleksandr Lazarev 175, Alexandra Landa 209r, Andrey Saprykin 156, Antoine Cupial 37, Arkady Chubykin 38, Arto 75, auremar 100, CROSS DESIGN 93, Danny Hooks 189, Dariusz Kopestynski 59, Diego Cervo 224r, Digishooter 134, Downunderphoto 17, drx 117, 206, drx 117, 206, Dusan Radivojevic 74, EcoView 140, Eldad Yitzhak 151, Eli Coory 78, Emmanuelle Combaud 26, Eray 177, Eric Isselée 120, Freefly 28, Gail Johnson 228, goodluz 32r, Harry HU 119, icholakov 147, imrek 172b, Jack 18, Jenny Thompson 122, Jim Parkin 212, Joe Gough 16, jscalev 7t, Kadmy 123, Kheng Guan Toh 174, 208, Kheng Guan Toh 174, 208, Kirsty Umback 172t, lamax 60, Lee Prince 114, Leonid Meleca 181, Les Cunliffe 230, lunamarina 142, Matthew Antonino 157, Max Blain 213, MAXFX 139, Michalis Palis 219, Midkhat Izmaylov 126b, Monkey Business 10, 11, 204, 209l, Monkey Business 10, 11, 204, 209l, Monkey Business 10, 11, 204, 209l, Monkey Business 10, 11, 204, 209l, munchkinmoo 110, Natalia Pavlova 12, naten 128, Olga Khoroshunova 2, olly 112, otisthewolf 33, Paul Cowan 126t, Paulus Rusyanto 34 (d), picsfive 6, pmphoto 52, poco_bw 35, Ralf Hasemann 68, recose 143, RedTC 56, robert lerich 1, Roman Milert 34 (a), 224l, Roman Milert 34 (a), 224l, rphotos 15, Ryan Long 90, Sandra van der Steen 226, Springfield Gallery 48, Stanislav Komogorov 32tl, stevem 148, styf 178, Sunny_baby 101, T^i^ 7b, Tan Kian Khoon 115, terex 21, Tomo Jesenicnik 144, Topone 207, visi.stock 199, William Burnett 170; **Pearson Education Ltd:** Debbie Rowe 9, 198, Debbie Rowe 9, 198, Dex Image. Yoshio Sawargai. Alamy 34 (c), Digital Stock 34 (b), 91, Digital Stock 34 (b), 91, Digital Vision 203, Haddon Davies 194, Jules Selmes 31, MindStudio 192tl, Naki Kouyioumtzis 23, New Holland 192r, Photodisc. Kim Steele 29, Photodisc. Malcolm Fife 192bl, Photodisc. Photolink. Annie Reynolds 51, Studio 8 32bl.

All other images © Pearson Education Ltd 2011.

The author and publisher would also like to thank the following for permission to reproduce copyright material:

p.9 from Thomas Cook Group plc strategy, reproduced with permission of Thomas Cook Group plc; p.10 from Unilever Mission Statement, reproduced with permission of Unilever; p.11 adapted from Boston Pizza Mission Statement, www.bpincomefund.com, copyright © Boston Pizza International, Inc.; p.22 from *Automotive News Europe 2006 Global Market Data Book* (2006) © copyright Automotive News Data Center and R.L. Polk Marketing Systems GmbH; p.36 adapted from 'Employment in agriculture, UK 1960 - 2007', International Comparisons of Annual Labor Force Statistics, 1 Oct 2009, source: US Bureau of Labor Statistics; p.36 from 'The numbers of people employed in manufacturing and services in the UK 1960 – 2007 (employment approximating U.S. concepts by economic sector)', International Comparisons of Annual Labor Force Statistics, 1 Oct 2009, Source: US Bureau of Statistics; p.40 from 'German Online Sales Rose Last Year' *emarketer*, 09/04/2009 (Karen von Abrams), www.emarketer.com, copyright © eMarketer; p.45 from 'Unemployment in Singapore' January 2008 to April 2009, www.tradingeconomics.com, copyright © Trading Economics; p.52 from 'US vehicle miles traveled and CO2 emissions from gasoline and diesel transportation use 1990-2008', www.eia.doe.gov, Source: U.S. Energy Information Administration (Oct 2008); p.54 from 'India's visible balance (April to September 2008/09)' source www.IndiaOneStop.com, copyright © Ontrack Systems Ltd, India; p.54 from 'Poland's imports and exports' January 2000 to March 2009; p.62 from 'Household waste recycling', AEA Energy and Environment; 'UK residents' holiday visits abroad', United Kingdom, 1971 to 2008, International Passenger Survey; and 'Source of greenhouse gas emissions: by selected UK Sector', United Kingdom, 1990 to 2007, Social Trends no. 40, 2010; p.66 from Tesco Customer Feedback Form, copyright © Tesco Stores Limited; p.99 adapted from 'Protection at Work' http://www.shaw-trust.org.uk/disability_and_employment_statistics. Reproduced with permission of The Shaw Trust; p.99 from 'Fatal injury rates to UK workers (1992/93 - 2008/09)' public sector information published by the Health and Safety Executive, Crown copyright © 2010; p.107 from *Motivation and Personality*, 3rd edition, New Jersey: Prentice Hall (Maslow, A.H, Frager, R.D. and Faidman, J. 1954) copyright © 1987. Adapted by permission of Pearson Education, Inc., Upper Saddle River, NJ; p.163 Office for National Statistics. Crown Copyright material is reproduced with permission under the terms of the Click-Use License; p.166 from 'Executive cars - 2009 market shares (UK)' *Motor Industry Facts 2010* (www.smmt.co.uk), copyright © The Society of Motor Manufacturers and Traders Ltd (SMMT), 2010; p.184 adapted from 'USA advertising by media 1997 and 2007 ($million)'. Source: The U.S. Census Bureau; p.187 from 'Percentage of followers using each medium to follow the Champions League', TGI Sport 2008, copyright © 2010 Kantar Media; p.191 from 'Online retail spending 2001 to 2007 and 2008 projections'. Source: The U.S. Census Bureau; p.194 from 'Top ten world brands', BrandZ Top 100 Most Value Brands, copyright © Millward Brown; p.227 from 'Casio Quality', http://world.casio.com, copyright © Casio Computer Co., Ltd.

Every effort has been made to contact copyright holders of material reproduced in this book. Any omissions will be rectified in subsequent printings if notice is given to the publishers.

Websites
The websites used in this book were correct and up to date at the time of publication. It is essential for tutors to preview each website before using it in class so as to ensure that the URL is still accurate, relevant and appropriate. We suggest that tutors bookmark useful websites and consider enabling students to access them through the school/college intranet.

Disclaimer
This material has been published on behalf of Edexcel and offers high-quality support for the delivery of Edexcel qualifications.

This does not mean that the material is essential to achieve any Edexcel qualification, nor does it mean that it is the only suitable material available to support any Edexcel qualification. Edexcel material will not be used verbatim in setting any Edexcel examination or assessment. Any resource lists produced by Edexcel shall include this and other appropriate resources.

Copies of official specifications for all Edexcel qualifications may be found on the Edexcel website: www.edexcel.com

Contents

About this book

This book has several features to help you with International GCSE Business Studies.

Getting started
Each chapter has a short introduction, usually including a case study, to help you start thinking about the topic and let you know what is in the chapter.

Questions
There are questions throughout each chapter, which help you to test your understanding of the material as you work through the book. Some require short answers, others need a paragraph or for you to draw a graph.

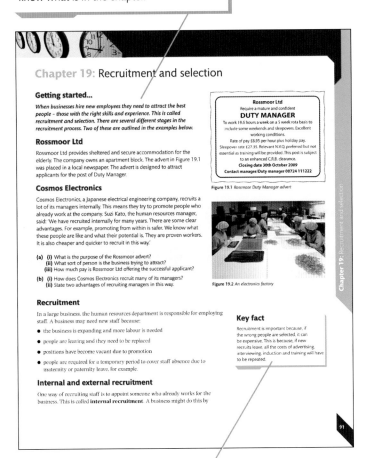

Margin boxes
The boxes in the margin give you extra help or information. They might explain something in a little more detail or guide you to linked topics in other parts of the book. The margin boxes include Did you know?, Key facts and Key terms.

Chapter review
This is a case study with questions to apply your knowledge of the material learned in the chapter. If you have any difficulties, try going over the chapter again, practising with the shorter question boxes.

Chapter 1: What is business activity?

Getting started...

Some people try to make money by setting up a business. They might do this because they want to work for themselves. Or they think they can make more money than working for someone else. Or perhaps they have been made redundant and cannot find another job. Running a business is hard work but the rewards can be worth it. Look at the example below.

Okkas Taverna

In Cyprus in 2008, Marios and Alexia Okkas opened Okkas Taverna, a restaurant catering for tourists. The couple no longer wanted to work for another employer. Both had previous experience in restaurants. Alexia had worked as a waitress in Limassol while Marios had been employed as a chef in Paxos. The couple used €15,000 of their own money to set up the business. Before they opened they had to:

- obtain a €10,000 bank loan
- find suitable premises and decorate the restaurant
- obtain a fire certificate to meet health and safety regulations
- buy furniture and kitchen equipment
- employ two part-time staff to help out when busy
- advertise the restaurant.

Once the restaurant was open, Marios and Alexia played different roles. Marios ran the kitchen. He was responsible for planning the menu, dealing with suppliers and preparing the food. Alexia ran the restaurant area. She waited on tables, settled bills and looked after the customers. Marios and Alexia worked long hours during the holiday season. However, it was worth it because in 2009 Okkas Taverna made a profit of €34,600.

(a) Why do you think Marios and Alexia opened a restaurant?

(b) State three resources used by Marios and Alexia when setting up their business.

(c) Why do you think businesses exist?

Figure 1.1 *A Greek restaurant*

Business activity

A **business** is an organisation which provides **goods** and **services**. The above example illustrates many features of business activity.

- Business activity produces an output – a good or service. A restaurant service is being provided by Marios and Alexia.

- Goods and services are consumed. Tourists consume the service provided by Marios and Alexia.

- Resources are used up. Food and drinks, furniture, people, gas and electricity are just a few of the resources used by Okkas Taverna. Money, such as the €10,000 bank loan and the €15,000 provided by Marios and Alexia, is also a resource. The resources used by businesses are often called the *four factors of production.* These are explained in Chapter 7.

- A number of business functions may be carried out. Production, marketing, human resources and financial control are examples of these functions. Production in the case of Okkas Taverna involved the provision of meals in a restaurant. Marketing involved advertising in the local area.

- Businesses can be affected by external factors. This means they are affected by things that they cannot control such as government laws, changes in consumer tastes and competitors. Marios and Alexia had to obtain a fire certificate because of government health and safety regulations.

- Businesses aim to make a profit. Most businesses are set up by people who aim to make money for themselves. In this case Okkas Taverna made a profit of €34,600 for Marios and Alexia in 2009.

Goods and services

Businesses provide a wide range of goods and services. Some are produced for consumers – ordinary people. These are called **consumer goods**. Products sold by one business to another are called **producer goods**. Examples are shown in Figure 1.2. Some businesses serve both consumers and producers. For example, the Taj Mahal hotel in Mumbai caters for both tourists and business people.

Satisfying needs and wants

Businesses have to satisfy people's **needs** and **wants**.

Needs are the requirements for human survival. Some are physical such as water, food, warmth, shelter and clothing. If these needs cannot be satisfied humans will die.

Humans also have other desires. These are called **wants** and include holidays abroad, a better house, a bigger car, more status, a better education and a cleaner environment. These wants are *infinite.* Most people want more than they already have. It is human nature. Unfortunately, the resources used by businesses are *finite.* This means there is a limited amount. Economists say that resources are **scarce**.

The purpose of business activity

Businesses exist to provide goods and services. However, different types of organisation provide goods and services for different reasons. Each type of organisation has a different purpose.

- **Private enterprise.** Most businesses are owned privately by individuals or groups of individuals. They are **private sector** businesses. The objective of a private enterprise is to make money – a *profit* for the owners. The objectives of private sector businesses are discussed in Chapter 2.

Consumer products	
Goods	**Services**
mp3 player	Health care
Magazine	Banking
Crisps	Air travel
Handbag	Education
Computer game	Garden design
Producer products	
Goods	**Services**
Delivery van	Market research
Office furniture	Insurance
Tools	Software design
Sugar cane	Industrial cleaning
Tractor	Printing

Figure 1.2 *The different products that businesses provide*

Figure 1.3 *Sugar cane – an example of a producer good*

- **Non-profit making organisations.** Some organisations in the private sector are non-profit making. Organisations such as charities, pressure groups, clubs and societies exist for other reasons. For example, charities such as Oxfam exist to raise money for 'good' causes. Clubs and societies, such as the scouting association and sports clubs, provide opportunities and facilities for people with common interests. Most of these non-profit making organisations are run like businesses. They:

  - need to raise money

  - try to minimise costs

  - market themselves

  - employ staff.

  Non-profit making organisations aim to meet the needs and wants of their members, or those which they aim to support.

- **Public enterprise.** Some goods and services are provided by organisations owned by central or local government. These are **public sector** organisations. In many countries public sector organisations often provide health care, education, postal services, protection and environmental services. The main purpose of public enterprise is to provide goods and services which private enterprise fails to provide adequately.

  Public sector organisations do not normally aim to make a profit. They try to provide good quality services.

QUESTION 1

The Li Ka Shing Foundation is a charity founded in 1980 by Hong Kong entrepreneur Li Ka Shing. Its mission is to develop 'a culture of giving' in Chinese society. The money raised by the Li Ka Shing Foundation is used for education and healthcare projects. For example, in 2005, the Foundation gave HK$1 billion to the University of Hong Kong. To date the Li Ka Shing Foundation, and other charities established by Mr Li, have donated HK$10.7 billion.

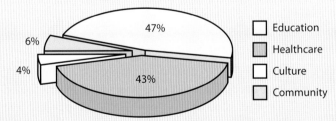

Figure 1.4 *Donations made by Li Ka Shing Foundation as of 15 April 2009 – by type*

(a) What is meant by a non-profit making organisation? (Use this case study.)

(b) What is the purpose of the Li Ka Shing Foundation?

Business stakeholders

Any individual or group that has an interest in the operation of a business is called a **stakeholder**. Owners have a financial 'stake' in the business. This is because they have invested some of their own money. Some stakeholders, such as employees, rely on the success of a business so that they can meet their needs and wants. Figure 1.5 shows the different business stakeholders.

Figure 1.5 *Business stakeholders*

Owners

A business belongs to its owners. Many small businesses are owned by individuals, families, or small groups of people. These people are often called **entrepreneurs.** They are responsible for setting up and running the business. Larger businesses, such as limited companies (see Chapter 4), are owned by *shareholders*. Shareholders invest money in a business and get a share of the profit called a *dividend.*

Customers

Customers buy the goods and services that businesses sell. Most customers are *consumers* who use or 'consume' goods and services. However, some may be other businesses. Customers want good quality products at a fair price. If they do not get this they will spend their money somewhere else.

Employees

Employees work for businesses. They depend on businesses for their livelihood. However, they have other needs. They will require training so that they can do their jobs properly. They want good working conditions, fair pay and benefits, job security and opportunities for promotion.

Managers

Most businesses have managers who help with their running. Managers are often employed to run the different departments in businesses such as marketing, production, finance and human resources. Managers have to show leadership, solve problems, make decisions, settle disputes and motivate workers. Managers are likely to help plan the direction of the business with its owners. They also have to control resources such as finance, equipment, time and people. Managers are also accountable to the owners. This means they have to take responsibility if things go wrong.

Financiers

Financiers lend money to a business. They may be banks but could be individuals such as family members or private investors such as *venture capitalists* (see Chapter 26). Clearly these stakeholders have a financial interest in a business and will be keen for it to do well.

Suppliers

Businesses which provide raw materials, components, commercial services and utilities to other businesses are called *suppliers*. Relations between businesses and their suppliers must be good because they rely on each other. Businesses want good quality resources at reasonable prices. In return suppliers will require prompt payment and regular orders.

The local community

Most businesses are likely to have an impact on the local community. A business may employ a lot of people that live in the local community. If the business does well the local community may prosper. There may be more jobs, more overtime and possibly higher pay. In contrast a business may be criticised by the local community. For example, if the owners of a noisy factory decide to introduce night shifts, there may be complaints from local residents.

The government

The government has an interest in all businesses. They provide employment, generate wealth and pay taxes. Taxes from businesses and their employees are used to fund government spending.

The changing business environment

All businesses operate in a changing business environment. This means that they may be affected by external factors that are likely to change over time. Such factors include the strength of competition, the economic climate, government legislation, population trends, demand patterns, world affairs and social factors.

To survive, businesses must produce goods and services that satisfy people's needs and wants. They must have clear objectives and recognise that the changing environment can bring new opportunities and impose new constraints.

Key terms

Business – an organisation which produces goods and services.

Consumer goods – goods and services sold to ordinary people (consumers) rather than businesses.

Entrepreneurs – people who take risk and set up businesses.

Goods – physical products like a mobile phone, packet of crisps or a pair of shoes.

Needs – basic requirements for human survival.

Private sector – business organisations owned by individuals or groups of individuals.

Producer goods – goods and services produced by one business for another.

Public sector – business organisations owned by central or local government.

Scarce resources – the amount of resources available is limited.

Services – non-physical products like banking, car washing and waste disposal.

Stakeholder – an individual or group with an interest in the operation of a business.

Wants – peoples' desires for goods and services.

Did you know?

In 2008/09 there was a global recession. This meant that many businesses had deal with very difficult trading conditions. Many adapted by freezing wages, closing down unprofitable divisions, laying off staff and improving efficiency.

QUESTION 2

Boart Longyear, one of the world's largest drilling contractors and manufacturers, operates in 40 countries. Examples of its products include diamond and hard rock drills, exploration equipment and environmental tools. In 2008, the Australian-based company scrapped its dividend after having cut 2,000 jobs due to a downturn in the mining sector. The number of people employed in the Asia–Pacific region in February 2009 was about 2,600, down from 3,200 in September 2008. Boart said the job cuts would save about $AUS123m. Further cuts were expected. The company has also imposed a wage freeze and reduced managerial salaries.

Boart plans to scrap the dividend.

(a) Which stakeholder will be affected by this decision?

(b) How will employees and managers be affected by Boart's recent actions as a result of the downturn in the mining sector?

Chapter review – SurgiCo

SurgiCo is a private sector business which designs and manufactures surgical instruments. The company aims to be the world's leading supplier of high quality and cost-effective instruments. In 2008, the business made a profit of $780,000 on sales of $4.3 million. This was an increase on the previous year when the profit was $685,000. In 2008, the business moved to new premises. This helped SurgiCo to improve its manufacturing processes. For example, since the move to new premises the business has bought some specialist machinery which has helped to improve the quality of its surgical instruments.

SurgiCo makes producer goods.

(a) What does this mean?   **(2 marks)**

SurgiCo is a private sector business.

(b) What does this mean?   **(2 marks)**

(c) Suggest how SurgiCo meets customer needs.   **(4 marks)**

(d) Identify two stakeholders in SurgiCo.   **(2 marks)**

Figure 1.6 *Surgical instruments*

SurgiCo operates in a changing business environment.

(e) Outline what this means.   **(4 marks)**

(f) Suggest how the objectives of SurgiCo might differ from those of the hospitals which it supplies.   **(6 marks)**

Chapter 2: Business objectives

Getting started...

Businesses exist to produce goods and services for consumers and other businesses. However, the owners of businesses will want to achieve certain objectives. Most business owners want to make a profit. They risk their own money when setting up a business and aim to make a financial return. However, there are other objectives which businesses might try to achieve. Look at the two examples below.

The Bahrain Central

The Bahrain Central is a three star hotel located in Manama, the capital of Bahrain. The owners of the hotel have recently met with the hotel manager and agreed a two-year plan to increase profitability. The owners want to raise profit from 120,000 to 200,000 Bahraini Dinars. The hotel manager hopes to cut costs and increase room occupancy by aiming more advertising at business customers.

British Airways

British Airways (BA) lost a record £401 million in 2009 and is struggling to survive. BA said it will ground aircraft, reduce the number of seats for sale and postpone the purchase of 12 A380 super jumbos as it faces a fall in passengers. BA also said that it was cutting the number of seats for sale by 3.5 per cent instead of the original 2.5 per cent.

In addition, BA staff voted for a pay cut to save jobs. However, senior managers turned them down. Unite, the union which represents 28,000 of BA's 40,000 workforce, put forward a pay plan to help BA save more than £200m. This was after managers wrote to all staff asking them to volunteer to work for nothing.

(a) What is **(i)** The Bahrain Central and **(ii)** BA trying to achieve?

(b) Describe briefly the measures being taken by **(i)** The Bahrain Central and **(ii)** BA to achieve their objectives.

Figure 2.1 *A hotel in the Middle East*

Figure 2.2 *British Airways aircraft*

The importance of clear objectives

Businesses are more likely to be successful if they set clear objectives. Businesses need to have objectives for the following reasons:

● Employees need something to work towards. Objectives help to motivate people. For example, sales staff might get bonuses if they reach certain sales targets.

● Without objectives owners might not have the motivation needed to keep the business going. Owners might lose grip and allow their business to 'drift'. This might result in business failure.

- Objectives help to decide where to take a business and what steps are necessary to get there. For example, if a business aims to grow by 10 per cent, it might decide that launching products overseas might be the best way to achieve this.

- It is easier to assess the performance of a business if objectives are set. If objectives are achieved it could be argued that the business has performed well.

Private sector objectives

In the *private sector,* where businesses are owned by individuals or groups of individuals, the following objectives are common:

- **Survival**: All businesses will consider survival as important. However, from time to time survival may be *the* most important objective. For example, when a business first starts trading it may be vulnerable. The owners may lack experience and there may be a shortage of resources. Therefore, an objective for a new business may be to survive in the first 12 months. The survival of a business might also be threatened when trading conditions become difficult. In 'Getting started' above, British Airways took a number of measures to ensure that the large airline survived the recession in 2009/10.

- **Profit:** Most businesses aim to make a profit because their owners want a financial return. Some businesses try to **maximise profit**. This means they make as much profit as they possibly can. For example, companies, which are owned by shareholders, may try to maximise profits. This is because shareholders often put pressure on companies to pay out large *dividends* (which come from profits).

- **Growth and wealth creation:** Some owners want their businesses to grow. This is because larger businesses enjoy a number of benefits. For example, they:

  - may enjoy lower costs

  - have a larger market share

  - enjoy a higher public profile

  - generate more wealth for the owners.

  The growth of a business might also benefit a wide range of stakeholders linked with the business. For example, employees are likely to benefit from the growth of a business because their jobs will be more secure.

- **Increase market share:** Businesses often want to build a larger market share. They may be able to do this if they can win customers from competitors. Businesses with a large market share may be able to dominate the market. They may be able to charge higher prices for example.

- **Image, reputation and social responsibility:** In recent years many businesses have tried to improve their image and develop a good reputation. One way of doing this is to take into account the needs of others such as customers, the local community and employees. If a business has a bad image or a poor reputation it may lose customers.

Did you know?

Owners of many small businesses are happy to make a satisfactory level of profit – just enough to fund a comfortable lifestyle, perhaps.

QUESTION 1

Thomas Cook Group plc is one of the world's leading leisure travel groups. In 2008, it had sales of £8.8bn, 22.3m customers and 31,000 employees. It has 93 aircraft, 3,400 travel stores and interests in 86 hotels and holiday resorts. Thomas Cook is a leader in its core markets and has a clear strategy for the future, which is to...

'improve performance in mainstream tour operating, make significant advances in independent travel, travel-related financial services and emerging markets, and grow overall revenue and profit.'

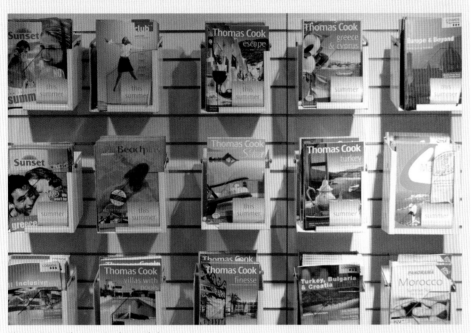

Figure 2.3 *A Thomas Cook travel shop*

(a) Describe two possible objectives of Thomas Cook.

(b) Do you think Thomas Cook will be concerned about its image and reputation as an objective?

SMART objectives

The setting of business objectives may achieve more if they are SMART. This means that they should be:

● **S**pecific – stating clearly what is trying to be achieved

● **M**easurable – capable of numeric measurement

● **A**chievable – attainable by the people involved

● **R**ealistic – able to be achieved given the resources available

● **T**ime specific – state a time by which they should be achieved.

An example of a SMART objective might be for a business to increase turnover by 8 per cent in the next 12 months.

Our mission

Unilever's vision is to work to create a better future every day. We help people feel good, look good and get more out of life with brands and services that are good for them and good for others. We will inspire people to take small everyday actions that can add up to a big difference for the world. We will develop new ways of doing business that will allow us to double the size of our company while reducing our environmental impact.

Figure 2.4 *Unilever mission statement*

Mission statements

Some businesses write a **mission statement** when setting objectives. This describes the purpose of a business. Mission statements are often directed at stakeholders such as customers, employees and shareholders. They:

● help a business to focus

● provide a plan for the future

● make clear to all stakeholders what the business is trying to achieve.

Figure 2.4 shows the mission statement for Unilever, the 'soups to soaps' company.

Public sector objectives

The objectives of public sector organisations are likely to be different from those in the private sector. For example, schools, hospitals, government departments and council-run services are not likely to make a profit. Generally, public sector objectives are linked to quality of service and reducing costs. Examples of public sector objectives may include:

● Increasing special needs provision in schools.

● Increasing response time by the emergency services.

● Reducing specific crime rates.

● Reducing waste sent to landfill.

● Increasing the number of students entering higher education.

QUESTION 2

The National Health Service in the UK has hit its target to treat patients within a maximum of 18 weeks from referral by their doctor. It said the average wait for treatment for admitted patients is now 8.6 weeks. For example:

● Cataract removal waiting times have halved – from 20 weeks in March 2007 to 10 weeks in January 2009.

● Waiting times for a heart bypass have halved from 14 to seven weeks.

● Audiology referral to treatment times now stands at around five weeks.

The Health Secretary at the time, Alan Johnson, said: 'Achieving the shortest waits since NHS records began is a tremendous achievement for staff and I congratulate them for all their hard work. Meeting the standard nationally five months before it came into effect, shows the commitment of the whole health service to improving patients' experiences.'

(a) What objectives are set by public sector organisations? (Use examples from this case.)

The National Health Service does not aim to make a profit like private sector health services.

(b) Why is this the case?

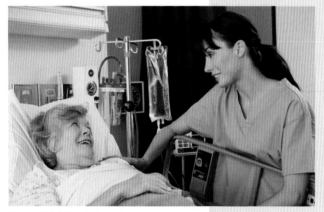

Figure 2.5 *A hospital ward*

Relationship between business objectives

Several of the business objectives described above are closely related to each other. For example, a business that aims to grow could make more profit in the future. This is because a larger firm will enjoy more revenue and this is likely to result in more profit. Similarly, a business aiming to grow is also likely to increase its market share. Also, if a business improves its image it may attract more customers and increase its market share.

Finally, a business may have more than one objective. For example, a business may try to grow and try to become a market leader. Also, long-term objectives may differ from short-term objectives. For example, in the early stages of the business start-up survival may be the main objective. But in the long term profit will become more important.

Key terms

Mission statement - a brief summary of a firm's aims and objectives.

Objectives - the goals or targets set by a business.

Profit maximisation - making as much profit as possible in a given time period.

Chapter review - Boston Pizza International

Boston Pizza International (BPI) operates a pizza franchise in Canada. It has over 300 restaurants and operates three of these as corporate restaurants. These serve as franchisee training centres and allow BPI to test new menu items and other policies. The following information about the company is given.

- BPI had sales of over $830m in 2008.
- Sales growth has averaged 5.7 per cent for the last 10 years.
- Menus include health check options.
- The Boston Pizza Foundation has raised over $9m for charities since 1990.
- It was named Franchisor of the Year by the Quebec Franchise Council in 2007.
- It was named No. 3 in Canada's 10 Most Admired Corporate Cultures.

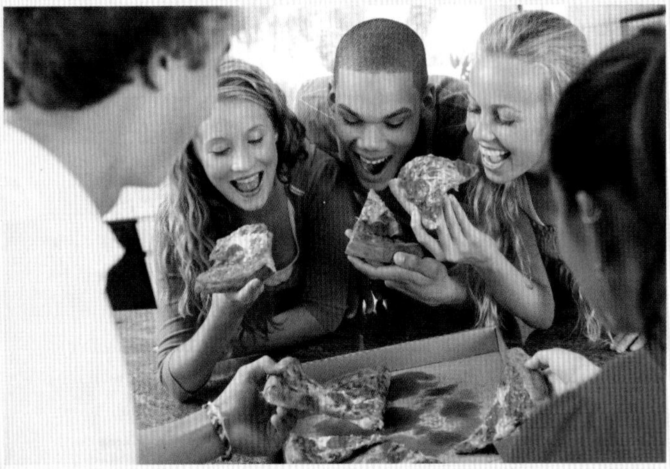

Figure 2.7 *People eating pizza*

our corporate mission statement

To be a world class franchisor through selecting and training people to profitably manage an outstanding foodservice business. To achieve this goal we are innovative and responsible in our approach to business. We work as a team providing attention to detail but never losing sight of the larger picture. We recognize the need to provide leadership in all areas of operations, marketing and restaurant development.

Figure 2.6 *Boston Pizza mission statement*

(a) What is meant by a business objective? (Use this case as an example.) **(2 marks)**

(b) Describe the purpose of a mission statement. **(4 marks)**

It is suggested that BPI is concerned about its image and reputation.

(c) What evidence is there in the case study to support this view? **(4 marks)**

(d) Assess why it is important to a company like BPI to have objectives. **(10 marks)**

Chapter 3: Sole traders, partnerships and franchises

Getting started...

There are several different types of business organisation. They vary according to size, type of ownership and legal status. Look at the examples below.

Luke's Kaffeestrube

Luke Burger is the owner of Luke's Kaffeestrube, a bakery and cafe located in Swakopmund, Namibia. He set up the business in 2001 when he bought a small disused bakery for 20,000 Namibian dollars. Two years later he decided to open a cafe by extending the premises. He thought the cafe would provide another outlet for some of the cakes and pastries produced in the bakery. The cafe serves shoppers, workers and tourists. It is busy and Luke employs two other staff. He recently invested 50,000 Namibian dollars of his own money to refurbish the cafe.

R & H Photography Services

Andrea Rolton and Gillian Hammond are business partners. They provide photography services in Darwin, Australia. Andrea has a degree in Photographic Art and is responsible for the production work. Gillian spends most of her time promoting the business. She develops contacts and handles the administration. Andrea and Gillian set up the business in 2005 by investing $AUS20,000 each. They used the money to buy photography equipment and a studio in central Darwin.

(a) Who owns the businesses in the above case studies?

(b) State **one** advantage and **one** disadvantage of owning a business with a partner.

Business owners have to take risks.

(c) What risks are taken in the above case studies?

Figure 3.1 *A female photographer at work*

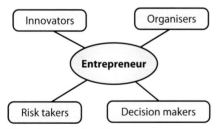
Figure 3.2 *The roles of the entrepreneur*

Entrepreneurs

People who set up businesses are called entrepreneurs. They are the owners and without them businesses would not exist in the private sector. The roles played by entrepreneurs in business are summarised in Figure 3.2.

● Entrepreneurs are *innovators* because they try to make money out of a business idea. Such ideas might come from spotting a gap in the market, a new invention or market research. However, many people set up a business by copying or adapting what another business does.

● Entrepreneurs are responsible for *organising* other factors of production. They buy or hire resources such as materials, labour and equipment. These resources are used to make their products. Organising involves giving instructions, making arrangements and setting up systems.

- Since entrepreneurs are the owners they have make all the key *decisions*. They may make decisions on how to raise finance, product design, choice of production method, prices, recruitment and wages.

- Entrepreneurs are *risk takers*. This is because they risk losing any money they put into the business if it fails. However, if the business is successful they will be rewarded with profit.

Unincorporated and incorporated businesses

Businesses vary according to the legal form they take.

- **Unincorporated:** These are businesses where there is no legal difference between the owner and the business. Everything is carried out in the name of the owner. These businesses tend to be small and owned by one person, or a small group of people.

- **Incorporated:** An incorporated business is one which has a separate legal identity from that of its owners. In other words, the business can sue, be sued, taken over or *liquidated*. Incorporated businesses are often called *limited companies* and the owners are shareholders. This is discussed in the next chapter.

Features of a sole trader

A **sole trader** or **sole proprietor** is the simplest form of business organisation. It has one owner but can employ any number of people. Sole traders may be involved in a wide range of business activity. In the primary sector they may be farmers or fishermen. In the secondary sector they may be small builders or manufacturers. However, most sole traders are found in the tertiary sector. Many are retailers running small shops. Others may offer services such as web design, tutoring, hairdressing, taxi driving, garden maintenance and so on.

Setting up as a sole trader is simple because there are no legal requirements. However, all sole traders have **unlimited liability**. This means that if the business fails a sole trader can lose more money than was originally invested. This is because a sole trader can be forced to use personal wealth to pay off business debts. The advantages and disadvantages of operating as a sole trader are summarised in Figure 3.3.

Advantages of a sole trader	Disadvantages of a sole trader
All the profit is kept by the owner.	Have unlimited liability.
They are independent – owner has complete control.	May struggle to raise finance – too risky for lenders.
It is simple to set up with no legal requirements.	Independence may be a burden.
Flexibility – e.g. can adapt to change quickly.	Long hours and very hard work.
Can offer a personal service because they are small.	Usually too small to exploit economies of scale.
May qualify for government help.	No continuity – the business dies with the owner.

Figure 3.3 *Advantages and disadvantages of a sole trader*

Features of a partnership

A **partnership** exists when between 2 and 20 people jointly own a business. The owners will share responsibility for running the business. They also share the profits. Partnerships are often found in professions such as accountants, doctors, estate agents and solicitors.

There are no legal formalities to complete when a partnership is formed. However, partners may draw up a **deed of partnership**. This is a legal document which states partners' rights in the event of a dispute. It states:

● how much capital each partner will contribute

● how profits (and losses) will be shared amongst the partners

● the procedure for ending the partnership

● how much control each partner has

● rules for taking on new partners.

The advantages and disadvantages of partnerships are summarised in Figure 3.4.

Advantages of partnerships	Disadvantages of partnerships
Easy to set up and run – no legal formalities.	Partners have unlimited liability.
Partners can specialise in their area of expertise.	Profit has to be shared.
The burden of running a business is shared.	Partners may disagree and fall out.
More capital can be raised with more owners.	Any partners' decision is legally binding on all.
Financial information is not published.	Partnerships still tend to be small.

Figure 3.4 *Advantages and disadvantages of partnerships*

Limited partnerships

It is possible to have a **limited partnership**. This is where some partners provide capital but take no part in the management of the business. Such a partner will have **limited liability** and can only lose the original amount of money invested. This type of partner is called a *sleeping partner*. However, even with a limited partnership there must always be at least one partner with unlimited liability.

In 2000, the law changed so that **limited liability partnerships** could be formed. This is where all partners have limited liability. However, to set up a limited liability partnership the business has to comply with a number of legal requirements such as filing annual accounts with the *Registrar of Companies*.

QUESTION 1

Mirza and Associates is a small firm of solicitors based in Lahore, Pakistan. There are four partners in the business and each one specialises in a specific area of law.

Figure 3.5 *A solicitor in Asia*

- Salim Hussain is an expert in property law and deals with property ownership disputes.

- Tariq Zaman deals with tax and corporate matters for business clients.

- Nasir Ahmed deals with wills.

- Salman Mirza is responsible for administration and also deals with criminal cases.

(a) Use this case study as an example to explain what is meant by a partnership.

(b) How does this case study illustrate **one** of the main advantages of partnerships?

Features of franchises

One approach to running a business is to buy a **franchise**. This may suit someone who wants to run a business but does not have their own business idea. Owners of franchises are called *franchisors*. They have developed a successful business and are prepared to allow others, the *franchisees*, to trade under their name. Franchisees pay fees to the franchisor. Examples of some international franchises are McDonalds, Subway, and Avis, the car rental business.

What does the franchisor offer the franchisee?

- A licence to trade under the recognised *brand name* of the franchisor.

- A start-up package including help, advice and essential equipment.

- Training in how to run the business and operate the systems used by the franchise.

- Materials, equipment and support services that are needed to run the business.

- Marketing support which is organised on behalf of all franchisees.

- An exclusive geographical area in which to operate. This means that the business will not face competition from other franchisees in the same franchise group.

In return for these services the franchisee has to pay certain fees.

- A start-up fee – a lump sum.

- An ongoing fee (usually based on sales).

- Contribution to marketing costs.

- Franchisors may make a profit on some of the materials, equipment and merchandise supplied to franchisees.

Advantages to the franchisee	Disadvantages to the franchisee
Less risk – a tried and tested idea is used.	Profit is shared with the franchisor.
Back-up support is given.	Strict contracts have to be signed.
Set-up costs are predictable.	Lack of independence – strict operating rules apply.
National marketing may be organised.	Can be an expensive way to start a business.

Figure 3.6 *Advantages and disadvantages to* **franchisees** *of franchising*

Advantages to the franchisor	Disadvantages to the franchisor
Fast method of growth.	Potential profit is shared with franchisee.
Cheaper method of growth.	Poor franchisees may damage brand's reputation.
Franchisees take some of the risk.	Franchisees may get merchandise from elsewhere.
Franchisees more motivated than employees.	Cost of support for franchisees may be high.

Figure 3.7 *Advantages and disadvantages to* **franchisors** *of franchising*

Key terms

Deed of partnership – a binding legal document which states the formal rights of partners.

Franchise – where a business (the franchisor) allows another operator (the franchisee) to trade under their name.

Incorporated businesses – where the business has a separate legal identity from that of its owners.

Limited liability – where a business owner is only liable for the original amount of money invested in the business.

Limited liability partnership – a partnership where all partners have limited liability.

Limited partnership – a partnership where some partners contribute capital and enjoy a share of the profit but do not take part in the running of the business.

Partnership – a business owned by between 2 and 20 people.

Sole trader or sole proprietor – a business owned by a single person.

Unincorporated business – those businesses where there is no legal difference between the owner and the business.

Unlimited liability – where the owner of a business is personally liable for all business debts.

QUESTION 2

Mr & Mrs Idly is an Indian franchise selling snacks from kiosks. It aims to provide customers with healthy and wholesome snacks at affordable prices. Mr & Mrs Idly is the only fast food franchise selling idly and dosai (Indian food) from a 'kiosk'. For an investment of between Rs2,00,000–Rs5,00,000 franchisees are provided with:

- A market and feasibility study
- Established brand name and logo
- Technical support and exclusive know how
- Operating manuals
- Access to cheap materials
- Negotiations and site selection help
- Assistance on hiring and training employees.

Figure 3.8 *Indian food*

Under the franchise agreement the kiosk space is to be owned or leased by the franchisee. Franchisees may only sell approved Mr & Mrs Idly products. Also, the kiosk and equipment are purchased by the franchisee. Franchisees are expected to maintain high standards of hygiene and look after the counters.

(a) How do franchisors make money? (Use this case study as an example.)

(b) Outline **three** advantages to a franchisee of taking out a franchise in Mr & Mrs Idly.

Chapter review – Marek Jonata

The fishing industry in Indonesia is very important. Marek Jonata is a fisherman and owns a sail boat which cost about $1,000. For five years, Marek worked most days of the week fishing for groupers, rabbitfish and slipmouth. He saved most of his profits because he wanted to buy a powered boat. This would have greater capacity and he could make more money.

Figure 3.9 *Indonesian fishing boats*

In 2009, Marek decided that he would never be able to save for a powered boat. He also found that banks would not lend him $4,000 to match his own savings to buy the new boat. Marek had his eye on a Searay 270 Sundancer with a 2003 quickload trailer, a 7.4 litre engine and all fishing equipment. The only way he could afford the boat would be to take on a partner. One of his fishing colleagues, Endang Witarsa, said he would join Marek as a business partner. However, Marek was not sure that going into business with someone else was the right thing to do.

Marek is an entrepreneur.

(a) What does this mean? **(2 marks)**

(b) State four roles of an entrepreneur. **(2 marks)**

Sole traders are unincorporated businesses.

(c) What does this mean? **(2 marks)**

Operating as a sole trader Marek has unlimited liability.

(d) Explain what this means. **(4 marks)**

(e) Discuss the advantages and disadvantages of operating as a partnership and suggest whether Marek should take on a partner. **(10 marks)**

Chapter 4: Limited liability companies

Getting started...

Limited companies have different features to sole traders and partnerships. They have different types of owners and raise capital in different ways. They are also set up and run differently. Look at the examples below.

Airport to Hotel

Airport to Hotel is a limited company. It was set up by Paul Stanyer when he lost his job at Thomas Cook, the travel and holiday company. It provides travel agents with transfer services between airports and hotels. Airport to Hotel operates in 70 countries and has links with Easyjet and other airlines. It sells its service through its websites. It is also launching a ski shuttle service to winter holiday destinations. Sales grew 84 per cent a year from £1.4m in 2004 to £8.6m in 2007. Half of the shares in Airport to Hotel are owned by Hong Kong-based Unifol International, a group of investors. The other half are owned by Paul Stayner.

Bank of East Asia (BEA)

BEA is run by the Chairman, Sir David Li, and 17 directors. The company is quoted on the Hong Kong stock exchange and owned by shareholders. BEA is the largest independent local bank in Hong Kong and operates more than 70 outlets in China. BEA also has branches in the United States, Canada, the UK, the British Virgin Islands, and Southeast Asia. Worldwide, BEA has 240 outlets and employs over 10,000 people. The bank's turnover was HK$6,793m in 2008.

(a) (i) Who owns limited companies? **(ii)** Who runs limited companies? (Use examples from the case studies.)

(b) Comment on the size of limited companies, such as those above compared to sole traders and partnerships.

Figure 4.1 *A branch of Bank of East Asia*

Limited companies

Limited companies are incorporated. This means that they have a separate legal identity from their owners. They can own assets, form contracts, employ people, sue and be sued. What are the other main features of limited companies?

- The owners have **limited liability.** If a limited company has debts, the owners can only lose the money they originally invested. They cannot be forced to use their own money to pay debts run up by the business.

- Capital is raised by selling shares. Each shareholder owns a number of these shares. They are the joint owners of the company. They are entitled to vote on important matters such as who should run the company. They also get dividends paid from profits. Those with more shares will have more control and get more dividends.

- They are run by directors elected by the shareholders. The board of directors, headed by a chairperson, is accountable to shareholders. He/she should run the company as the shareholders wish. If the company performs badly, directors can be 'voted out' at an *Annual General Meeting (AGM)*.

- Whereas sole traders and partnerships pay income tax on profits, companies pay corporation tax.

- To form a limited company it is necessary to follow a legal procedure. This is outlined below.

Forming a limited company

Some important documents must be sent to the *Registrar of Companies* before a limited company can be formed. The two most important ones are the Memorandum of Association and the Articles of Association (see Figure 4.2).

A limited company must have a minimum of two members, but there is no upper limit.

If these documents are acceptable the company will get a *Certificate of Incorporation*. This allows it to trade as a limited company. The shareholders have a legal right to attend the AGM and must be told of the date and venue in writing.

Memorandum of Association
This sets out the constitution and gives details about the company.
The following details must be included:
- name of the company;
- name and address of the company's registered office;
- objectives of the company and the nature of its activities;
- amount of capital to be raised and the number of shares to be issued.

Articles of Association
This document deals with the internal running of the company.
The Articles include details such as:
- rights of shareholders depending on the type of share they hold;
- procedures for appointing directors;
- length of time directors should serve before re-election;
- timing and frequency of company meetings;
- arrangements for auditing company accounts.

Figure 4.2 *Memorandum of Association and Articles of Association*

Private limited companies

Most private limited companies tend to be small or medium-sized. However, a small minority are large. Some features of private limited companies are as follows:

- Their business name ends in *Limited* or *Ltd.*

- Shares can only be transferred 'privately' (from one individual to another). All shareholders must agree on the transfer and they cannot be advertised for sale. Shares in private limited companies cannot be traded on the **stock market**.

- They are often family businesses owned by family members or close friends.

- The directors of these firms tend to be shareholders and are involved in the running of the business.

Advantages of private limited companies	Disadvantages of private limited companies
Shareholders have limited liability.	Financial information has to be made public.
More capital can be raised.	Costs money and takes time to set up.
Control cannot be lost to outsiders.	Profits are shared between more members.
Business continues if a shareholder dies.	Takes time to transfer shares to new owner.
Has more status – e.g. than a sole trader.	Cannot raise huge amounts of money like plcs.

Figure 4.3 *Advantages and disadvantages of private limited companies*

QUESTION 1

Sir Anwar Pervez founded Bestway as a single grocery store in 1963. Since then Bestway has grown to become one of the largest cash-and-carry operators. The group's other interests include food processing, cement factories in Pakistan and a 31 per cent stake in a Pakistani bank.

Bestway is an example of a large private limited company. It employs over 5,000 staff and sales reached £1,895m in 2008. Sir Anwar Pervez and his family own 66 per cent of the company. The rest is owned by managers.

(a) Who controls the Bestway Group?

(b) Analyse two advantages to Bestway of operating as private limited company.

Public limited companies

Public limited companies (plcs) tend to be larger than private limited companies. Their shares can be bought and sold by the public on the stock exchange. Any person or organisation can buy shares in plcs.

'Going public' can be expensive because:

- The company needs lawyers to ensure that the prospectus is 'legally' correct.
- The prospectus has to be printed and circulated.
- A bank may be paid to process share applications.
- The company must insure against the possibility of some shares remaining unsold, therefore, a fee is paid to an *underwriter* who must buy any unsold shares.
- There are advertising and administrative expenses.
- The plc must have a minimum of £50,000 share capital.

Key fact

When *'going public'* a company is likely to publish a *prospectus*. This advertises the company to potential investors. It also invites them to buy shares before a **flotation**.

Advantages of public limited companies	Disadvantages of public limited companies
Large amounts of capital can be raised.	Setting up costs can be very expensive.
Shareholders have limited liability.	Outsiders can take control by buying shares.
Plcs can exploit economies of scale.	More financial information has to be made public.
May be able to dominate the market.	May be more remote from customers.
Shares can be bought and sold very easily.	More regulatory control due to Company Acts.
May have a very high profile in the media.	Managers may take control rather than owners.

Figure 4.4 *Advantages and disadvantages of public limited companies*

Joint ventures

A **joint venture** is where two or more companies share the cost, responsibility and profits of a business venture. Most joint ventures involve two firms and the costs and profits are shared equally.

What are the advantages of joint ventures?

- They allow companies to enjoy some of the advantages of mergers, such as higher turnover, without having to lose their identity.

- Each business can specialise in aspects of the venture to suit its expertise.

- Takeovers are expensive. Takeovers often incur heavy legal and administrative costs.

- Mergers and takeovers are often unfriendly. Most joint ventures are friendly. The companies commit their funds and share responsibility. This may help to improve the success of the venture.

- Competition may be eliminated. If companies co-operate in a joint venture they are less likely to compete with each other.

There are some disadvantages to joint ventures.

- Some joint ventures do not work out. There may be control struggles. For example, who should have the final say in a 50:50 joint venture?

- Disagreements may occur about the management of the joint venture. As with any joint venture there may be different views on which direction to take.

- The profit from the venture is split between the investors. This obviously reduces profit potential.

Key terms

Flotation – the process of a company 'going public'.

Joint venture – where two or more companies share the cost, responsibility and profits from a business venture.

Limited company – a business organisation which has a separate legal identity from that of its owners.

Stock market – a market for shares in plcs.

QUESTION 2

Fiat, the Italian car company, is to make cars and engines in China from 2011. It has formed a joint venture with Guangzhou Automobile Group (GAC). Each will invest €400m in a 50:50 joint venture. They plan to build a large production plant in Hunan province. Fiat and GAC said the plant will produce 140,000 cars and 220,000 engines per year. However, it could be expanded to produce up to 250,000 cars and 300,000 engines. The venture with GAC will launch Fiat into a highly competitive market with more car manufacturers than America's.

(a) Using this case study as an example, explain what is meant by a joint venture.

(b) Outline two advantages of joint ventures.

Chapter review – homeofficeplus.com

Nathan Edwards is the majority shareholder in Nathan's Home Offices Ltd. The three other shareholders are family members. They all work in the business. The company is based in Australia and serves the Brisbane area. It specialises in office fitting for people that work

Figure 4.5 *A newly furnished office*

at home. The business was started in 2001 when Nathan operated as a sole trader. However, in 2004 he invited family members to take a stake in the business and formed Nathan's Home Offices Ltd. They contributed some capital and the business expanded.

The family is now considering raising more money by 'going public'. Nathan wants to expand the business further and needs $10m. This will be used to:

- develop an online business

- build two warehouses as distribution centres

- develop a fleet of delivery vehicles to serve the whole of Eastern Australia

- buy stock to supply a full range of office equipment and accessories.

The company also plans to change its name to homeofficeplus.com.

Nathan's Home Offices Ltd is a private limited company.

(a) What evidence is there to support this view? **(2 marks)**

When Nathan's Home Offices Ltd was formed, Nathan had to produce a Memorandum of Association.

(b) What information would this document contain? **(2 marks)**

(c) What is the purpose of a prospectus? **(2 marks)**

Share issues have to be underwritten.

(d) What does this mean? **(2 marks)**

(e) Outline why going public is expensive. **(4 marks)**

(f) Discuss whether Nathan should convert his business to a public limited company. **(8 marks)**

Chapter 5: Multinational companies

Getting started...

*In the last 30 years or so, some businesses have developed large operations in many different countries. They serve global markets and provide jobs and other benefits for the countries in which they locate. They are called **multinationals**. Look at the example below.*

The global car industry

The global car industry is dominated by a few large multinationals such as Toyota, General Motors (GM), Ford, Volkswagen, Honda and Nissan. All of these firms produced over 3 million cars each in 2007. Two of them, Toyota and GM, produced over 9 million. These companies have a global outlook. They sell their cars anywhere and set up production wherever costs can be minimised. For example, Ford has factories in many countries such as the US, UK, Spain, Brazil, Mexico, France and Thailand.

Fifty years ago three large US car makers – GM, Ford, Chrysler – dominated the global car industry. Now their market share has fallen as new, leaner producers like Toyota have entered the market. GM and Ford are cutting thousands of jobs and closing plants. In contrast, Toyota is building one new plant each year. Toyota is worth 10 times as much as GM and is now the world's largest carmaker.

(a) What do you think is meant by a global market?

It is suggested that the US is becoming less important in the global car industry.

(b) What evidence is there to support this view?

(c) State one possible reason why car production is rising in Asia.

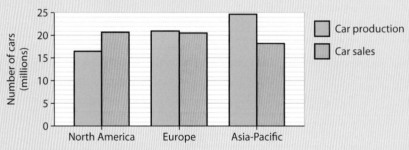

Figure 5.1 *World car production by region*

Globalisation

Many markets today are global. This means that some firms expect to sell their products anywhere in the world. Firms and people are behaving as though there is just one market in the whole world. This development is called **globalisation**. What are the key features of globalisation?

- Products are traded freely across international borders. There are no government restrictions which prevent firms from selling in overseas markets.

- In some areas, such as the EU, people are free to live and work in any country they choose. People from many different nations often live and work in the same city.

- There is a high level of interdependence between nations. This means that events in one economy are likely to affect other economies. For example, the financial crisis in the US in 2008 had an impact on many economies all over the world.

- Capital can flow freely between different countries. This means, for example, that a firm or consumer in Australia can put their savings in a bank in the US. It also means that firms and investors can buy shares in foreign companies.

Did you know?

It is not unusual for a firm to have a head office in London, borrow money from a Japanese bank, manufacture goods in China, deal with customers from a call centre in India and sell goods to countries in Europe and the Americas.

The importance and growth of multinationals

Multinationals play a large and growing role in the world economy. They contribute about 10 per cent to world GDP and about two thirds to global exports. Figure 5.2 provides a summary of information about the world's five largest multinationals.

	Company	Sector	Turnover	Year	HQ
1	ExxonMobil	Oil & gas	$390.3 bn	2007	US
2	Wal-Mart Stores	Retailing	$374.5 bn	2008	US
3	Royal Dutch Shell	Oil & gas	$355.8 bn	2007	UK/Netherlands
4	British Petroleum	Oil & gas	$292.0 bn	2007	UK
5	Toyota	Automotive	$264.8 bn	2008	Japan

Figure 5.2 *The world's five largest multinationals*

Why have multinationals been created?

- **Economies of scale:** Multinationals can exploit *economies of scale*. This means they enjoy lower costs because of their size (see Chapter 44). Businesses that sell to global markets will produce more than those who just sell to domestic markets. Therefore their costs will be lower. Multinationals are powerful and can put pressure on suppliers to lower their prices. Also, multinationals have access to cheap global resources such as labour, capital and commodities.

- **Marketing:** Some firms have become multinationals by relying on effective marketing. Firms such as Starbucks and MacDonald's are good examples. These are low-tech firms that have developed a successful brand at home and then exploited it globally. Both companies face fierce competition in their markets. However, they have protected their brand with patents and use heavy advertising and innovative marketing to attract customers globally.

- **Technical and financial superiority:** Most multinationals have developed into large businesses over a period of time. They have developed advanced technologies and built up a huge bank of knowledge. They can also afford to invest heavily in research and development. They are experienced and can afford to employ the most talented people available. They also have the resources to take risks and diversify. As a result they can take on business ventures that small firms could never dream of.

QUESTION 1

HSBC is one of the largest banks in the world. It has around 9,500 offices in 86 countries in Europe, the Asia-Pacific region, the Americas, the Middle East and Africa. HSBC has an international network linked by advanced technology. It also makes increasing use of online banking. HSBC provides a wide range of financial services for individuals, commerce, corporations and investors. In 2008, HSBC had a turnover of nearly £50bn and employed over 300,000 people.

HSBC is a multinational.

(a) What evidence is there to support this view?

In common with many other banks, HSBC offers an online banking service.

(b) How would this help the company to reach the global market?

Figure 5.3 *An HSBC branch*

Advantages of multinationals

- **Increase in income and employment:** When multinationals set up operations overseas income in those countries rises. Multinationals create new jobs in developing countries. For example, according to an IBM database, a report said that, in 2007, around 10,000 new foreign business projects created 1.2 million jobs around the world. Local suppliers are also likely to get work when a multinational arrives. The extra output and employment generated by multinationals will increase economic growth and raise living standards for people in these countries.

- **Increase in tax revenue:** The profits made by multinationals are taxed by the host nation. This increases tax revenue for the government in that country and this can be used to improve government services.

- **Increase in exports:** The output produced by a multinational in a particular country is recorded as output for that country. Therefore, if this output is sold out of the host country it is counted as an export. This helps less developed countries to increase their foreign currency reserves.

- **Transfer of technology:** Multinationals often provide foreign suppliers with technical help, training and other information. They may also help local suppliers to purchase resources and modernise production facilities.

- **Improvement in the quality of human capital:** Multinationals provide training and work experience for workers in less developed countries. Also, governments in less developed countries often spend more on education to help attract multinationals. This happened in India where the government invested heavily in IT education and training.

- **Enterprise development:** The arrival of multinationals has encouraged more people to set up businesses in less developed countries. Multinationals may have provided the skills and motivation needed for enterprise. For example, a new multinational may encourage locals to supply services such as transport, accommodation, maintenance, cleaning and leisure activities.

QUESTION 2

Coca-Cola is a multinational and is the world's largest beverage company. Along with Coca-Cola, the world's most valuable brand, other brands include Diet Coke, Fanta, Sprite, Coca-Cola Zero, Vitaminwater and Powerade. People in more than 200 countries consume nearly 1.6bn servings a day. Coca-Cola has more than 300 bottling plants around the world which manufacture, package, distribute and merchandise their brands. In 2008, Coca-Cola had a turnover of $31.9bn and made a profit of $7.4bn.

(a) How might the following benefit from Coca-Cola locating a bottling plant in their country? **(i)** residents; **(ii)** the government.

Disadvantages of multinationals

- **Environmental damage:** Many environmentalists are suspicious of multinationals because they may cause environmental damage. One reason is because multinationals are heavily involved in the extraction industries such as coal, oil and gold mining. Mining is often destructive.

- **Exploitation of less developed countries:** It is sometimes argued that multinationals may exploit developing nations.

  - Some multinationals may encourage developing countries to rely on producing primary products. This is risky because the prices of primary products can change sharply, which causes variations in income. Relying on one industry also makes developing nations vulnerable.

Did you know?

Oil spills and waste dumping have seriously damaged agricultural land in the Niger Delta in Nigeria. According to Amnesty International this has undermined the livelihood of many locals in the area.

- Multinationals often pay low wages. They may also employ child labour and working conditions are often very poor.

- Resources are extracted and sold with little money going to the host nation.

- Taxes paid to the host nation are often minimal.

- As little as possible is put back into the country because this would reduce the amount of profit made by the multinational.

However, although such exploitation does occur, many multinationals have good records when developing business interests in less developed countries.

- **Repatriation of profits:** The profits made by multinationals abroad are often *repatriated*. This means that profits are returned to the country where the multinational is based. As a result the host country loses out. This suggests that multinationals bring more benefits to developed countries than to less developed countries. This is because the headquarters of most multinationals are based in developed countries.

- **Lack of accountability:** Some argue that because multinationals are so large and powerful they lack accountability. This means they may be able to evade the law – especially in countries where the government is weak or corrupt. Also, multinationals may be keener to operate where regulation is inadequate or non-existent. However, multinationals may be monitored by pressure groups. This helps improve accountability.

Key terms

Globalisation – the growing integration of the world's economies.

Multinational – a large business with markets and production facilities in several different countries.

Repatriation (of profit) – where a multinational returns the profits from an overseas venture to the country where it is based.

Chapter review – Newmont Mining Corp

Newmont Mining Corporation is mainly a gold producer. Based in Colorado (USA), it has operations in the US, Australia, Peru, Indonesia, Ghana, Canada, New Zealand and Mexico. The company also has 34,000 employees worldwide.

Newmont owns mines in Indonesia and claims that over a seven-year period one mine (now shut) paid the Indonesian government $500m. Another Newmont mine currently pays $35.90m a year in taxes and other fees to the government. Newmont says it buys $183m of goods and services from Indonesian businesses. It also pays $55m to Indonesian employees and spends $2.3m in community development.

However, there have also been some negative impacts which include:

- loss of life in mining accidents

- contamination of lakes in Sulawesi

- loss of water for farming

- damage to forests.

In 2006, some protestors were shot by police near one of Newmont's mines. The protests centred in Newmont's activities in forests near Sumbawa. Local people wanted the company to leave. They said that Newmont had caused environmental damage and loss of livelihood. Locals were prevented from collecting honey, candlenut and palm sugar from the forests. The water supply has decreased, and crops such as rice and cucumber have failed due to drought.

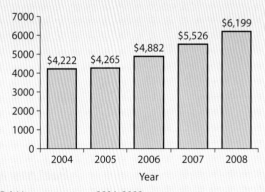

Figure 5.4 *Newmont revenue 2004-2008*

(a) What is meant by a multinational? (Use this case study as an example.) **(2 marks)**

(b) How do you think Newmont's shareholders have benefited from its involvement in other countries in the world? **(2 marks)**

(c) State two reasons why multinationals such as Newmont are created. **(2 marks)**

(d) How has Indonesia benefited from Newmont's business ventures in the country? **(4 marks)**

(e) Analyse the disadvantages to Indonesia of Newmont's business developments in the country. **(10 marks)**

Chapter 6: Factors influencing the choice of organisation

Getting started...

The type of organisation that owners choose for their business will depend on a number of factors. For example, there is a relationship between the objectives of a business and the type of business organisation. Generally, as a business grows the legal status of the business changes. Look at the examples below.

Marco Valdez

Marco Valdez is a self-employed taxi driver. He works in Mexico City and owns his own vehicle. He operates as a sole trader and made a profit of 150,000 Mexican peso in 2008. Marco is happy with his current business situation and does not want to expand. He enjoys operating as a sole trader and is making sufficient profit to fund a comfortable life style. As long as he can maintain his current market share, he is happy with his business. He does not want to take on the extra responsibility that growing the business might bring.

Cemex

Cemex is a large Mexican multinational. The company was set up in 1906 and supplied the north of Mexico with cement. Today Cemex is a global building materials company. It has customers in the Americas, Europe, Africa, the Middle East, Asia and Australia. It produces and sells cement, ready-mix concrete and other building materials in more than 50 countries. Cemex has 64 cement plants, 2,200 ready-mix factories, 493 quarries, 253 distribution centres and 88 marine terminals.

Marco Valdez is happy operating as a sole trader.

(a) Give two reasons why he might be happy.

(b) Why could Cemex not really operate as a sole trader?

(c) Why might businesses in general be forced to change their legal status as they grow?

Figure 6.1 *Traffic in Mexico City*

Factors affecting the choice of business organisation

- **Growth:** Many businesses start small and gradually get bigger. Most businesses change their legal status as they grow. This is because they need to raise more capital. For example, sole traders often find it difficult to raise additional finance. However, by taking on a partner, or becoming a private limited company, they can raise more money. This is because more owners can generate more capital. Similarly, if the owners of a private limited company want to raise even larger amounts of capital they may have to become a public limited company.

  Many small businesses are sole traders or partnerships. Public limited companies are much larger with thousands of employees and huge turnovers. It could be argued that a very large business could only be run if it were a limited company.

- **The need for finance:** Finance is the main reason why owners change the legal status of their businesses. Quite often the only way to get more money is to change the type of organisation. See **Growth** above.

- **Control:** Some owners like their independence. They like to have complete control of their business. This is why many owners remain as sole traders. Once new partners or shareholders join the business, some control is lost because it is shared with the new owners. It is possible to keep control of a limited company by holding the majority of shares. However, even if one person holds 51 per cent of shares in a limited company, the wishes of the holders of the other 49 per cent cannot be ignored.

- **Limited liability:** Owners can protect their own personal financial position if the business is a limited company. Sole traders and partners have unlimited liability. Because of this they could be forced to use their own money to meet business debts. Therefore, some owners become limited companies to give themselves more financial protection.

Other factors

- The type of business activity may influence the choice of legal status. For example services such as plumbing, decorating and gardening tend to be provided by sole traders, while professional services such as accountancy, legal advice and surveying are usually offered by partnerships. Relatively small manufacturing and family businesses tend to be private limited companies and large banks, retail chains and manufacturers are usually plcs. It must be remembered that there are many exceptions to these general examples.

- The way in which a business plans to use its profits may be important. For example, plcs usually pay dividends to their shareholders. Therefore a growing business which prefers to reinvest a lot of its profit may choose to remain as a private limited company.

- Finally, the different stakeholders such as employees and shareholders might influence the choice of organisation. For example, influential employees in a private limited company might discourage the shareholders from going public. They may argue that the company operates more effectively without external owners.

Objectives and the type of organisation

It is likely that the different types of business organisation will have different objectives. Some examples are given below.

- Small sole traders might be happy to make a modest amount of profit – just enough to fund a comfortable lifestyle. They may not want the responsibility associated with other objectives such as growth. This is sometimes called *profit satisficing*.

- Family businesses and other medium-sized private limited companies are often reluctant to go public because they are afraid of losing control to outsiders. As a result their growth might be limited and other objectives are more important.

- Most multinationals want to grow. Their aim is often to get bigger and bigger so that they can dominate global markets.

Did you know?

Some business activity, such as oil processing and chemical manufacturing, requires large-scale production. This could not be managed effectively by sole traders or partnerships.

Did you know?

Entrepreneurs such as Richard Branson (Virgin) and Alan Sugar (Amstrad) have changed the legal status of their organisations from public limited companies back to private limited companies. After operating as plcs for some time they found that they did not like sharing control. Their own objectives may have been different from those of the other shareholders.

Chapter review – ADgirlsport.com

Amanda Duval has run her sports shop business, ADgirlsport.com, first as a sole trader, then a partnership and now a limited company. Set up in 1999, the business first traded from a back bedroom where she supplied sportswear for girls by mail order. But now it has a shop and a growing internet business. Amanda said: 'When I started, I started small, operating from home, and never needing outside funding, so being a sole trader seemed the simplest option.'

Three years later Amanda decided to open a shop. However, she needed money for premises, stock and marketing. After a few months there was a strain on her cash flow. Therefore she decided to take on her best friend as a partner. This helped to share the burden of running the business and raised $20,000 much needed cash. However, after 18 months Amanda fell out with her partner. Her partner wanted to take more profit from the business whereas Amanda wanted to use it for expansion. The break-up of the partnership was bitter and Amanda ended up having to pay her friend off. Amanda said: 'I was a fool really. I should have drawn up a Deed of Partnership in case we disagreed.'

Immediately after the break-up Amanda formed a private limited company. Amanda had 51 per cent of the shares because she wanted control. Her mother bought 29 per cent and she allowed two of her staff to buy the remaining 20 per cent. She wanted to reward them for their loyalty and also keep them motivated. Some of the money raised from selling the shares was used to set up an online business. This is now expanding fast and Amanda thinks she could develop a small chain of shops. A major sports retailer has recently put a number of stores up for sale. However, to buy, convert and stock them would cost $5m. The only way she could raise this money is by going public.

Figure 6.2 *Sportswear for girls*

(a) Why was a sole trader organisation suitable for Amanda's business when she first started? **(2 marks)**

(b) **(i)** Why did Amanda form a partnership? **(2 marks)**
(ii) Outline the importance of drawing up a Deed of Partnership when forming a partnership. **(2 marks)**

Amanda formed a private limited company after the break-up of the partnership.

(c) Do you think it was appropriate? **(4 marks)**

(d) Discuss whether Amanda should form a public limited company to buy the shops. **(10 marks)**

Chapter 7: Factors of production

Getting started...

Businesses use a range of resources to make goods or deliver services. Examples include raw materials, components, buildings, energy, tools, equipment, machinery and people. Businesses will try to make the best use of these resources to improve efficiency. For example, workers often specialise in one task so that they become highly proficient in that task. Look at the resources used in the example below.

JCB

JCB is one of the world's top manufacturers of construction equipment. The company employs around 7,000 people on four different continents and sells products in 150 countries. JCB has a reputation for innovation and high-quality products. It has some of the finest engineering facilities across the globe. It produces a range of over 300 machines and has a record of effective customer service.

(a) Identify four resources used by JCB.

(b) To what extent do you think JCB relies on the use of machinery in its production of construction equipment?

Figure 7.1 *A production line*

What is production?

Production involves converting resources into goods or services. These goods and services are provided to satisfy the needs and wants of people. Some examples of production might be:

- a baker using flour, yeast, salt and water to make bread

- a large manufacturer using people to assemble components to make laptop computers

- a dentist using dental instruments to extract a diseased tooth

- a taxi driver using a car and petrol to transport a family from their home to an airport.

All of these examples involve using resources to produce goods or provide services. These resources are called the **four factors of production**. They are summarised in Figure 7.2.

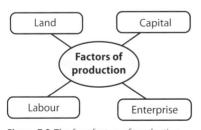

Figure 7.2 *The four factors of production*

Key facts

- Some land resources are *non-renewable*. This means that once they have been used they cannot be replaced. Examples include coal, oil, diamonds and gold.
- *Renewable* land resources are those like fish, forests and water which are replaced by nature. These resources should not run out. However, there is a risk that if some of them are not protected they could disappear.

Land

Businesses will need a 'plot of land' to locate their premises. For example, the developers of a large shopping mall may look for several acres of land on the outskirts of a town to locate the stores and car parking facilities. However, land also includes natural resources such as coal, oil, iron ore, rainwater, forests, rivers and fertile soil.

Labour

The workforce in the economy is the **labour**. Manual workers, skilled workers and managers are all part of a nation's workforce. The quality of individual workers will vary considerably. Each worker is unique, possessing a different set of abilities, characteristics, skills, knowledge, intelligence and emotions.

Capital

Capital is often said to be an artificial resource because it is made by labour. There are two types of capital.

- **Working capital** or **circulating capital** refers to stocks of raw materials and components that will be used up in production. It also includes stocks of finished goods that are waiting to be sold.

- **Fixed capital** refers to the factories, offices, shops, machines, tools, equipment and furniture used in production. Fixed capital is used in production to convert working capital into goods and services.

Enterprise

Entrepreneurs are responsible for setting up and running businesses. Without them production would not take place. What is the role of entrepreneurs?

- They come up with a *business idea*. This might involve the production of a completely new product. However, this is unusual. Most new businesses supply goods or services that are currently produced by others.

- They are business *owners*. They usually provide some money to help set up a business and are responsible for its direction.

- Entrepreneurs are *risk-takers*. For example, they risk their own money in the venture. If the business collapses they may lose some or all of the money. However, if the business is successful they may make a lot of profit. But when they start up they do not know what will happen – they are taking a risk.

- Entrepreneurs are responsible for *organising* resources. They have to buy and hire resources such as raw materials, tools, equipment and labour. Entrepreneurs need to use skills such as decision-making, people management, time management and financial judgment to organise resources effectively.

QUESTION 1

Alonso Cortez set up a small bus company to provide an express passenger transport service from Madrid city centre to the airport. He invested €40,000 in the venture and recruited two drivers to help him out. He spent €80,000 on a 50-seater coach and rented a small office in the Bus Station. He also purchased a computer, mobile phones for his drivers and some office furniture.

(a) State two examples of capital that Alonso will use.

Alonso Cortez is an entrepreneur.

(b) What evidence is their in this case study to support this view?

Figure 7.3 *A coach about to leave Madrid city centre for the airport*

Labour-intensive and capital-intensive production

Businesses have to manage resources effectively. They have to choose a suitable combination of materials, tools, equipment, machinery and labour for production. Some businesses use **labour-intensive** production. This means that they use relatively more labour than capital. Labour-intensive production is common in Far Eastern countries such as China where labour is cheap.

In contrast, some businesses use **capital-intensive** production methods. This means that production relies more on the use of plant and machinery. Production in the West tends to be more capital intensive.

Specialisation and the division of labour

One feature of modern business is **specialisation**. This is the production of a limited range of goods by an individual, business, region or nation. For example, Coca-Cola specialises in soft drinks, Toyota makes cars and Emirates provides air travel. Specialisation inside a business is also common. Departments specialise in different activities such as marketing, production, finance, personnel (human resources) and purchasing.

Workers will also specialise in certain tasks and skills. This is called the **division of labour**. It allows people to concentrate on a limited range of tasks. For example, in construction an architect will draw up plans, a bricklayer will build walls, a roofer will lay the roof, and so on. The division of labour will increase productivity because:

● Workers concentrate on the task that they do best.

● Workers' skills improve as they continually repeat the same task.

● Time is saved because workers are not switching from one task to another.

● The organisation of production is easier.

Although specialisation is likely to improve productivity, it does have drawbacks. For example, work can become tedious and boring because of repetition. Also, when one stage of production depends on another, there may be delays if one stage breaks down.

Key terms

Capital-intensive production – production methods that make more use of machinery relative to labour.

Division of labour – specialisation in specific tasks or skills by an individual.

Entrepreneur – an individual who organises the other factors of production and risks their own money in a business venture.

Factors of production – the resources used to produce goods and services. They include land, labour, capital and enterprise.

Fixed capital – the stock of 'man-made' resources such as machines and tools used to help make goods and services.

Labour – the people used in production.

Labour-intensive production – production methods that make more use of labour relative to machinery.

Production – the transformation of resources into goods or services.

Specialisation – in business, the production of a limited range of goods.

QUESTION 2

The Dublin Construction Company is based in Ireland. It has 37 employees, eight of whom are general labourers. The remainder are skilled workers. Details of three are outlined below:

● **Brendan O'Hagan** is 26 years old and has worked for the company since leaving school. He is a bricklayer and learnt his trade from one of the experienced bricklayers in the company.

● **Mary O'Mara** is 27 years old and has only just started working for the company. She is a qualified electrician. She spent three years at college and has an NVQ Level 3 in Electrical Installation.

● **Ahab Patel** is a self-taught plumber. He spent time working with his father and then became self employed. However, after doing some contract work for Dublin Construction Company, he was invited him to join them full time.

Figure 7.4 *Employees at work for the Dublin Construction Company*

(a) What is meant by the division of labour? (Use an example from this case study.)

(b) How might such specialisation benefit Dublin Construction Company?

Did you know?

Modern production techniques often require workers to be more flexible. They may be expected to learn a variety of skills, work in different parts of the organisation, make decisions for themselves and solve problems.

The changing relationships between enterprise, capital and labour

Over time the types of resources used by a business, and the way they are used, is likely to change. For example, rapid advances in technology have resulted in more capital-intensive production worldwide. Fifty years ago computers were undeveloped and not widely used. Workers in a wide range of different jobs are likely to use computers today. There is also more large-scale production because it is more efficient. This often results in more capital-intensive methods and a greater division of labour.

Chapter review – Dragon Toys

Dragon Toys, a Chinese company, manufactures plastic toys such as pedal tractors. The business was set up in 1994 by Yang Chen. He invested $10,000 of his own money and produced small plastic toy tractors using a simple moulding machine. The business was successful but a breakthrough came in 2001 when he was asked to produce a pedal tractor that a child could actually drive. A retailer placed a very big order and in 2004 the business was forced to move to a larger factory near Shanghai.

Figure 7.5 *A child's pedal tractor*

The workforce increased from 12 to 160 in just a few years. Production is labour-intensive. Machines can mass produce the plastic components but they have to be assembled by hand. Yang Chen is about to introduce a new product and has recruited another 40 workers to help in the assembly department.

(a) What is meant by production? (Use this case study as an example.) **(2 marks)**

Yang Chen is an entrepreneur.

(b) Outline his role at Dragon Toys. **(6 marks)**

(c) Suggest two examples of land used in production at Dragon Toys. **(2 marks)**

(d) What might be the drawbacks of labour specialisation at Dragon Toys? **(2 marks)**

Production at Dragon Toys is labour intensive.

(e) What does this mean? **(2 marks)**

'Production at Dragon Toys is likely to become more capital intensive in the future.'

(f) To what extent is this statement true? **(6 marks)**

Chapter 8: Primary, secondary and tertiary activity

Getting started...

Businesses operate in different sectors. In developed countries such as the US and Germany most businesses provide services. They may be fitness centres, insurance brokers, retailers, or provide services for businesses such as market research or IT support. In some countries, such as China, there are large numbers of manufacturers. Finally, in less developed countries most businesses will concentrate on producing agricultural goods. Look at the businesses below.

Figure 8.1a *A shopping mall*

Figure 8.1b *Computer production*

Figure 8.1c *Rice cultivation*

Figure 8.1d *Interior of an airliner*

(a) Which of these businesses are concerned with **(i)** agriculture **(ii)** manufacturing **(iii)** services?

(b) Which of these businesses are **most likely** to be common in **(i)** Africa **(ii)** Western Europe?

Primary sector

Business activity is classified into three sectors. In the **primary sector** business activity involves extracting raw materials from the earth. Here are some examples.

● **Mining and quarrying,** where raw materials such as coal, iron ore, copper, tin, salt and limestone are dug out of the ground. This sector also includes the extraction of oil and gas. Saudi Aramco, the largest oil producer in the world, is an example of a business that extracts oil.

● **Fishing,** which involves netting, trapping, angling and trawling fish. It also includes catching or gathering other types of seafood such as mussels, prawns, lobsters, crabs, scallops and oysters. China is the world's largest fish producer.

● **Forestry,** which involves managing forests to provide timber for wood products. Modern forestry also involves protecting the natural environment, providing access and facilities to the public and managing wildlife habitats.

● **Agriculture,** which involves a range of farming activities, is probably the most important primary sector activity for most countries. Most agriculture is concerned with food production. However, other examples include ornamental or exotic products such as cut flowers, nursery plants and tropical fish.

Secondary sector

In the **secondary sector** business activity involves converting raw materials into finished or semi-finished goods. All of manufacturing, processing and construction lies within this sector. Secondary sector business activities include metal working, car production, textile production, chemical and engineering industries, aerospace manufacturing, energy utilities, engineering, food processing, construction and shipbuilding. In many countries this sector has declined in recent years.

Tertiary sector

The **tertiary sector** involves the provision of a wide variety of services, such as:

- **Professional services:** accountancy, legal advice and medical care
- **Transport:** train, taxi, bus and air services
- **Household services:** plumbing, decorating, gardening and house maintenance
- **Leisure services:** television, tourism, hotels and libraries
- **Financial services:** banking, insurance, investment advice and pensions
- **Commercial services:** freight delivery, debt collection, printing, and employment agencies.

Figure 8.2 *Root vegetables on sale*

QUESTION 1

Jill and Ronnie Sanchez have owned a farm for 40 years. They grow a range of root vegetables such as carrots, swedes, turnips and parsnips. They have a contract to supply two local supermarkets and also sell to other shops in the area. In the 1970s, Jill and Ronnie employed up to 12 workers, but due to mechanisation they now just employ three.

(a) What is the difference between the primary and the tertiary sectors? (Use examples from this case study.)

Look at Figure 8.3.

(b) What has happened to the number of people employed in agriculture in the UK since 1960?

(c) Outline **one** possible reason for the pattern described in **(b)**.

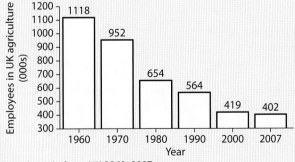

Figure 8.3 *Employment in agriculture, UK 1960–2007*

Interdependence

Businesses in each of the three sectors above are likely to be *interdependent*. This means that they rely on each other. For example, in the primary sector cereal farmers rely on bakers in the secondary sector for their sales of wheat. Bakers may depend on advertising agencies in the tertiary sector to produce newspaper adverts for their products. The transport industry in the tertiary sector relies on the oil industry in the primary sector to provide fuel for its vehicles. Workers in both the secondary and tertiary sectors rely on the primary sector for their food. In modern developed economies this interdependence is huge.

Changes in sectors

The number of people employed in each sector does not stay the same. Different sectors grow and decline over time. In the UK, before the Industrial Revolution began in the late 18th century, most production was in the primary sector. During the 19th century secondary production expanded rapidly as manufacturing grew during the Industrial Revolution.

However, in the last 60 years the tertiary sector has started to expand at the expense of manufacturing. The decline in manufacturing is called **de-industrialisation**. Figure 8.5 shows the pattern of employment in manufacturing and services in the UK between 1960 and 2007. Similar patterns can be identified in other developed nations.

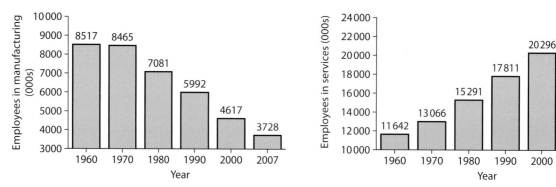

Figure 8.4 *The numbers of people employed in manufacturing and services in the UK 1960-2007 (employment approximating US concepts by economic sector)*

Key terms

De-industrialisation – the decline in manufacturing.

Primary industry – production involving the extraction of raw materials from the earth.

Secondary industry – production involving the conversion of raw materials into finished and semi-finished goods.

Tertiary industry – the production of services in the economy.

Why has manufacturing declined in developed countries while services have grown?

- People may prefer to spend more of their income on services than manufactured goods. There has also been a decline in demand for the goods produced by some of the traditional industries in manufacturing such as shipbuilding and textiles.

- There is some fierce competition in the production of manufactured goods from developing countries such as India, China and Brazil.

- As countries develop the public sector grows. Since the public sector mainly provides services, this adds to the growth of the tertiary sector.

- Advances in technology means that employment in manufacturing falls because machines replace people.

Chapter review – Business sectors

Banco Santander

In 2008, Banco Santander, the third largest bank in the world, made a profit of €8,876bn. The Spanish-based bank also has operations in Europe and Latin America. It has grown rapidly recently since buying other banks or financial organisations such as Alliance & Leicester and Bradford & Bingley in the UK. In 2008, it doubled its number of retail outlets and served 90m customers.

V T Garments

Thailand is one of the world's largest textile manufacturers and V T Garments is one of the largest producers in the country. It produces a range of clothes such as padded jackets, ski jackets, pants; shorts, jogging suits and T-shirts. Some of its customers include The North Face, Nike, Patagonia and Nautica. The

business has grown rapidly in the last 20 years. In 1981 it employed 120 people. By 2007 this had increased to 3,500.

Wagagai Ltd

Wagagai Ltd is a flower farm in Uganda. The company began in 1998 by exporting roses to Holland. Soon after, the farm diversified into producing chrysanthemum cuttings. Today, about 260m chrysanthemum cuttings are produced in more than 22 acres of greenhouses. In 2005,

Figure 8.5 *Flower farm in Uganda*

the owners stopped producing roses and approached German company Selecta First Class about producing cuttings. This was a success and Selecta and Wagagai formed a joint venture to supply international markets.

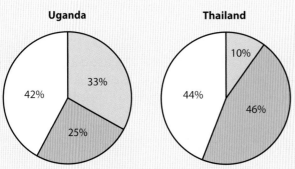

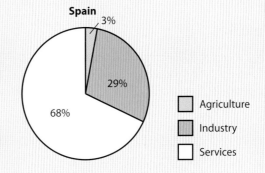

Figure 8.6 *Sector output in Uganda, Thailand and Spain (GDP %)*

Source: adapted from World Development Report, World Development Indicators, World Bank

(a) What is meant by **(i)** secondary and **(ii)** tertiary production? (Use examples from the case study.) **(4 marks)**

Look at Figure 8.6.

(b) Which nation relies most on the secondary sector for its output? **(2 marks)**

(c) Explain the interdependence that exists between the different sectors of business activity. **(2 marks)**

(d) (i) What is meant by de-industrialisation? **(2 marks)**
(ii) Which of the countries in Figure 8.6 have been subject most to de-industrialisation? **(2 marks)**

(e) Evaluate the main causes of de-industrialisation. **(8 marks)**

Chapter 9: Business location

Getting started...

Businesses have to decide where to operate from. Should they choose a site in the town centre, on an industrial estate, close to a motorway, by a port or in the countryside? Businesses may be located in a wide range of different places and the choice of location will be influenced by the changing business environment. Look at the examples below.

Prawn farming

Thailand has around 20,000 prawn farms. Its tropical climate and abundance of suitable coastal locations have made prawn farming one of its biggest industries. Prawn farms need plenty of clean water, which has to be introduced into the ponds throughout the rearing period. Hatchery sites should not be located by cities, harbours and industrial centres, or other activities which may pollute the water supply. There must also be enough soil available for pond construction and it is best to site the farm where the soil is fertile.

Figure 9.1 *Output from a Prawn farm*

Matisse Textiles

Matisse Textiles is a large producer of underwear garments based in Lyon, France. In 2008, the directors decided that, in order to remain competitive, costs must be reduced by 40 per cent. To achieve this challenging objective production was moved to Bangladesh. Wages in Bangladesh are very low compared with those in the West. Factory wages in Bangladesh were about 25 per cent of those in Lyon.

(a) Outline two factors that must be taken into account when locating a prawn farm.

(b) Describe how the changing business environment affected Matisse Textiles when locating their factory.

Factors affecting business location

Historically, many businesses were located near to the sources of power and raw materials. Heavy industries such as steel and chemicals were located close to power sources such as coal and raw materials such as water and iron ore. This is why the steel industry flourished in the Ruhr and Rhine valleys in Germany. Today, electricity and gas can be supplied to most locations and therefore businesses do not have to be located close to the power sources. Today businesses are more likely to be influenced by the factors below.

- **The cost of premises or land:** Many businesses require large areas of land to locate factories, stores, staff car parks and other facilities. As a result they look to minimise land and property costs. For example, they may set up in areas where:

  - premises are cheap – perhaps in a business park or on an industrial estate; these are often located away from expensive residential areas

  - *business rates* (a tax paid by businesses to the local authorities) are low

  - land has been earmarked for business development such as **brownfield sites** or **greenfield sites**.

- **Transport:** Some manufacturers locate their factories close to effective transport networks. This makes it easier for distributors and suppliers. For example, a British manufacturer that exports goods to the EU may choose a site close to the Channel Tunnel. Businesses that sell in national markets may locate their premises next to a motorway.

- **Cost and availability of labour:** Businesses needing large numbers of workers have to consider wage costs and labour skills. Wage rates may vary in different regions and large companies may also consider locating in countries where labour is very cheap. Also, labour skills are not evenly distributed throughout a country. If a firm needs a particular type of skilled labour a certain location may be more suitable than others.

- **Proximity to the market:** Some businesses locate their premises close to customers. For example, manufacturers that make bulky or heavy products may locate close to their customers so as to keep transport costs down. Also, the manufacturers of components, e.g. car parts, often locate close to their customers.

  Many service providers have to locate their premises close to their markets. This is because many services are sold direct to consumers. For example, restaurants, cafes, shops, hair salons, opticians, taxis and dry cleaners have to be located in towns and cities. This is where customers live and shop.

- **Government constraints and opportunities:** Governments may try to influence location decisions. They do this for the following reasons.

  - To avoid congestion where there is already enough or too much development.

  - To encourage firms to locate where unemployment is high.

  - To attract foreign businesses into the country.

  Some governments use **regional policy** to help develop 'run-down' areas. Regional policy provides opportunities for businesses. For example, governments use incentives such as quick planning permission, investment grants, tax breaks, employment subsidies and rent-free factory space, to attract businesses. However, sometimes business development may be constrained in certain areas because of congestion or to help protect the environment. Governments can do this by denying planning permission.

Did you know?

In India, Bangalore has a reputation for good IT professionals. Firms in Bangalore employ about 35 per cent of India's 1 million IT professionals. Many multinationals have IT operations in Bangalore for this reason.

Did you know?

In the car industry, firms making components such as braking systems, light fittings, car seats and other parts may locate close to a car assembly plant. The use of just-in-time (see Chapter 47) production has encouraged this trend. It is easier for suppliers to make several deliveries per day, for example, if they are located 'next door' to their main customer.

QUESTION 1

Guangxi Yuchai Machinery Company Ltd (GYMCL) makes diesel engines for trucks, construction equipment, buses, and cars in China. In 2009, it completed phase one of its new diesel engine assembly factory. The factory is located in the Xiamen Automobile Industry City in Guannan Industrial Park, near to Xiamen Port. This is a major auto-parts, bus and construction equipment area. This will allow the business to increase its scale of operations, shorten its supply chain and lower production costs. Xiamen is a popular and growing business development area. Locating a factory there will help to improve the firm's competitiveness and strengthen its customer relations.

GYMCL located its new factory in the heart of the Xiamen Automobile Industry City in Guannan Industrial Park.

(a) Discuss possible reasons for this decision.

Business location and the changing environment

Location decisions will be affected by the changing business environment. Over time, certain changes will provide new opportunities and impose new constraints on business. As a result location decisions may be influenced. Some examples are given below.

- **More home-based businesses:** In recent years there has been a growth in the number of home-based businesses. For example, many small service providers can operate from home. Examples include mobile hairdressers, mobile mechanics, freelance writers, consultants, designers, accountants, tutors, wedding planners, child carers and translators.

- **The internet:** Many people are switching to the internet when shopping rather than going to stores. This means that retailers, for example, can serve national markets and operate in premises away from their customers. For example, an online clothes retailer could operate from a warehouse near a motorway and serve a national market. Figure 9.2 shows the growth in online sales in Germany between 2003 and 2008. Sales have more than doubled over this period.

- **Legislation:** Government legislation is changing all the time. One recent trend is the growing concern about the environment. Governments are providing more protection for the environment. This has put constraints on some businesses when trying to locate new operations.

- **Changes in factor costs:** The cost of resources such as raw materials and labour do not remain constant. Businesses will be attracted to locations where resources are cheap. For example, many manufacturers in the West have moved production to the Far East where wages are considerably lower.

- **New markets:** A multinational may decide to locate in a particular country because it wants to sell goods into a new market. This is a reason why many companies are trying to locate in China. China has the largest population in the world and its economy has been booming for many years now.

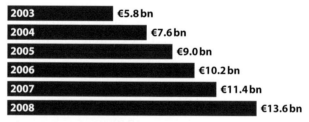

2003	€5.8bn
2004	€7.6bn
2005	€9.0bn
2006	€10.2bn
2007	€11.4bn
2008	€13.6bn

Figure 9.2 *Online sales in Germany 2003–2008*

QUESTION 2

In August 2010, plans to develop a bauxite mine on sacred tribal land in India were blocked. Vedanta Resources was prevented by India's environment ministry from mining aluminium ore in the eastern state of Orissa. A government enquiry said that mining would destroy the way of life of the area's 'endangered' and 'primitive' people, the Kutia and Dongria Kondh tribes. A local subsidiary of Vedanta was also accused of violating forest conservation and environment protection regulations.

The value of shares in the company dropped by 6 per cent and almost £300m was wiped off the value of the business. Campaigners against the mining giant's plans described the move as a 'stunning victory'. Monty Python star Michael Palin who, along with Joanna Lumley, had backed the campaigners expressed 'absolute delight' in the news, adding: 'I hope it will send a signal to the big corporations that they can never assume that might is right. It's a big victory for the little people.'

The government can have an impact on business location.

(a) How does this case study illustrate this impact?

(b) How was Vedanta Resources affected by the government's decision?

International location

Multinationals have business operations all over the world. When locating a new operation a multinational will take into account many of the factors discussed above. However, there are some additional factors to consider.

- **Avoiding trade barriers:** Some countries put up trade barriers, such as tariffs and quotas. This is to protect domestic businesses from foreign competition. One way a multinational business can get round such trade barriers is to locate within the country.

- **Financial incentives:** Businesses may be attracted to a particular country if financial incentives are offered. Some of the regional aid available in parts of Europe may have influenced the location of Asian multinationals in the 1990s. Governments may offer cash, sometimes called 'sweeteners', to businesses if they locate in their country.

- **Cost of labour:** A number of multinationals have located plants in countries where labour is cheaper, such as India or China. Cheap labour gives them a competitive advantage. Labour is so cheap in certain Asian countries that production methods tend to be labour-intensive rather than capital-intensive. This can help to reduce costs.

- **Proximity to markets or suppliers:** Transport costs can be much greater over longer distances. Therefore, multinationals locate near their markets or their suppliers to remain competitive. A car component manufacturer, for example, may have to set up a factory in the Far East to be near a car manufacturer.

- **Political stability:** Some countries, such as African states, are unpopular with multinationals because of political instability. Also, some countries are avoided by multinationals because of their poor human rights record. To locate in these countries could result in consumer boycotts or shareholder disapproval.

- **Language barriers:** Language can be an important factor in location decisions. For example, much of the foreign investment over the past ten years in China has been by companies owned by Chinese people living outside of China.

Key fact

Japanese car producers set up car plants in Europe and the USA in the 1980s and 1990s partly to avoid trade barriers designed by Europe and the USA to keep Japanese cars out of their markets.

Key terms

Assisted areas – areas that are designated by the UK or EU as having economic problems and are eligible for support in a variety of forms.

Brownfield site – areas of land which were once used for urban development.

Greenfield sites – areas of land, usually on the outskirts of towns and cities, where businesses develop for the first time.

Regional policy – measures used by the government to attract businesses to 'depressed' areas.

Chapter review – CompComp

Germany-based CompComp makes computer components. It plans to build a new factory in south-east Asia. It has a growing number of customers in China, South Korea, Japan and India. CompComp has found two sites where a new factory could be located. Details about the locations in Shanghai, China and Busan, South Korea are summarised in Figure 9.3.

- **Shanghai:** Shanghai is the largest centre of commerce and finance in China. It has been described as the 'showpiece' of the world's fastest-growing major economy. It is a high-profile business centre and has excellent communication links. However, with a population of over 20m the city is becoming congested and suffers from serious pollution problems.

- **Busan:** Busan is the fifth busiest seaport in the world, with transportation and shipping an important part of the local economy. Busan can handle up to 13.2m shipping containers per year. It is also well served by rail links and has an airport. The factory site proposed is on a purpose-built brownfield site with excellent amenities. However, there could be a problem finding suitable suppliers in the area.

	Shanghai	Busan
Rent per month	$20,000	$17,500
Unemployment	6.5%	9%
Hourly wage rate	$4.20	$3.60
Government support	None	$500,000

Figure 9.3 *Information about Shanghai and Busan*

The German company CompComp wants to locate a factory in south-east Asia.

(a) What is the reason for this? **(2 marks)**

Governments may try to influence business location.

(b) Suggest two reasons for this influence. **(2 marks)**

(c) What is meant by a brownfield site? **(2 marks)**

(d) Analyse two factors that must be taken into account when locating operations overseas. **(4 marks)**

(e) Which site do you think CompComp should choose for its new factory? **(10 marks)**

Chapter 10: Government influence on businesses – economic policy and regional policy

Getting started...

Businesses are likely to do well if the economy is stable. This means that prices should not be rising too quickly, unemployment should be low and the economy should be growing steadily. Governments use economic policy to help keep the economy stable. Such policies can provide opportunities for, and impose constraints upon, businesses. Look at the example below.

2008–2009 Recession

In 2008, many countries were hit by a recession. It was caused by a financial crisis which started in America. The main problem was that banks cut back on their lending. This caused problems for businesses. Businesses need to borrow money to fund their activities. Also, consumers borrow money to buy certain goods and services. As a result, many governments took measures to encourage lending, ease the recession and help businesses. Some examples used by the UK government are outlined below.

1. Value added tax (VAT), a tax on spending, was reduced from 17.5 per cent to 15 per cent.

2. Interest rates were slashed from 4.5 per cent to 0.5 per cent.

3. A 'scrap and save' scheme was introduced (£2,000 off the price of a new car if the old one was scrapped – provided it was over 10 years old).

4. LloydsTSB, Northern Rock and Royal Bank of Scotland (RBS) were taken into public ownership to prevent them from collapsing.

(a) How might a restaurant benefit from the reduction in VAT?

(b) How might a house builder be affected by the cut in interest rates?

(c) What effect might the 'scrap and save' scheme have on a motor car manufacturer?

Government influences on business activity and objectives

In many countries, the government has an important influence on business activity. The diagram in Figure 10.1 provides a summary of the main ways in which this occurs. This chapter looks at the way a government's economic and regional policies can influence business activity. The next chapter will show how legislation and competition policy affects businesses.

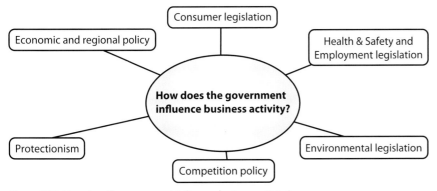

Figure 10.1 *How does the government influence business activity?*

The role of the government in the economy

It is the job of the government to manage the economy. As a result most governments have economic objectives. The main ones are outlined below.

- **Promote economic growth:** An increase in national income in the economy is called **economic growth**. It is good for the economy to grow because living standards rise. Economic growth also provides businesses with opportunities because people's incomes and demand will rise.

- **Maintain price stability:** The government will want to keep **inflation** low. Inflation means that prices are rising and this can harm the economy. For example, it means that business costs will rise and people will have to pay more for their shopping.

- **Reduce unemployment: Unemployment** occurs when people cannot find a job. Unemployment is bad for the economy because it is a waste of resources. Also, the government has to pay benefits to the unemployed and the funds for these benefits are drawn from taxes.

- **Control the balance of payments:** Some governments get concerned if *imports* are much higher than *exports*. It might mean that a country is relying too heavily on foreign goods and services. Also, a country has to pay its way. It cannot import more than it exports indefinitely.

- **Reduce the gap between the rich and the poor:** Many governments believe that a better society is created if the gap between the rich and the poor is reduced. It is not desirable if some groups in society are very poor while others live in luxury. It can lead to social problems such as crime, poverty and homelessness.

Why do governments influence businesses?

- **Boom and recession:** Over time economies will grow. For example, most western economies grow at a rate of around 2 per cent a year. However, the pattern of growth is often uneven. This uneven pattern is illustrated by the *business cycle or trade cycle* shown in Figure 10.2. It shows the two main phases in the cycle. This uneven pattern of growth means that governments have to intervene in the economy.

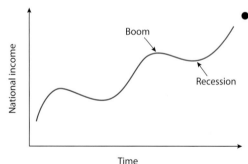

Figure 10.2 *The trade cycle or business cycle*

> **Boom** This is the peak of the cycle where national income is growing fast. Demand will be rising, jobs will be created, wages will be rising and the profits made by firms will be rising. However, prices may also be rising.

> **Recession** If national income is flat or starts to fall, the bottom of the cycle may be referred to as a recession. Demand will start to fall for many goods and services. Unemployment rises sharply, business confidence is low, bankruptcies rise and prices become flat or even fall.

- **Control the impact of businesses:** Governments may influence businesses to protect people and the environment.
  - **Employees** may need protection to ensure that their working environment is safe and not exploited. In many countries, government legislation exists to provide such protection. This is discussed in the next chapter.

Key fact

During a recession the government may try to 'kick-start' the economy. The government will want to stop unemployment from rising and help businesses to recover. On the other hand, during a boom the government might intervene to reduce inflation.

- **Consumers** may need protection from businesses. Sometimes businesses can become very powerful. They may develop a **monopoly**. This means they will have very little competition. Governments might use *competition policy* to ensure there is sufficient competition in markets. They might also use *consumer legislation* to prevent businesses from exploiting consumers. Competition policy and consumer legislation is discussed in the next chapter.

- Some business activity may damage the **environment**. For example, a business might lower its costs by dumping waste into a river. This could kill plant and animal life. Many governments use legislation to help protect the environment from businesses. This is discussed in more detail in the next chapter.

Examples of government influence on business activity

Government involvement can affect businesses in different ways. It may restrict business activity or provide opportunities. Some examples are shown in Figure 10.3.

Subsidies may be given to businesses that make 'green products' such as solar heating systems. This should encourage businesses to produce 'green products'.
A council may offer firms rent-free units if they locate on a local industrial estate. This would affect business location decisions.
Employment subsidies may be given to firms that create jobs in a depressed area. This would influence business decisions relating to recruitment and location.
New legislation may force construction companies to increase the energy efficiency of buildings. This would influence the decision on which materials to use in production.
Free government advice and training may be given to businesses that launch products overseas. This might affect the decision whether to risk exporting or not.

Figure 10.3 *Examples of government influence on business activity*

One of the most important ways in which the government influences business decision making is through **fiscal policy** and **monetary policy**. This is discussed below.

QUESTION 1

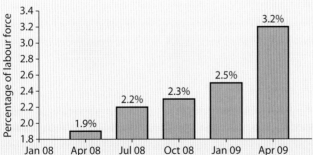

Figure 10.4 *Unemployment in Singapore*

It is suggested that Singapore went into recession in 2008–2009.

(a) What evidence is there in Figure 10.4 to support this view?

(b) How might a Singapore holiday company selling luxury cruises react to the pattern shown in Figure 10.4?

Key terms

Economic growth – an increase in income, output and expenditure over a period of time.

Fiscal policy – using changes in taxation and government expenditure to manage the economy.

Inflation – a rise in the general price level.

Interest – the price of borrowed money.

Monetary policy – using changes in interest rates and the money supply to manage the economy.

Monopoly – where one business dominates the whole market.

Unemployment – when people are out of work and cannot find a job.

Did you know?

In 2010 some governments around the world planned to cut public expenditure very sharply. This was because government borrowing had reached unsustainable levels. Such measures are likely to influence business objectives. For example, many businesses began to prepare for lower levels of demand. Surviving government cuts became an important objective for many businesses.

Key fact

Generally, lower taxes are better for businesses than higher taxes. This is because high taxes will reduce demand and discourage work and enterprise.

Fiscal policy

Governments can influence businesses when using fiscal policy. Fiscal policy involves changing the levels of taxation and government spending to adjust the level of demand in the economy. Governments can use changes in taxes and government spending to help achieve their aims. For example, a government might lower taxes to help create more jobs. Such a move would affect businesses because there would be more demand from people who have more money to spend.

Government expenditure

In the public sector the government is likely to provide a range of services. These might include healthcare, education, defence, policing, a judicial system and transport networks. The amount of money spent by governments on these services will vary enormously. For example, in less developed countries governments will tend to spend less because they are relatively poor. Sweden, however, has a reputation for very high levels of public expenditure.

Government spending levels will influence businesses. Generally, higher levels of spending will be welcomed by businesses. However, it often depends where the money is spent. For example, if a government decides to build a new motorway, businesses in the construction industry are likely to benefit the most.

Taxation

Taxes are paid by businesses and individuals. Different countries have different sorts of taxes. Some taxes are *direct*, which means they are charged on income. Examples include income tax, which is paid on personal income, and corporation tax, which is paid on company profits. Some taxes are *indirect*, which means they are put on spending. Value Added Tax (VAT), which is paid when buying goods and services, is an example.

Examples of the way changes in taxes might influence businesses are outlined below.

- If income tax is lowered, there would be more spending in the economy. Businesses may respond by increasing production or raising prices.

- Businesses may respond to higher corporation tax by cutting investment or reducing dividends.

- An increase in VAT may raise prices so demand might fall. However, businesses may decide to cut profit margins to keep prices the same.

QUESTION 2

In 2009, the New Zealand government announced some tax changes to help businesses. They were expected to save small and medium-sized businesses $480 million over four years. The changes were also designed to help businesses manage their cash flows. This is because businesses could delay paying their tax. The measures included:

- reducing the amount of tax that businesses pay in advance

- reducing interest rates on underpaid and overpaid tax

- lifting the GST (goods and services tax) registration threshold from $40,000 to $60,000. This means that small businesses do not have to charge GST until their turnover is $60,000.

(a) How will the tax measures introduced in New Zealand support businesses?

(b) Why do businesses prefer lower taxes?

Monetary policy

Monetary policy involves the government adjusting the money supply to control demand in the economy. This often means that **interest** rates are changed. Interest is paid when money is borrowed. Higher interest rates mean that consumers and firms will borrow less so demand in the economy will fall. In contrast, lower interest rates will increase demand in the economy because it will be cheaper to borrow.

Changes in the interest rate can influence businesses. Generally, high interest rates are bad for businesses for the following reasons.

- Costs rise when interest charges increase. This will reduce profit.
- The purchase of capital goods funded by borrowing is discouraged because it is more expensive.
- People's mortgage payments rise so they have less to spend.
- Demand for goods bought with borrowed money will fall because it is dearer.

Changes in the interest rate will have a bigger impact on those businesses which have lots of debt. These changes will also affect those which produce goods bought with borrowed money such as cars, houses, and consumer durables.

Regional policy

Regional policy (see Chapter 10) is designed to solve regional problems such as unemployment, congestion and regional income inequality. In some countries there is often a tendency for certain industries to congregate in a particular area or region. When these industries decline the whole region suffers. Unemployment rises and levels of business activity are low. A lot of regional policy aims at attracting new businesses into these 'run-down' areas. Therefore, regional policy will influence location decisions made by businesses.

Did you know?

Monetary policy has been used in many countries recently to help businesses during the world recession. For example, interest rates have been reduced substantially to make borrowing cheap. This should increase consumer demand and make it cheaper for businesses to invest.

Did you know?

For the period 2007–2013, the EU's regional policy is the EU's second largest budget item, with an allocation of €348 billion. Money is distributed through the Structural and Cohesion Funds. These are designed to support social and economic restructuring across the EU. They are divided into three separate funds:

- European Regional Development Fund (ERDF), which provides money for the development of human resources – to fund training for example.
- European Social Fund (ESF), which provides money in the most disadvantaged regions for infrastructure development.
- Cohesion Fund, which provides money to strengthen the economic and social cohesion of the EU.

Chapter review – Government influences on businesses

Most governments set a *budget* each year which outlines their spending plans for the future. It also states how revenue is to be raised from taxes. In 2009, a government budget contained some measures to help businesses. Some examples are outlined below.

- Tax allowances on investment were increased (this makes investment cheaper).
- Loss relief was extended. This means that a business loss can be offset against profits in a certain period. This reduces the tax paid by businesses.
- Money was provided to firms investing in renewable energy such as wind farms and solar power.
- Dividends paid by multinational businesses to foreign investors will be exempt from tax.

A manufacturer is considering the construction of a new warehouse.

(a) How might the decision be affected by the 2009 budget measures? **(2 marks)**

Some businesses have foreign investors.

(b) How might these be affected by the budget? **(2 marks)**

(c) Outline the role of the government when managing the economy. **(4 marks)**

(d) Analyse why businesses prefer lower interest rates. **(4 marks)**

(e) Evaluate the need for government intervention in the economy. **(8 marks)**

Chapter 11: Government influence on businesses – legislation and other controls

Getting started...

Chapter 10 showed that a government's economic policies can influence business activity. However, a government can also influence business objectives and decisions by passing legislation that is intended specifically for businesses. Much of this legislation is designed to protect people and the environment from the impact of business activity. Look at the example below.

Vehicle glass cartel

In 2008, the European Competition Commission imposed a record fine of €1.38 billion on four car glass manufacturers for operating a cartel (where a group of firms secretly join together and exploit customers) and sharing commercial secrets. The four companies were found guilty of running a cartel between 1998 and 2003. They discussed target prices, market-sharing and customer allocations during secret meetings in hotels and airports. The European Commission said these companies cheated the car industry and car buyers in a market worth €2 billion in the last year of the cartel.

(a) How have customers been affected in this case?

(b) How have the authorities influenced businesses in this case?

Figure 11.1 *A car windscreen*

Consumer protection

Consumers want to buy good quality products at a fair price. They want information about products that is accurate, clear and with good customer service. They do not want to buy goods which may be dangerous, overpriced or sold to them on the grounds of false claims.

The activities of monopolies and markets which are dominated by a few large firms have to be monitored. Without government regulation some firms would exploit consumers by using **anti-competitive practices** or **restrictive practices**. Such practices might include:

● **Increasing prices:** Prices are increased so that they are higher than they would be in a competitive market. For example, some manufacturers supply goods to retailers and insist that they are retailed at a fixed price.

● **Restricting consumer choice:** A manufacturer might refuse to supply a retailer if that retailer stocks rival products. This will reduce choice for the consumer.

● **Raising barriers to entry:** For example, some companies might spend huge amounts of money on advertising, which smaller companies couldn't afford to spend. A dominant firm might also lower its price for a specific product for a temporary period. This would make it difficult for a new business to break into the market. If the new business disappears as a result of this, the dominant firm would increase its prices again.

● **Market sharing:** This might occur if there is *collusion*. This is what happened in the above example in the market for glass. If a market is shared between the dominant firms, choice is restricted and price rises.

How does legislation protect the consumer?

Some countries have a lot of consumer legislation. It covers a variety of consumer issues and aims to protect consumers from some of the practices mentioned above. Figure 11.2 shows some examples.

Figure 11.2 *Consumer issues covered by legislation*

Legislation exists to prevent businesses from activities such as making false claims about the performance of their products, selling goods that are not fit for human consumption and selling goods that are not 'fit for purpose'. If businesses break consumer laws they may be fined and have to compensate consumers for any loss.

The growth in consumer legislation is likely to influence businesses. Many have responded by focusing more effectively on the needs of consumers. Many businesses now aim to match or exceed customer expectations and the terms of the legislation. Complying with consumer legislation also imposes costs on businesses. For example, they may have to spend more money informing consumers about their rights.

Key facts

Some examples of UK consumer legislation are as follows:
- **Sale of Goods Act, 1979:** This states that products sold by businesses must be of a merchantable quality and fit for the purpose. For example, customers cannot be sold paint which peels off in the sun after one month or a waterproof coat that lets in the rain.
- **Food Safety Act, 1990:** This law means that food should be fit for human consumption and comply with safety standards. For example, a business should not sell frozen food if it has thawed out and refrozen or fresh produce that is decaying.
- **Trade Descriptions Act, 1968:** This law is designed to prevent businesses from making false claims about the performance of their products. For example, a producer of herbal remedies cannot claim that a particular product cures an illness if it does not.

QUESTION 1

In January 2010, all restaurants and cafes in the UAE were ordered to stop adding any service charges to their bills. The Director General of the Ministry of Economy, Ahmed Bin Abul Aziz Al-Shehi, said that it was illegal for non-tourist restaurants to add service charges. Restaurants and cafes operating inside hotels and those paying taxes to the local governments are the only exception. He also said that inspection teams will be employed to ensure that the law was not broken.

The law prohibiting this practice is Consumer Protection Law Number 24/2006. The enforcement followed a flood of complaints about surcharges from consumers nation-wide. Consumers said that illegal service charges of between 5 per cent and 20 per cent were imposed on bills by most restaurants and cafes in the country.

(a) Outline how consumers are being exploited in this case study.

(b) How has the government influenced businesses in this case study?

Key facts

Two examples of UK legislation to protect consumers are:

- The **Fair Trading Act, 1973** stated that a monopoly is said to exist if a business has at least a 25 per cent market share. The Act set up the Office of Fair Trading (OFT) whose responsibility it is to oversee all policy relating to competition and consumer protection.
- The **Competition Act, 1998** outlaws agreements, cartels or practices which prevent, restrict or distort competition. It also set up the Competition Commission which carries out enquiries into mergers and anti-competitive practices.

Did you know?

Business start-up schemes can be used to provide funds for new businesses. **Business Links** provide information and advice on running a business and obtaining finance. These services are usually provided by the government. Taxes are also lower for small firms.

Did you know?

Many countries use minimum wages to protect employees from exploitation. If a minimum wage is imposed, it means that no employer is allowed to pay a wage rate which is below the minimum wage. This helps to raise the incomes and living standards of those in poorly paid jobs.

Competition policy

One of the roles of the government in the economy is to promote competition. This helps to prevent anti-competitive practices and consumer exploitation. How might they do this?

- **Encourage the growth of small firms:** If more small firms are encouraged to join markets there will be more competition. With more small firms the market is less likely to be dominated by one very large firm. Several measures can be used to help the growth of small firms.

- **Lower barriers to entry:** If **barriers to entry** are lowered or removed then more firms will join a market. This will make it more competitive. For example, in some countries public transport was provided solely by the public sector. However, laws have been changed to allow private companies to provide public transport services.

- **Introduce anti-competitive legislation:** Many countries have laws which help to promote competition. Such laws are often designed to protect consumers from exploitation by monopolies, mergers and restrictive practices. Some countries have special bodies or agencies that are responsible for overseeing all policy relating to competition and consumer protection. They may also carry out enquiries into mergers, takeovers and anti-competitive practices.

Health and Safety legislation

In some jobs the working environment can be dangerous. For example, it is reckoned that in India nearly 50,000 workers die from work-related accidents or illness every year. Because of the danger to employees, governments aim to protect workers by passing legislation which forces businesses to provide a safe and healthy workplace. This is discussed in Chapter 20.

Employment legislation

Governments often pass legislation to protect peoples' rights at work. Without such protection some businesses would exploit their workers. For example, they might pay low wages, make them work long hours, discriminate against certain groups and dismiss them unfairly. In addition to providing a healthy and safe working environment businesses have other legal obligations. This is discussed in Chapter 20.

Environmental legislation and other controls

Business activity can have a serious negative impact on the environment.

- **Pollution:** There are different types of pollution. Water pollution may be caused by businesses dumping waste into rivers, streams, canals, lakes and the sea. An example would be warm water or chemicals being leaked into rivers. Air pollution may be caused by businesses discharging waste or gases into the air. Noise pollution can also be a problem. Noise from factory machinery, loud music from pubs and night clubs, and low flying aircraft by airports are examples.

- **Destruction of wildlife habitats:** When businesses develop on greenfield sites plant and animal life is often destroyed. Also, a new business development can spoil an area of outstanding natural beauty.

- **Traffic congestion:** Extra traffic caused by commercial vehicles or workers travelling to and from work can cause congestion resulting in delays and accidents.

- **Wasted resources:** Some businesses waste resources. For example, many argue that some of the packaging used by businesses is unnecessary. It is also argued that many businesses do not make enough use of recycled materials.

Environmental legislation

One approach used by many governments to minimise the damage done by businesses to the environment is to pass new laws. Much of the pressure for environmental legislation has emerged due to the growing concerns about global warming. If businesses fail to comply with environmental laws they may be fined or forced to close until the problem is resolved.

Taxes and subsidies

Taxation can also be used to help reduce pollution. For example, if a tax is imposed on a firm that produces harmful emissions, production costs will increase and the prices charged by the firm will rise. This should reduce demand for the firm's product and therefore reduce pollution.

Governments can offer grants, tax allowances and other subsidies to firms as an incentive to reduce pollution and encourage 'greener' practices. For example, a firm might receive a subsidy if it builds a plastics recycling plant. This might encourage households and firms to recycle their plastic waste instead of dumping it.

QUESTION 2

In 2009, Thames Water was fined £125,000 and ordered to pay £21,335 in costs after polluting the River Wandle. Sodium hydroxide had been accidentally released into the river in September 2007. Over 7,000 fish were killed on a stretch of the river which is a popular fishing spot. The prosecution said when staff at a Thames Water's sewage treatment works realised the chemical had escaped they thought it would only cause 'limited damage'. Thames Water said the death of the fish had been caused by a 'juvenile' error.

Figure 11.3 *Results of river pollution*

(a) Describe the impact that this accident has had.

(b) How has the government intervened in this case?

Key terms

Anti-competitive practices or restrictive trade practices – an attempt by firms to prevent or restrict competition.

Barriers to entry – obstacles that make it difficult for new firms to enter a market.

Government influence and business objectives

As a result of government influence on business in the form of legislation and controls, some businesses have made adjustments to their objectives. Many have become more socially responsible and want to improve their image. One way of doing this is to take into account the needs of other stakeholders. If a business has a bad image or a poor reputation it may lose customers.

Chapter review – Seattle Logistics

Chuck Rivers runs a transport company and warehousing operation called Seattle Logistics. He owns a fleet of haulage trucks and a large warehouse where 210 workers are employed. Chuck has been struggling to keep his business alive in recent years and blames the minimum wage for rising costs. Minimum wages in the US are, at the time of writing, $8.55 per hour. By law all businesses must pay their workers **at least** the minimum wage. Chuck says: 'I could pay my labourers $6 per hour in this neighbourhood. Wage costs are killing this company. I used to make good profits but now my main aim is to stay in business.'

Another issue that concerns Chuck is the threat of legislation to restrict carbon emissions in the US. President Obama wants to introduce legislation to cap carbon emissions to reduce the volume of greenhouse gases produced by the nation. Chuck fears that if legislation is introduced he will have to scrap more than half of his fleet because they are old and produce too much carbon.

(a) (i) Why do governments impose minimum wages? **(2 marks)**
    (ii) How has employment legislation influenced Seattle Logistics? **(4 marks)**

(b) (i) How does the graph in Figure 11.4 support President Obama's view that there should be a cap on carbon emissions? **(2 marks)**
    (ii) How might the proposed environmental legislation influence Seattle Logistics? **(4 marks)**

(c) How have the business objectives of Seattle Logistics been influenced by the government in this case? **(2 marks)**

(d) Do you think it is right for the government to influence businesses? **(6 marks)**

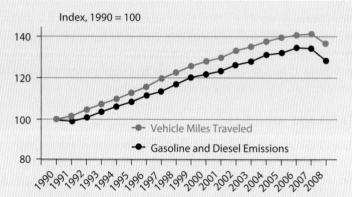

Figure 11.4 *US vehicle miles travelled and CO$_2$ emissions from gasoline and diesel transportation fuel use, 1990–2008*

Figure 11.5 *US haulage truck*

Chapter 12: International trade and exchange rates

Getting started...

Businesses operate in an international environment. For example, many businesses sell their products overseas. They may also buy resources from abroad. Trade between nations has grown a lot in recent years. One reason for this is because many countries have become more open. There has also been a growth in the size and number of multinationals. Look at the example below.

Samsung

Samsung is one of the world's largest multinationals. Based in South Korea it has many international businesses including:

- Samsung Electronics, the world's largest electronics company

- Samsung Heavy Industries, one of the world's largest shipbuilders

- Samsung Engineering & Construction, a major global construction company.

Samsung accounts for more than 20 per cent of South Korea's total exports. It is the leader in many domestic industries, such as chemical and retail industries. Samsung currently sponsors the English Premier League football club, Chelsea.

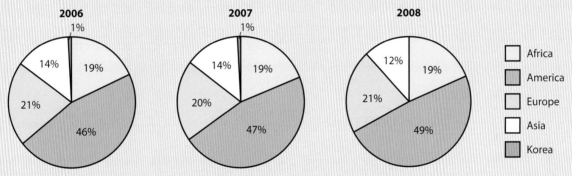

Figure 12.1 *Samsung – geographical analysis of turnover*

Look at Figure 12.1.

(a) Why is international trade important to Samsung?

(b) How might international trade help a business like Samsung grow?

International trade

International trade benefits the world. It creates opportunities for business growth, increases competition and provides more consumer choice. However, there are some specific reasons why countries trade with each other.

- **To obtain goods that cannot be produced domestically:** Many countries are unable to produce certain goods. This is because they lack the natural resources needed for such production. For example, most northern European countries cannot produce foods like tropical fruits because they do not have the right climate.

- **To obtain goods that can be bought more cheaply from overseas:** Some countries can produce goods more efficiently than others. This may be because they have cheaper resources. For example, China can produce cheap manufactured goods because labour is cheap.

- **To improve consumer choice:** International trade provides more choice for consumers. One reason is because some countries both buy and sell the same products. For example, Nestlé (Switzerland) and Mars (US) both produce confectionery. They also sell their products in both countries.

- **To sell off surplus commodities:** Some countries have so much of a resource they could never use it all themselves. For example, Saudi Arabia has huge reserves of oil. It produces far more than it can use.

Visible and invisible trade

Goods and services sold overseas are called **exports**. Those bought from other countries are called **imports**. Economists distinguish between **visible trade** and **invisible trade**.

- Visible trade involves trade in physical goods. For example, India sells textiles, leather goods, gems and jewellery overseas. These are visible exports for India. On the other hand, India buys oil, fertiliser and chemicals from overseas. These are examples of visible imports for India. The difference between total visible exports and imports is called the **visible balance** or the **balance of trade**. Figure 12.2 shows India's visible trade in 2008–2009. The balance of trade is −$69,181 million ($96,732−$165,913). It has imported more goods than it has exported.

- Invisible trade involves trade in services. For example, the money India gets from tourists is recorded as an invisible export. On the other hand, India pays foreign carriers to transport goods to other countries. Payments for this service are recorded as invisible imports.

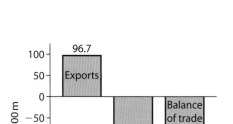

Figure 12.2 *India's visible balance (April to September 2008-2009)*

QUESTION 1

Poland became an open economy after the break-up of the Soviet Union in 1991. In the last decade, Poland's foreign trade has increased almost ten-fold. Poland exports processed fruit and vegetables, meat, dairy products, vehicles, aircraft and vessels. Most of Poland's imports are capital goods and inputs for manufacturing. Examples include machinery, chemicals, minerals, fuels and lubricants.

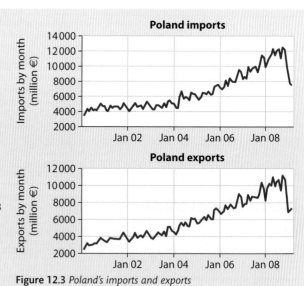

Figure 12.3 *Poland's imports and exports*

(a) (i) Describe the pattern of international trade in Poland over the period shown.
(ii) What might account for the pattern identified in **(i)**?

(b) Why do you think Poland imports **(i)** capital goods; **(ii)** resources such as minerals and fuels?

Benefits and opportunities resulting from international trade

More and more countries encourage **free trade**. This is where a country allows foreign businesses access to its markets and the government does not restrict imports. The main benefits of free trade are summarised in Figure 12.4.

- **More consumer choice:** For example, consumers in Norway will be able to buy goods:

  - that are impossible to produce, such as tropical fruits and wine

  - made from materials that are not available in Norway, such as gold and diamonds

  - that other countries produce more cheaply, such as cars and consumer durables.

- **Competition:** Competition increases because most countries import goods that they can also produce themselves. For example, Germany both imports and exports cars. With overseas competition businesses will have to keep costs down, produce high-quality goods and be more innovative.

- **Growth:** Domestic markets may become saturated so by selling overseas businesses can generate more sales and more profit. This helps multinationals to develop.

- **Less risk:** Risk may be reduced when trading conditions become poor. For example, a multinational may survive poor trading conditions in Europe if it has growing markets in the Far East.

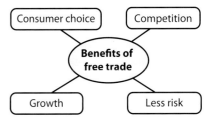

Figure 12.4 *Benefits of free trade*

Protectionism

Despite the benefits of international trade, countries sometimes believe that it is in their interests to restrict trade. For example, governments may think it is necessary to protect their domestic producers from overseas competition. Or they may give financial help to exporters. This approach is called **protectionism**. Governments can use a number of measures to restrict trade. They are called **trade barriers** and some examples are outlined below.

Methods of protectionism

- **Tariffs:** One way to restrict imports is to make them more expensive. This will reduce demand for imports and increase demand for home goods. Imports can be made more expensive if the government imposes a special tax on them. Taxes on imports are called **tariffs**. Tariffs also raise revenue for the government.

- **Quotas:** Another way of reducing imports is to place a physical limit on the amount allowed into the country. This is called a **quota**. By restricting the quantity of imports, domestic producers face less of a threat. They will have more of the market for themselves.

- **Subsidies:** Quotas and tariffs aim to reduce imports. Another approach to protectionism is to give a **subsidy** to domestic producers. This involves giving financial support, such as grants or tax breaks, to exporters or domestic producers that face fierce competition from imports.

Key fact

An extreme form of quota is an embargo. This is where imports are completely banned from a country. Most embargoes are imposed for political reasons. For example, America has had an embargo on trade with Cuba for political reasons for around 50 years.

- **Administrative barriers:** Some countries restrict imports by insisting that imported goods meet strict regulations and specifications. For example, a shipment of toys from the Far East might be returned if it fails to meet strict health and safety regulations. Goods that fail to reach cultural or environmental standards may also face administrative barriers.

- **Depreciating exchange rate:** It may be possible for the government to reduce imports and increase exports by allowing the exchange rate to fall. This may be called a **devaluation.** A lower exchange rate means that exports are cheaper and imports are dearer. As a result the demand for exports rises and the demand for imports falls. Exchange rates are discussed below.

What is an exchange rate?

Most countries in the world do not use the same currency. For example, China has the yuan, India has the rupee, America uses the US dollar and Britain has the pound. When countries use different currencies, transactions between people and firms in different countries are affected. For example, an Indian visitor to the US cannot use rupees when making payments. The Indian visitor would have to buy some US dollars.

How many dollars could the visitor get for 20,000 rupees? This depends on the **exchange rate** between the rupee and the dollar. If it were $1 = Rs50 the visitor would get $400 (Rs20,000 ÷ Rs50). The exchange rate shows the price of dollars in terms of rupees. When businesses buy goods from other countries payments are often made in another currency. Some more examples are given below.

Example 1 How much will it cost a French firm to buy goods from a British firm which cost £400,000 if £1 = €1.10? The cost to the French firm in euros is given by:

$$£400,000 \times 1.1 = €440,000$$

Example 2 How many US dollars will be needed by a British firm buying £55,000 of goods from an American firm if £1 = US$1.50? The cost to the British firm in US dollars is given by:

$$£55,000 \times \$1.50 = \$82,500$$

Example 3 How much will it cost a British firm in pounds to buy $300,000 of goods from a US firm if £1 = US$1.50? The cost in pounds is given by:

$$\$300,000 \div \$1.50 = £200,000$$

Figure 12.5 *A food processing plant*

QUESTION 2

British-based Miskin plc manufactures machines and other equipment for production lines in the food processing industry. About 40 per cent of its output is sold to American producers. However, Miskin buys materials and components from Germany and Spain. In May 2009, there were three important international transactions.

- A US firm bought machines from Miskin costing £3,600,000.

- Miskin bought components from a German firm for €2,500,000.

- Miskin bought materials from a Spanish firm for a sterling price of £200,000.

(a) Calculate the price in US dollars of the machines sold by Miskin to the US firm (assume £1 = $1.50).

(b) Calculate the amount paid in pounds by Miskin for the €2.5m components bought from Germany (assume £1 = €1.10).

(c) Calculate the amount in euros received by the Spanish supplier for the £200,000 of materials sold to Miskin (assume £1 = €1.10).

The impact of a depreciation in the exchange rate on imports and exports

Changes in the exchange rate can have an impact on the demand for exports and imports. This is because when the exchange rate changes the prices of exports and imports also change. Look at what happens when the exchange rate falls from £1 = US$1.50 to £1 = US$1.20.

- **Impact on exports:** If a UK firm *sells* goods worth £2m to a US customer, the dollar price at the original exchange rate is $3m (£2m × $1.50). When the exchange rate falls the dollar price of the goods also falls to $2.4m (£2m × $1.20). This means that demand for UK exports is likely to rise because they are now cheaper than they were.

- **Impact on imports:** If another UK firm *buys* goods worth $600,000 from a US supplier, the price in pounds at the original exchange rate is £400,000 ($600,000 ÷ $1.50). When the exchange rate falls the sterling price to the importer rises to £500,000 ($600,000 ÷ $1.20). This means that demand for imports is likely to fall because they are dearer.

The impact of an appreciation in the exchange rate on imports and exports

A rise in the exchange rate will have the opposite effect on the demand for exports and imports. Look at what happens when the exchange rate rises from £1 = $1.50 to £1 = $2.

- **Impact on exports:** If a UK firm sells goods worth £2m to a US customer, the dollar price at the original exchange rate is $3m (£2m ×$1.50). When the exchange rises the dollar price of the goods also rises to $4m (£2m × $2). This means that demand for UK exports is likely to fall because they are now dearer.

- **Impact on imports:** If another UK firm *buys* goods worth $600,000 from a US supplier, the price in pounds at the original exchange rate is £400,000 ($600,000 ÷ $1.50). When the exchange rate rises the sterling price to the importer falls to £300,000 ($600,000 ÷ $2). This means that demand for imports is likely to rise because they are cheaper.

The effects of changes in the exchange rate on the demand for exports and imports are summarised in Figure 12.6.

Exchange Rate	Price of Exports	Demand for Exports	Price of Imports	Demand for Imports
Falls	Falls	Rises	Rises	Falls
Rises	Rises	Falls	Falls	Rises

Figure 12.6 *A summary of the effects of changing exchange rates*

Key terms

Balance of trade or visible balance – the difference between visible exports and visible imports.

Devaluation – the depreciation or fall in the value of a currency.

Exchange rate – the price of one currency in terms of another.

Exports – goods and services sold overseas.

Free trade – trade between nations that is completely without government restrictions.

Imports – goods and services bought from overseas.

Invisible trade – trade in services.

Visible trade – trade in physical goods.

Protectionism – an approach used by a government to protect domestic producers.

Quota – a physical limit on the quantity of imports allowed into a country.

Subsidy – financial support given to a domestic producer to help compete with overseas firms.

Tariff – a tax on imports to make them more expensive.

Trade barriers – measures designed to restrict trade.

Key fact

Another problem is that it costs money to switch from one currency to another. There is a usually a commission charge of around 2 per cent. This represents a cost to importers and therefore reduces profit.

How are businesses affected by exchange rates?

The examples above show what happens to the prices of imports and exports when exchange rates appreciate and depreciate. Sometimes these changes will benefit a business, other times they will not. For example, if the value of the rupee falls, Indian exporters will benefit because the price of exports falls and demand should increase. However, Indian importers will lose out because their purchases will be more expensive.

Fluctuating exchange rates cause uncertainty. Businesses do not know what is going to happen to exchange rates in the future. This means that it is difficult to predict demand for exports and the cost of imports. This makes planning and budgeting more difficult.

Chapter review – Nampak

South Africa has benefited from international trade since its economy became more open in 1994. It has lots of mineral resources and is a major exporter of gold, platinum, coal and diamonds. South Africa also has a growing tourist industry. In contrast, South Africa imports machinery, foodstuffs, chemicals, petroleum products and scientific instruments.

Nampak is an emerging multinational based in Sandton, Johannesburg. It manufactures packaging such as drinks cans, aerosol cans, bottles, labels, tubes, crates and drums. It also makes packaging products for confectionery and snack foods. Nampak has operations in 10 African countries and has markets in Europe. It is one of the leading manufacturers of folding cartons for the food industry in Europe and makes cartons, leaflets and labels for the healthcare market.

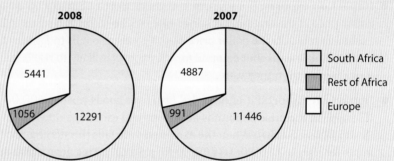

Figure 12.7 *Nampak turnover 2007–2008 (Rm)*

(a) State two reasons why nations trade. (Use examples from this case study.) **(2 marks)**

(b) What is meant by an invisible export? (Use an example from this case study.) **(2 marks)**

(c) Outline two methods of protectionism a government might use to reduce imports. **(4 marks)**

(d) **(i)** How will Nampak be affected by exchange rates? **(2 marks)**

(ii) If €1 = R10, how much would a European customer have to pay in euros for R124m of packaging? **(2 marks)**

(iii) If the exchange rate rose to €1 = R12 how might Nampak be affected? **(2 marks)**

(e) Discuss the problems businesses like Nampak are likely to have with fluctuating exchange rates. **(6 marks)**

Chapter 13: External influences

Getting started...

Business decisions are influenced by external factors other than those set by the government. These include economic, social, ethical, environmental and technological factors. Over time these change and create opportunities and constraints for businesses. Look at the example below.

Electric vehicles

Most car manufacturers are trying to develop alternatives to petrol-fuelled vehicles. This is because of the high price of oil and the damage done by cars to the environment. Most big carmakers plan to launch an electric car by 2012. For example, Honda and Toyota have already produced their hybrid cars which run on a combination of petrol and electricity.

Nissan has recently launched an electric vehicle (EV) prototype. The car will use a battery that will recharge in four hours. The car is expected to cost about 4 cents a mile to run. Nissan said that several hundred new jobs would be created in Sunderland (UK) where it planned to make the batteries for the car.

(a) What external factors have contributed to the development of electric cars?

(b) Outline two advantages to consumers of electric vehicles.

(c) How might Nissan benefit from the launch of its electric vehicle?

Figure 13.1 *An electric vehicle*

The economic environment

The state of the economy will influence the decisions made by businesses. This includes local, national and world economies. In Chapter 10 we saw how the economy grows. However, the pattern of growth is uneven. For example, between 1990 and 2007 most countries in the world enjoyed strong economic growth. This provided lots of opportunities for businesses. Many were able to expand, invest in new facilities, develop new products, take on more staff and enjoy more profit. However, in 2008 there was a global recession and, although there was a recovery at the end of 2009 and in 2010, fears were growing about the possibility in some countries of another recession. During a recession many businesses struggle to survive. Demand for many goods and services falls because unemployment rises. Businesses lose confidence, make cutbacks and place more emphasis on survival rather than profitability.

The social environment

Changes in society

Businesses have to adapt to any changes that occur in society. Some examples of changes that have occurred in recent years are outlined below.

- **More consumer awareness:** Consumers have higher expectations than ever before. They have easy access through the internet to lots of information about products and are more aware of their rights. As a result many businesses have become more customer-focused.

- **Changing demand patterns:** Changes in society bring about changes in demand for products. For example, modern lifestyles mean many people expect goods to be delivered to their doors. Consequently there has been a growth in home delivered goods such as takeaway food, rented DVDs and a whole range of personal, domestic and other services.

- **Increased numbers of women at work:** In many countries more and more women have abandoned the traditional child-rearing role and have combined family life with employment and running businesses. This has increased the supply of labour for businesses and helped to increase the number of business start-ups.

- **More part-time workers:** In many countries there has been a huge increase in the number of people taking on part-time work. This has helped to improve flexibility in business organisations because part-time labour is more flexible.

- **Urbanisation:** In some countries such as India, Brazil and China, very large numbers of people have left rural areas to live in towns and cities. This has provided businesses with more labour and created additional markets where goods and services can be supplied.

Did you know?

Businesses are more likely to behave ethically if they are challenged by **pressure groups**. These are organisations or groups of people who try to influence business decision making. For example, environmental pressure groups, such as Greenpeace, campaign to prevent businesses from damaging the environment. Local communities, consumer groups and employees may form pressure groups. Trade unions are an important pressure group. They represent the rights of employees in the workplace.

Business ethics

Businesses often have to make ethical decisions. **Business ethics** is about morality – 'doing the right thing'. For example, should a business:

- make more use of recycled materials even though profits will fall?

- test its products on animals?

- buy goods from suppliers that employ child labour?

- use a bribe to secure an overseas contract in a country where bribery is a part of the culture?

Often, if businesses adopt unethical practices they will make more profit. However, more and more businesses want to be 'good corporate citizens'. Therefore, they are more likely to behave more ethically. One way of doing this is to follow an ethical code of practice. This lays down guidelines on how employees should respond in situations where ethical issues arise. The code helps businesses to meet ethical standards.

Figure 13.2 *A flower picker*

QUESTION 1

Workers picking and packaging flowers in Kenya are no longer forced to work overtime or to accept casual contracts. This is a result of companies signing up to ethical codes of conduct. Pay slips are now available to staff, as are employment contracts, better medical facilities, improved housing and increased maternity leave. Better training in the use of pesticides and the stricter controls on the spraying of pesticides have also been introduced. More women have been promoted to supervisory roles and staff welfare committees have been established. Workers are also joining trade unions in increasing numbers.

(a) What is an ethical code of conduct?

(b) How have the Kenyan flower pickers benefited from an ethical code of conduct?

The environment and sustainability

Evidence suggests that as economies grow environmental damage increases. Businesses are often blamed for pollution and congestion (see Chapter 11). Some examples of other environmental issues are outlined below.

- **Global warming:** Governments are becoming concerned about global warming, which may be affecting weather patterns and climates. Some of the greenhouse gases which contribute to global warming come from factories. Also, economic development means that car ownership and air travel increases. The emissions from cars and aircraft also add to global warming.

- **Habitat destruction:** Some business development destroys wildlife habitats and spoils the natural environment. For example, around half of the forests that once covered the planet are now gone. Forests are important for the survival of the planet. At least 120 out of 620 living primate species will be extinct in the next 10 to 20 years. Many other species are under threat such as tigers, mountain gorillas and pandas.

- **Resource depletion:** In addition to the loss of forests many other resources are at risk. Here are some examples.

  - Oil, coal, gas and minerals are non-renewable resources and, therefore, cannot be replaced. Because of this, as business development gathers pace these resources are depleted.

  - Fish stocks are falling. The world's marine catch increased from 18.5m tons in 1950 to 82.5m tons in 1992. This staggering growth is threatening millions of people who depend on fishing for their livelihoods.

  - Fertile soil, which is needed to grow food, is being lost. This is due to deforestation, poor farming practices, over-grazing, urban sprawl and land pollution.

- **Sustainable development:** Many governments are talking about **sustainable development**. This means that people should satisfy their needs and enjoy better living standards without reducing the quality of life of future generations. Business development that denies future generations of resources is not sustainable. This means that the use of resources by businesses and consumers needs to be reduced. If businesses take a sustainable approach they will also find it easier to comply with regulations, reduce costs, improve their image and increase profits.

Technology

The development of new technology continues to have a huge impact on businesses. New technology results in new products which in turn provide new market opportunities. Also, new technology means production becomes more capital-intensive and costs are reduced. Here are some examples:

- In the primary sector the use of tractors, mechanical harvesters, grain-drying machines and automatic feeding systems have helped to lower costs in agriculture. Chemicals and pesticides have also helped to increase crop yields.

- In the secondary sector the introduction of robots on production lines has reduced costs. They are cheaper to employ than people because they can

Did you know?

To help reduce resource depletion businesses could:

- design packaging that can be reused or recycled
- use more energy-efficient equipment or renewable energy sources
- explore ways of selling waste to other businesses as a by-product
- reduce business travel and use video conferencing for meetings.

Key terms

Business ethics – ideas, in business, about what is morally right or wrong.

Pressure groups – groups of people without political power who seek to influence decision makers in politics, society and businesses.

Sustainable development – the idea that people should satisfy their basic needs and enjoy improved living standards without compromising the quality of life of future generations.

work 24/7. In some factories production is entirely automated. Computers are used to design products and the information is then fed into CNC (computer numerically controlled) machines which can carry out tasks such as cutting, milling, sewing, moulding and welding.

● The use of technology in service industries, i.e. the tertiary sector, has reduced costs. For example, the use of Automatic Teller Machines (ATMs) for dispensing cash has reduced costs in the banking industry. Internet banking has also helped to reduce costs because customers can manage their accounts online.

● The use of IT has helped to reduce administration and communication costs in business. For example, many routine tasks can be carried out quickly by computer. Huge amounts of data can be gathered, processed, manipulated, stored and retrieved using computer databases. A wide range of different information can be sent electronically anywhere in the world instantly.

The impact of technology in business, and the development of e-commerce, is discussed in detail in Chapter 48.

Chapter review – Recycling, holidays abroad and the environment

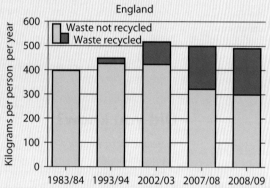

Figure 13.3 *Household waste recycling*

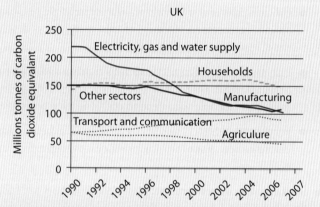

Figure 13.5 *Source of greenhouse gas emissions*

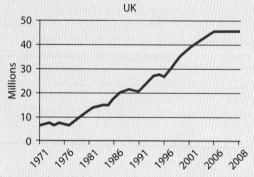

Figure 13.4 *UK residents' holiday visits abroad*

(a) **(i)** What does the graph in Figure 13.3 show? **(2 marks)**
(ii) What contributions might businesses have made to the reduction of waste in society? **(4 marks)**
(iii) What is meant by sustainable business development? **(2 marks)**

(b) Outline one possible reason for the trend shown in Figure 13.4. **(2 marks)**

Look at Figure 13.5.

(c) Which source of greenhouse gas emission has increased the most over the time period? **(2 marks)**

The government could impose a tax on air travel to help reduce greenhouse gas emissions.

(d) Evaluate the case for and against such action. **(8 marks)**

Chapter 14: Judging success

Getting started...

Business owners want their businesses to be successful. However, how can owners measure and judge that success? A lot depends on the objectives of the business. For example, if a company's main objective is to maximise profit, the amount of profit made by a business can be used to measure its success. Look at the example below.

Huawei Technologies

Huawei is China's largest manufacturer of telecommunications equipment. It employs over 87,000 people and makes a broad range of products. These include mobile phone handsets and videoconferencing systems. In the last year Huawei has:

- built a leading position in wireless, it is now ranked second in global market share of radio access equipment
- reduced resource consumption by more than 20 per cent. It also has over 3,000 sites powered by alternative energies that promote the sustainable development of the industry and society.

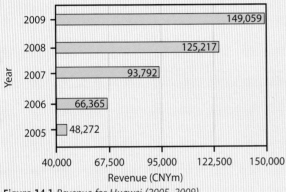

Figure 14.1 *Revenue for Huawei (2005–2009)*

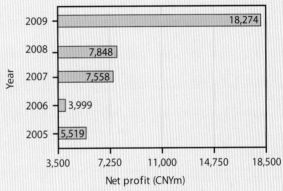

Figure 14.2 *Net profit for Huawei (2005-2009)*

(a) What evidence is there to suggest that Huawei is a successful business?

(b) What other information might be helpful to make an improved judgment about the success of Huawei?

Measures of success

The success of a business can be judged in different ways. The main approaches are outlined below.

Profit

Most private sector businesses aim to make a profit. Therefore rising profits should signal improving success. However, a number of factors have to be taken into account.

- It is possible to make higher profits if there is no competition in the market. Therefore, profits made by a monopoly are not as impressive as profits made in a competitive market.

- The amount of profit made by a business will often depend on its size. For example, a large multinational company is likely to make more profit than a sole trader. It is possible to take into account the size of a business when measuring profit. One approach is to compare the profit to the amount of money invested in the business by calculating the *return on capital employed*. Another is to compare the profit with the size of turnover by calculating the *profit margin*. Both of these approaches are discussed in detail in Chapter 46.

● Profit should also be compared with that made by other businesses in the same industry. This will provide a better indication of success because different industries often expect different profit levels. For example, it may not be appropriate to compare the profit made by a farmer with that made by an insurance company.

● Profit can only be used to measure success if the objective of the business is to maximise profit. For example, some small business owners are often content to make a 'modest' amount of profit. They may not want the responsibility or the hard work that often comes with striving for higher profits.

Size

Many businesses aim to grow, therefore the size of the business is important when judging success. However, there are several different ways of measuring size. The main ones are:

● **Turnover:** The turnover of a business could be used to measure size. For example, Lenovo, the Chinese computer company, is a large business. Its turnover in 2009 was over $14bn.

● **The number of employees:** A business with thousands of employees may be considered large. For example, Ford, the US car giant, employed over 280,000 people in 2008.

● **Market share:** It could be argued that a business with a 43 per cent market share is more successful than one which has a 9 per cent market share in the same industry. Coca-Cola, for example sells over 50 per cent of all cola drinks worldwide.

● **The amount of capital employed:** *Capital employed* is the amount of money invested in a business. The more money invested the larger the business.

● **EU definitions of size:** The EU defines the size of firms according to turnover, the number of employees and the capital employed. The definitions are summarised in Figure 14.3.

	Small	Medium-sized	Large
Turnover	Less than €10m	€10m to €50m	Greater than €50m
No. of employees	Less than 50	50 to 249	Greater than 249
Capital employed	Less than €10m	€10m to €43m	Greater than €43m

Figure 14.3 *The size of firms as defined by the EU*

Did you know?

In 2008, Ergon Energy, the Australian energy company, had capital employed of AUS$2,523.8 million. In contrast, Kresta Holdings, the Australian window and soft furnishings company, had capital employed of AUS$20.48 million. Clearly, Ergon is the larger business.

QUESTION 1

The Tata Group is an Indian-based business. It produces steel, motor cars, chemicals, electricity and watches. It also provides services such as telecommunications, IT consultancy, hotels and hospitality. The company employs more than 360,000 people and has operations in over 80 different countries. In 2008, Tata had a turnover of $62.5bn and made a profit of $5.4bn.

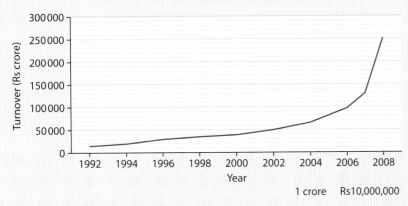

Figure 14.4 *Tata Group turnover 1992–2008*

(a) Using evidence from the case study, and the information in Figure 14.4, determine whether Tata Group is a small, medium-sized or large business.

(b) Do you think Tata Group has been successful?

Product quality

Some businesses are extremely focused on their products. They strive for very high quality and technical excellence. Their success will often be judged by measures of product quality and innovation. Product quality might be reflected by:

- awards and prizes won by businesses

- media reports

- customer surveys

- sales levels when new products are launched

- certification by international quality standards.

Product quality is discussed in more detail in Chapter 49.

Social responsibility

An increasing number of businesses are making an effort to become good corporate citizens. This means they try to meet the needs of a wider range of stakeholders, such as employees, suppliers, the local community and the environment. Many large companies carry out a **social audit** to judge the social impact and ethical behaviour of the business. This may involve an independent body judging whether social and ethical targets have been met.

Did you know?

With an annual turnover of over US $2.3 bn, Jindal Steel & Power Limited (JSPL) is a leader in steel, power, mining, oil and gas, and infrastructure. The company operates in Asia, Africa, South America and Georgia. It is committed to supporting local communities and employs an environment management department to take care of all the activities related to environmental safeguards. Some of its responsibilities include:

- assessing new projects and determining their impact on the environment
- seeking clearances in matters of environmental issues from government bodies
- constant monitoring of emissions/ discharges and their control
- ensuring compliance with statutory obligations on all environmental issues
- increasing awareness among the workforce about safeguarding the environment
- keeping plant areas clean through mechanised housekeeping initiatives.

Did you know?

Tour operators often get holidaymakers to fill in questionnaires on their homeward flights. The information from these questionnaires is then used to find out how well customers have been served. This allows firms to build on strengths and address weaknesses.

Consumer satisfaction

Many businesses will look at how consumers' needs and wants have been satisfied when judging success. If its customer service is good, a successful business will find that it has loyal customers and a growing customer base.

Many businesses are becoming more customer-focused and make efforts to get feedback from their customers. They monitor customer complaints very carefully. They might do this by having an effective complaints procedure. Such a procedure should encourage customers to record complaints without them feeling uncomfortable or threatened. Many businesses recognise that it takes a lot of effort for customers to complain. Therefore, the subject of any complaint should be taken seriously and action should be taken to make improvements.

QUESTION 2

How did we do?
Please give us your feedback...

Date of visit

DD   MM   YYYY

Time of visit

☐ am
☐ pm

Comments: (Please use **BLOCK CAPITALS**)

Please leave any preferred contact details

I wish to be contacted ☐

Remember you can also visit **www.tescocomments.com**

9553

Every little helps

Terms & Conditions. By sending us a text message we may identify your phone location. You may be located once and this will be done immediately for us to best action your comment. It will not cost you anything. No other terms or conditions apply. For further details visit www.tescocomments.com/terms. We will not disclose your phone number or email address to any third parties. Calls are free from a BT (or eircom in RoI) landline. Other providers may charge.

ECHRF6 **POWERED BY FIZZBACK**

Figure 14.5 *Tesco customer feedback form*

(a) What is the purpose of the form shown in Figure 14.5?

(b) How else does Tesco gather information from customers?

(c) Suggest how such information can be used to judge the success of Tesco.

The importance of targets when judging success

Many owners set objectives (targets)when running their businesses. This makes it easier to judge success. For example, a business might plan to grow its market share by 5 per cent. If, by the end of the trading year, market share has grown by 6.5 per cent, the business would be judged successful. Targets might also be used to motivate staff. If targets are met or exceeded they may be given bonuses. Another advantage of setting targets is that they can be adjusted to take into account the current circumstances of the business. For example, during a boom a business might set more challenging targets. Finally, setting targets is very similar to the use of SMART objectives. (See Chapter 2)

Judging success in the public sector

When judging the success of public sector organisations it is important to recognise that objectives are likely to be different from those in the private sector. For example, schools, hospitals and government-run services that are not likely to make a profit. Generally, public sector objectives are linked to quality of service and reducing costs. Some governments set targets for public sector performance and publish the results. Examples of these results include:

- examination results in schools
- the punctuality and reliability of public transport systems
- the response time of the emergency services
- crime rates
- the amount of waste sent to recycling units.

Business failure

It is not uncommon for businesses to fail. This means that they are no longer able to trade because they are making a loss or they run out of cash. Why might a business collapse?

- The people running the business may not have the necessary skills. To be successful skills such as people management, financial management, purchasing, marketing, administration and planning are required. It is hard work running a business and if they do not possess all of these skills business owners often fail.
- Businesses often fail because they run out of cash. Without cash a business cannot survive. Cash shortages may be caused by factors such as inadequate start-up capital, taking on too much business too quickly, poor *cash flow* management, non-payment by customers and unexpected expenditure.
- A sharp fall in sales. This might be caused by new competition, sudden changes in consumer tastes, a recession, poor product quality or customer service or a failure to meet changing market needs.

Did you know?

In 2010, Japan Airlines (JAL) Asia's biggest air carrier collapsed in one of the country's biggest business failures. Some 15,600 jobs were cut and all board members resigned. The failure was caused by the inability to control escalating costs and trading difficulties in the aviation industry. JAL was taken over by a state-backed organisation which provided ¥300bn to keep the airline trading.

When a large company is about to fail it may go into *administration*. This means that an independent group of specialists is appointed to run the business (the administrators). They try to save the business by making changes such as selling off unprofitable sections and laying off workers. However, if the business cannot be saved the business might go into *liquidation*. This means the business will be closed down and all of its assets sold off. Any cash raised from the sale of assets is then distributed among the firm's creditors.

Chapter review – Ganno Holdings

Ganno Holdings manufactures a range of rubber products such as concentrated latex. It also markets latex examination gloves, high-pressure hydraulic hoses, injection plastic and rubber moulded parts and escalator handrails.

In 2009, the Thai company won two prestigious industry awards for the quality of its latex products. This was the result of its commitment to product development and investment in a $50m research centre in 2007.

Also in 2009, Ganno Holdings was the subject of an investigation by environmental officers about emissions from one of its factories. This was in response to complaints from people in the local community who claimed that their eyes were being irritated by fumes from the factory. A spokesperson from Ganno said: 'We are aware of the complaints but we can assure everyone that there is no physical threat from the emissions. We comply with all environmental legislation.' However, around 60 local people have been treated for eye infections over the last two years. The results of the investigation have not yet been released.

Figure 14.6 *Pollution from factory chimney*

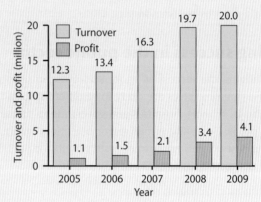

Figure 14.7 *Turnover and profit for Ganno Holdings 2005–2009*

(a) Comment on the financial success of Ganno Holdings between 2005 and 2009. **(4 marks)**

(b) Examine why targets are important when judging the success of a business. **(4 marks)**

(c) (i) How important is product quality to Ganno holdings? **(2 marks)**

(ii) State two ways in which product quality can be judged. **(2 marks)**

In 1999, Ganno Holdings almost collapsed. The company was trying to grow too quickly and nearly ran out of cash.

(d) Analyse two other reasons why businesses might fail. **(4 marks)**

(e) Do you think Ganno Holdings is a good corporate citizen? **(4 marks)**

Chapter 15: Internal organisation

Getting started...

As businesses grow they need to be formally organised. This means that workers must be placed into groups, teams or departments. Each group must have a leader who is responsible for the whole group and is able to control its activities. Every person in the business must understand their role in the organisation and be accountable to someone. Look at the example below.

Cerrillos Auto Hire

Cerrillos Auto Hire is a car hire business based in Santiago, Chile. It is an established business and serves local business people. The business has 65 vehicles, employs nine staff and is divided into four departments. The chart in Figure 15.1 shows how the business is organised.

- **General manager:** Carlos is in charge of the whole business. His main task is to buy and sell the cars. He works closely with Juan, the mechanic. Carlos is accountable to the owners.

- **Bookings and Administration:** Gabriela runs this department but is helped by Gina and Patricia. It deals with customers when cars are booked, collected and returned. It deals with all the paperwork and provides customer service.

- **Car maintenance and preparation:** Two people are employed in this department to maintain and prepare the cars. Juan is a mechanic and is in charge while Jesus prepares the cars.

- **Finance and accounts:** Charles is in charge of accounts. He also processes wages, deals with staff problems and responds to complaints. Julia is his part-time assistant.

- **Marketing:** Veronica is responsible for promoting the business and tries to develop new customers. She has recently designed a questionnaire to gather feedback from customers.

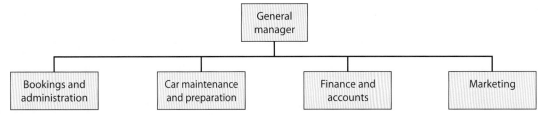

Figure 15.1 *Organisational chart for Cerrillos Auto Hire*

(a) Who is in control of Cerrillos Auto Hire?

(b) Describe briefly how Cerrillos Auto Hire is organised.

(c) What is Gabriela's role in the organisation?

(d) To whom is **(i)** Veronica **(ii)** Jesus accountable?

Formal organisation

Running a business involves planning, decision making, co-ordination and communication. These tasks are easier if workers are organised into a structure made up of different functions or departments. The internal structure of a business is known as its **formal organisation**. Small businesses rarely need a formal organisation. This is because the workforce is small and everyone will know what the others are doing. They will all be accountable to the same person – probably the owner.

However, businesses that employ thousands of people need a formal organisation. Without it the business would be difficult to control. Communications may break down, mistakes might occur and staff may become confused about their roles.

The formal organisation can be represented by an **organisation chart** which shows:

● how the business is split into functions or departments

● the roles of employees and their job titles

● who has responsibility

● to whom people are accountable

● communication channels

● the relationships between different positions in the business.

An organisation chart for Denham plc, a manufacturer, is shown in Figure 15.2. It is a traditional organisation chart and the person in charge is the chairperson. The chairperson, at the top of the **hierarchy**, is accountable to the shareholders. The roles played by all other employees in the chart are outlined below.

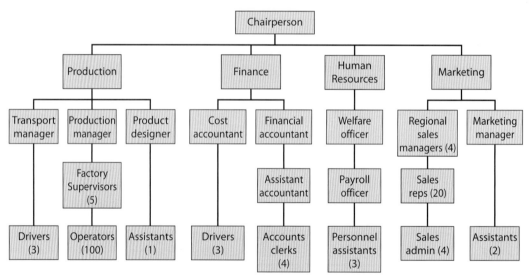

Figure 15.2 *Organisation chart for Denham plc*

Employee roles and responsibilities

The roles played by employees vary depending on the size and type of business. The roles outlined here relate to the chart in Figure 15.2.

Directors

Directors are appointed by the owners to run the business. Together with the chairperson they form the *Board of Directors*. They make all the important decisions in the business. Figure 15.2 shows that Denham plc is divided into four departments – Production, Marketing, Human Resources and Finance. Each of these departments is run by a director. These four directors are accountable to the chairperson. They also have **authority** over the managers in the layer below them.

Managers

Managers have a number *of functions*. They are responsible for planning, controlling, organising, motivating, problem solving and decision making. However, their overall *role* is to achieve the objective of the owners. They are employed to 'get things done' using the resources of the business as effectively as possible. They are also leaders and help to guide and shape the business. The manager in each department is accountable to the departmental director. In Figure 15.2 there are several managers in each department.

- The production department has a transport manager and a production manager. There is also a product designer who has the same *status* as a manager in the chart. They are on the same level in the hierarchy.

- In the finance department the cost and financial accountants both have managerial status. This is because they are responsible for the work of others.

- The welfare officer in the personnel department also has managerial status. He or she is responsible for the work of the payroll officer and three assistants.

- The sales department has four regional sales managers and a marketing manager. Each regional manager has five sales staff working for them.

Supervisors

Supervisors monitor the work in their particular area. They have authority over operatives and general workers. At Denham plc five factory supervisors are employed in the production department. Each of them has authority over 20 operatives. Supervisors may carry out managerial duties, but at a lower level. For example, Figure 15.2 shows that the assistant accountant, the payroll officer and the sales reps are all at the same level in the hierarchy.

Operatives

Operatives are skilled workers. They are involved in the production process. For example, they may operate machines, assemble products, work with tools or carry out maintenance. In Figure 15.2, 100 operatives are employed in the production department. They are accountable to supervisors or managers. They are shown at the bottom of the hierarchy in Figure 15.2. However, they may have more status than general workers because they are often skilled.

General staff

Businesses often employ staff that do not have any specific skills. However, with training they can perform a variety of tasks and gain promotion to other positions. Examples of general staff in Figure 15.2 include drivers, assistants, accounts clerks and people with administration jobs. They are shown at the bottom of the hierarchy in Figure 15.2. General staff do not have any authority.

Professional staff

Professional staff are skilled and highly trained. Examples include lawyers, accountants, doctors, pilots and dentists. In places where lots of professionals are employed, organisation charts may be different.

QUESTION 1

Chittagong Textiles Ltd manufactures towels and related products in Bangladesh. The company employs 200 staff and serves retailers, hotels, hospitals and other customers. The factory is based in Green Valley, Chittagong, and operates three production lines – A, B and C. Each line produces a 'family' of products. Figure 15.3 shows part of the company's organisation chart.

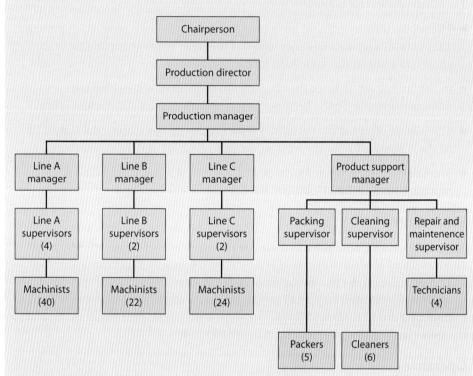

Figure 15.3 *Chittagong Textiles Ltd – organisation chart for production*

(a) Give two examples of operatives at Chittagong Textiles Ltd.

(b) Define the terms: **(i)** formal organisation; **(ii)** hierarchy.

(c) Outline the roles of: **(i)** the production director; **(ii)** line supervisors at Chittagong Textiles Ltd.

Features of organisational structures

Chain of command

Organisation charts show the **chain of command** in a business. This is the route through which orders are passed down in the hierarchy. In Figure 15.2, each layer in the hierarchy is like a link in a chain. Orders will pass down through the layers from the top to the bottom. Information may also flow back from the bottom to the top. If the chain of command is too long:

● messages may get lost or confused as they pass up and down the chain

● making changes might meet with resistance lower down the chain. Therefore, if there are lots of links in the chain, resistance is more likely.

Span of control

The number of people, or **subordinates**, a person directly controls in a business is called the **span of control**. For example, in Figure 15.2 the Finance Director is responsible for two people – the cost accountant and the financial accountant. Therefore the director's span of control is two. In the sales department each regional manager is responsible for five sales reps. Their span of control is five.

If a business has a *wide* span of control it means that a person controls relatively more subordinates. Someone with a *narrow* span of control controls fewer subordinates. If the span of control is greater than six, difficulties may arise.

Flat and tall structures

Organisation structures may be flat or tall. Examples are shown in Figure 15.4. A flat structure means there are a fewer layers in the hierarchy. In Figure 15.4 the flat structure only has two layers in the hierarchy. The chain of command is short but the span of control is wide. With flat structures:

- communication is better because the chain of command is short
- management costs are lower because there are fewer layers of management
- control may be friendly and less formal because there is more direct contact between layers.

With tall structures:

- communication through the whole structure can be poor because there is a long chain of command
- management costs will be higher
- there may be a clear route for promotion which might help to motivate staff
- control tends to be more formal and less friendly because of all the layers in the hierarchy.

Delegation

In some situations a manager may hand a more complex task to a subordinate. This is called delegation. The manager will still have responsibility for the overall task. However, time can be saved if a subordinate completes the task. Sometimes delegation can motivate workers. This is because they feel as though they are being trusted to carry out a more difficult work.

QUESTION 2

Marks & Spencer (M&S) is a very large clothing retailer. It has over 800 stores in more than 40 countries. It sells clothing, food, home wares, furniture and some electrical goods. In recent years the company has struggled financially. M&S developed a reputation as an ageing and bureaucratic company. Critics said it was losing touch with younger customers. As a result in 2004, M&S began a review of the business and made some changes. These changes created a business with a flatter organisational structure. M&S lost a number of layers of authority. This meant that employees had more accountability than before.

(a) What is meant by a 'flatter organisation structure'?

(b) Why did M&S adopt a flatter structure?

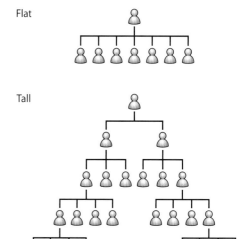

Flat

Tall

Figure 15.4 *Flat and tall organisational structures*

Key terms

Authority – the right to command and make decisions.

Chain of command – the route through which orders are passed down in the hierarchy.

Delegation – authority to pass down from superior to subordinate.

Formal organisation – the internal structure of a business as shown by an organisation chart.

Hierarchy – the order or levels of responsibility in an organisation from the lowest to the highest.

Organisational chart – a diagram that shows the different job roles in a business and how they relate to each other.

Span of control – the number of people a person is directly responsible for in a business.

Subordinates – people in the hierarchy who work under the control of a senior worker.

Key fact

One change in recent years has been a switch to flatter structures. This has helped to cut managerial costs. It has also given more responsibility to other workers which may help to motivate them.

Organisational charts and growth

As businesses grow the formal organisation is likely to change.

● Most businesses, because they start small, have an *entrepreneurial structure*. This means that decisions are made centrally – by the owner or 'key' workers.

● As businesses grow they may opt for a traditional structure. This is where the structure is based on a hierarchy and decision making is shared throughout the business. The chart in Figure 15.2 is an example.

● In some businesses a *matrix structure* is favoured. This is where employees are put into teams which cut across departmental roles. They may work together on a specific project – designing a new product, for example.

Chapter review – Ceylan Pumps

Ceylan Pumps make a range of pumps and valves. It is a family business based in Ankara, Turkey. Emre Ceylan is the chairman of the company. It has a traditional structure and the following information is given about the finance department.

● The finance director is in charge of the finance department.

● The department is divided into four sections each of which is run by a manager. These managers are the financial accountant, the cost accountant, the purchasing manager and the credit controller.

● The financial accountant has two assistant accountants each of which have three accounts clerks working for them.

● The cost accountant has one assistant cost accountant but no clerks.

● The purchasing manager has one supervisor and two purchasing clerks.

● The credit controller has no supervisor or assistant but does have two clerks.

(a) Draw an organisational chart for the finance department at Ceylan Pumps. **(6 marks)**

(b) What is the span of control for: **(i)** the credit controller; **(ii)** the cost accountant? **(2 marks)**

Figure 15.5 *Pumps and valves*

(c) What is meant by the chain of command? (Use this case study as an example.) **(2 marks)**

The financial accountant often delegates work to the assistant accountants.

(d) Outline what this means. **(4 marks)**

'Having a formal organisational structure helps to control a business.'

(e) Analyse this statement. **(6 marks)**

Chapter 16: Departmental functions

Getting started...

The way businesses are divided into departments will vary according to the size and needs of the business. For example, a small engineering business might have just two departments- production and sales. However, as businesses grow many are likely to divide their organisation into four traditional departments. These are production, marketing, human resources and finance. Employees working in each of these departments will specialise in a particular range of tasks. Look at the example below.

The Colombo Hotel

Thilak is in charge of the finance department. He is responsible for all the staff and meets with other managers every day. He is also responsible for producing important financial statements such as cash flow forecasts and the profit and loss account.

Chandrika works in the finance department of the Colombo Hotel. Examples of the tasks carried out by Chandrika include the following:

- preparation of customer bills and processing payments
- keeping financial records of all the hotel's purchases and sales
- preparation of wage slips and payment of wages to the hotel's 122 employees
- providing currency exchanges for hotel guests
- paying cash into the bank
- providing cover for reception when they are busy.

(a) Describe the role of a finance department. (Use examples from the case study.)

(b) Name three other possible departments in the hotel.

Figure 16.1 *An employee working in the finance department at the Colombo Hotel*

The need for departments

Small businesses can operate without being divided into **departments**. This is because they are often run informally. However, larger organisations, ones which employ tens of thousands of people for example, need to be broken down into smaller units. Each department in a business will specialise in one particular function. Everyone in a department will focus on a narrower range of activities and have a common purpose. Traditionally, a business may be divided into four departments. These are production, marketing, finance and human resources.

Production department

Production involves making goods and providing services. In many businesses the majority of workers are employed in the production department. In the primary sector they may be tractor drivers, shepherds and miners. In the secondary sector they may be machine operators, packers, assembly workers, welders, printers or managers. In the tertiary sector they may be receptionists, shop workers, sales assistants, porters, nurses, teachers, police workers, hairdressers, mechanics and solicitors. Other activities that may be carried out in the production department are shown in Figure 16.2.

Design Some firms design products for individual customers. Others are continually innovating by designing new products to meet changing customer needs.
Purchasing This involves buying the resources needed by the business such as raw materials, components, energy, tools, equipment and packaging.
Stock control This involves storing, controlling, issuing and handling stocks of resources and providing information about stocks. There will be close links between purchasing and stock control.
Maintenance Some production departments have a team of maintenance workers. They might be responsible for cleaning and the maintenance of machinery and business property.
Research and development (R & D) In some industries such as pharmaceuticals, automotive, electronics and computers, firms employ large R & D centres. They are responsible for the investigation and discovery of materials, processes and products.

Figure 16.2 *Other production department activities*

Marketing department

Most businesses today are *market orientated*. This means that the main focus for businesses is the customer. Consequently, marketing has grown in importance. In addition to selling products, the marketing department may be involved in the following activities.

- **Market research:** People may be employed gathering, processing and presenting data about customer needs, markets and competitors. This information will be used by the business to help make decisions. For example, it may use the information to improve existing products or create new ones.

- **Product planning:** This involves deciding which products should be marketed. For example, should old products be re-launched or withdrawn and replaced with new ones?

- **Pricing:** The marketing department has to decide what prices should be charged for the range of products sold by the business. Costs, competitors, the state of the market and the type of product will influence this decision.

- **Sales promotion:** People working in this area have to develop interesting and effective methods of promotion. Examples might be free gifts, coupons, discounts, buy-one-get-one-free offers, competitions and loyalty cards.

- **Advertising:** Businesses have to create innovative and effective adverts. People in this area might also be employed to buy advertising space from the media.

- **Packaging:** The marketing department will play a key role in the design of packaging. Packaging is important because it often says a great deal about the product itself.

- **Distribution:** Marketing people will be employed to make sure that products are made available to customers in the right place at the right time. This may involve organising transportation and securing contracts with retailers and wholesalers for example.

Finance department

The finance department is responsible for administering and monitoring all financial transactions carried out by the business. In a large business the following tasks may be carried out.

- **Recording transactions:** Details of every single purchase and sale must be recorded by a business. These records are used to produce important financial statements.

- **Wages and salaries:** This involves processing wages and salaries for all workers. The department will provide workers with wage slips, ensure that payment is made on time, deal with wage queries and make payments to the tax authorities.

- **Credit control:** This involves monitoring the amount of money owed by customers. It often requires staff to chase outstanding debts.

- **Cash flow forecasting and budgets:** The finance department is responsible for controlling the firm's money. Such control is aided by producing *budgets* and *cash flow forecasts.* These are discussed in Chapters 28 and 29.

- **Accounts:** One important job done by the finance department is producing the business's accounts. These are financial statements which show how well the company has performed. They include the *profit and loss account* and the *balance sheet.* These are discussed in Chapters 32 and 33.

Human resources (HR) department

The human resources (or personnel) department is responsible for the welfare of employees. The main tasks undertaken by the department include the following:

- **Recruitment and selection:** The HR department will help plan the numbers and types of workers needed, place job adverts, provide application forms, select appropriate candidates for interview, interview candidates and select the best employees for the job.

- **Training:** The HR department is likely to organise induction and most other training that employees will need during their employment.

- **Conditions and terms of service:** It is important to clarify the pay, hours and place of work, job descriptions, holiday entitlements, non-financial incentives and any other conditions of service for new employees.

- **Employment contracts:** This involves drawing up contracts of employment for employees, explaining the contents and ensuring that both the employer and the employee sign copies.

- **Industrial relations:** The HR department may have to maintain good communications with trade unions. They may also have to organise, and be involved in, negotiations between employers and employees.

- **Disciplinary and grievance procedures:** Sometimes workers may have to be disciplined due to poor conduct, or they may have a problem with a work issue. The HR department will have to provide information to employees on procedures in such matters and deal with the whole process.

● **Dismissal:** The HR department is responsible for issuing warnings to workers and dealing with any legal requirements when laying off staff. Workers may be forced to leave a job through dismissal or redundancy.

QUESTION 1

Monica works in the marketing department for a large Brazilian soft drinks producer. She is responsible for public relations (PR). This involves:

● dealing with the media by answering questions and providing company information

● organising company presentations to shareholders, potential investors and customers.

Monica is also employed to negotiate sponsorship deals on behalf of the company. For example, she recently secured a contract for her company to sponsor a national football competition in Brazil.

Figure 16.3 *Football in Brazil*

(a) Outline two other activities that might be carried out in the marketing department.

Marketing departments play an increasingly important role in businesses today.

(b) What might account for this development?

(c) What is Monica's job in the marketing department?

Relationships and interdependence between departments

It is very important for departments to work together. They are interdependent, which means that they rely on each other for their success. There must be good communication between departments to ensure that the business runs effectively. Some examples of relationships and interdependence between different departments are:

- The production department may have to meet with the marketing department to discuss modifications to a customer's order.

- The welfare officer from the personnel department may have to meet the sales director to discuss customer complaints about one of the sales people.

- The HR department will need to communicate regularly with the finance department to discuss wages and salaries.

- The finance department may have to communicate with the production department to ensure that designs for a new product are profitable.

There are many more examples of the interdependence between departments in a business. A business may struggle if there is no co-operation between departments.

Key term

Department – a section in a business where all employees have similar skills and specialise in particular activities.

Chapter review– Wan Ng

Wan Ng is a Chinese manufacturer based in Shanghai. The company makes agrochemicals for farmers. It is made up of four traditional departments with a senior manager and two deputy managers in each department.

The Chairman, Wan Ng, is becoming concerned about the sales trend for Nitrogrow, one of its leading products. The sales figures for this product are shown in Figure 16.4. Wan Ng also believes that there is some friction between the production department and the finance department. This is because the production department is overspending on its labour budget. The production department argues that more skilled labour is needed to maintain quality. However, the finance department argues that expenditure budgets should not be exceeded. Communication between the two departments has almost broken down and some important data needed for a financial report has not been provided by the production department.

(a) Draw a simple organisation chart for the management team at Wan Ng. **(4 marks)**

(b) Which departments at Wan Ng would be responsible for the following activities?
  (i) Chasing customers for late payment.
  (ii) Dealing with the dismissal of an employee with a very poor attendance record.
  (iii) Placing adverts in farming magazines.
  (iv) Setting output targets for processing plants. **(4 marks)**

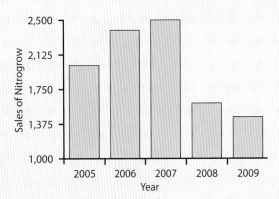

Figure 16.4 *Sales of Nitrogrow (2005–2009)*

(c) How might the marketing department find out the reasons for the trend in sales of Nitrogrow? **(4 marks)**

(d) Outline two possible functions of the Wan Ng production department in addition to making agrochemicals. **(4 marks)**

(e) Outline the importance of interdependence between departments in a business. (Use examples from this case study.) **(4 marks)**

Chapter 17: Communication in business

Getting started...

People in businesses exchange information all the time.

- *A sales manager may telephone the production manager to ask if a customer order is ready.*
- *A credit controller may write to a customer explaining that their account is overdue.*
- *An operative may ask a technician to repair a fault with a machine.*

Look at the examples of communication below.

A team meeting

We have to increase sales this month. Every person who meets their sales target will get a bonus of $200.

Figure 17.1 *A team meeting*

Customer email

> Customer Service Centre
> Apollo Airways
> 12/10/08
>
> Dear Mr Husain,
> Please note that the time of your flight from London to Dubai has been brought forward by one hour. The new flight itinerary is shown below. We apologise if this causes any inconvenience.
>
> **Outward**
> London Flight A102 Dep:13.05   12.11.08
> Dubai   Flight A102 Arr: 21.25 12.11.08
> **Return**
> Dubai   Flight A103 Dep: 14.05   19.11.08
> London Flight A103 Arr: 22.55 19.11.08
>
> Please remember to arrive at the airport three hours before departure.
>
> Yours sincerely
>
> **Waleed Abbas** (customer services)

Figure 17.2 *An email to a customer*

(a) Identify the:
  (i) sender;
  (ii) receiver(s);
  (iii) message in the above examples of communication.

What is communication?

Communication is about sending and receiving information. Figure 17.3 shows how communication might work in business. It shows who is involved, the message and the feedback. Communication begins with a *sender*. In Figure 17.3 the sender is an applicant for a job. The *message* being sent is a job application form for a clerical assistant. The *receiver* is the personnel manager. The *feedback* is a letter inviting the applicant for an interview. Note that the personnel manager becomes the sender when the interview invitation is sent back. Therefore, the applicant now becomes the receiver.

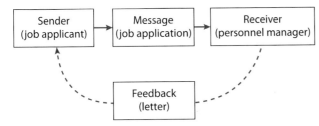

Figure 17.3 *The process of communication*

How does communication take place?

Inside a business messages can be passed vertically (upwards or downwards) and horizontally. These routes are called **channels of communication**.

Downward communication usually involves managers giving information or instructions to their subordinates. Downward communication is important because:

- subordinates look to their managers for leadership and guidance

- it allows the decisions made by management to be carried out by employees

- it allows managers to command, control and organise.

Upward communication often involves workers giving feedback to managers. However, it might also involve requests by workers. They may need more resources, for example. Upward communication is helpful because it:

- helps managers to understand the views and needs of subordinates

- may alert managers to problems

- helps staff to feel that they are valued

- provides managers with information to help make decisions.

Horizontal communication occurs when workers on the same level in the hierarchy exchange information. Horizontal communication is common within a department. For example, operatives are likely to discuss their work with each other.

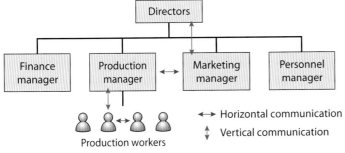

Figure 17.4 *Vertical and horizontal communication*

QUESTION 1

Didier Bonnet is the regional manager of La Femme, a French clothes retail chain. He is responsible for the performance of six stores in the south of France. The table in Figure 17.5 contains financial information about the performance of the stores in June 2009. The table has been sent to the finance director who is compiling a report for a board meeting.

	Nice	Marseille	St Tropez	Cannes	Toulon	Nimes	Total
Turnover	98,500	133,400	87,600	94,900	76,900	83,400	574,700
Profit	23,200	34,600	21,400	19,700	−1,200	16,800	114,500

Figure 17.5 *Financial information for La Femme*

(a) Who is the sender of the information in this example?

(b) What is meant by vertical communication? (Use an example from the case study.)

(c) What sort of information is being sent in this example?

(d) Outline why upward communication is helpful.

Formal and informal communication

Formal communication in business is when people use recognised channels. **Informal communication** is through non-approved channels. Most informal communication is done through the *grapevine*. This means that unofficial information is passed on through gossip and rumours. It can both help and hinder communications. Information passed on through the grapevine may become distorted and misleading. This is unhelpful.

Communication often takes place between groups. These can be both formal and informal. *Formal groups* are those set up by the business. They are often shown on organisation charts as departments, for example. Examples of *informal groups* might be:

● employees who meet outside work at sports clubs, local churches or social clubs

● families and very close friends who work in different departments

● groups of workers that started together or trained together.

Communication between informal groups is helpful if it keeps people informed and encourages co-operation. However, it can also be disruptive. One reason for this is because leaders of informal groups often have more power than those of formal groups. Therefore, formal communication may be undermined by informal communication.

The importance of good communication in business

If internal communication is poor problems can arise. As a result, efficiency and profitability may suffer. Poor communication can lead to mistakes, wasted resources and confusion. It can lead to workers not understanding what they have to do, poor motivation and a duplication of effort.

Did you know?

The *grapevine* can be used by management to find out what people 'feel'. Some firms 'leak' information on the grapevine to see what reaction it gets. The reactions might then affect management decisions.

Poor external communication can make the business look foolish and may cost it money. For example, if prices on a company's website are set too low by mistake, this could lead to a flood of online orders. These may have to be accepted at a loss. Poor communication with outsiders could also damage the image of the company. The main effects of poor communication on a business are summarised with examples in Figure 17.6.

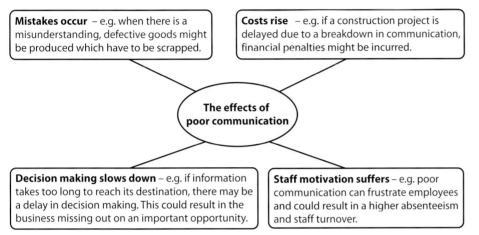

Figure 17.6 *The effects of poor communication*

Barriers to communication

Communication is only effective if the message sent is understood by the receiver. Things that get in the way of good communication are called **barriers to communication**. Some examples are given below.

- **Message is unclear:** If a message is not clear it may be misinterpreted or ignored.

- **Technological breakdown:** A lot of business communication is done electronically. If technology is faulty, communication may be distorted or break down. For example, emails cannot be sent if broadband connections are lost. Mobile telephone conversations can often be distorted by a weak signal. Sometimes mobile phones cannot be used because there is no signal.

- **Poor communication skills:** Some people may have poor communication skills. For example:
    - when communicating verbally, some people may have a limited vocabulary or may not be able to make themselves understood
    - some people may be poor listeners and may 'switch off' during the communication process
    - written messages may contain poor spelling or weak grammar.

- **Jargon:** Sometimes people use jargon when communicating. Jargon is terminology that is used and understood by people in a specific group. However, outside that group it may be meaningless. Clearly, jargon should not be used when communicating with people outside such a group.

Key fact

Information is more likely to be understood if:
- there is not too much information
- clear and precise language is used
- it is delivered at a reasonable pace
- the receiver is familiar with the sender and method of communication
- the message only contains relevant information.

Did you know?

In Arabian countries it is common to spend time discussing trivial matters before a business meeting gets under way. This may not be acceptable in the west and may slow down communication. There may also be time differences between countries.

Key terms

Communication – the sending and receiving of messages.

Communication barriers – things that get in the way of communication.

Communication channels – routes along which information might travel in a business.

Communication media – the different methods by which information can be sent.

Formal communication – the use of recognised channels when communicating.

Informal communication – the use of non-approved channels when communicating.

- **Long chain of command:** If there are too many layers in the organisational hierarchy the chain of command will be longer. This means messages take longer to pass through the chain and may become distorted on the way.

- **Using the wrong medium:** The different methods by which messages can be sent are called **communication media**. These are discussed in the next chapter. However, if the sender uses an inappropriate medium an important message may be missed.

- **Different countries, languages and cultures:** In multinationals people may be working in different countries where languages and cultures vary. Such differences may hamper communications.

QUESTION 2

Eric Demsey left school and got a job as an apprentice in a market research agency. On his first day he asked about lunch arrangements. He was told that most team members ate at Al Desco. At 1 o'clock Eric spent a fruitless 45 minutes looking for a restaurant by the office called Al Desco. When he returned he discovered that Al Desco was not a restaurant but meant eating at your desk.

On the fourth day when Eric arrived at work, he was asked by his team leader why he missed the team briefing the previous afternoon. Eric explained that he did not know about it. His leader said that the notice was quite clear on the staff notice board.

(a) (i) What is meant by jargon? (Use an example from this case study.)
(ii) Why should jargon be avoided when communicating?

(b) Do you think the communication medium used to notify people about a meeting in this case was effective?

(c) What steps can be taken to ensure that messages are clear?

Overcoming the barriers to communication

- **Training:** Businesses must overcome barriers to communication. One way is to train staff in communication. For example, staff can be trained to improve verbal communication skills when dealing with customers on the telephone.

- **Recruitment:** Businesses should recruit staff with good communication skills. The quality of people's written communication in job applications may provide some guide. Also, people's verbal communication skills can be assessed in interviews.

- **Technology:** If communication barriers result from faulty technology a business may have to repair or replace equipment.

- **Chain of command:** If this is too long, a business may decide to remove some of the management levels in the organisation. A shorter chain of command means that information can pass through an organisation more quickly.

- **Social events:** Internal communication may improve if social events are organised for staff. These provide opportunities for workers from different departments to come together, which may be helpful.

Chapter review – SASB

SASB is a South American satellite television broadcaster based in Lima, Chile. It broadcasts programmes to Chile, Argentina, Uruguay and Peru. Recently, many customers have cancelled their subscriptions because of poor customer service. SASB lost $1.5m in subscriptions in a single month. There are two problems.

● Because there is a technical fault on the switchboard, customers hang up because they cannot get through to a helpline. Some of the equipment is too old.

● Workers employed in one call centre based in Argentina have complained that they are not equipped to give out the information asked for by customers. This was the result of inadequate training.

Generally, communications at SASB are poor. It has been suggested that the chain of command is too long. Workers at SASB do not know each other very well and are not given enough opportunities to mix with their colleagues. As a result staff turnover is high and money is being wasted on constant recruitment.

An urgent meeting was organised for all Level 6 divisional managers to discuss communication at SASB.

(a) What is meant by communication? (Use an example from this case study) **(2 marks)**

(b) What is meant by horizontal communication? **(2 marks)**

(c) Describe two communication barriers at SASB. **(4 marks)**

(d) How does this case highlight the importance of good communication in business? **(4 marks)**

(e) Evaluate the measures that might be taken to overcome the communication problems at SASB. **(8 marks)**

Chapter 18: Communication methods

Getting started...

Businesses use a variety of methods to communicate information. For example, communication might be verbal or written. Information can be sent electronically or distributed using the postal system. Communication may also be formal or informal. Look at the examples below.

- **Case 1:** A business wants to inform a customer that an order will be delayed because an item is out of stock.

- **Case 2:** A member of staff has to be informed that they have been promoted to a senior position and will be entitled to higher pay.

- **Case 3:** A general worker needs permission from a supervisor to finish work 15 minutes early to take her daughter for a hospital appointment.

Figure 18.1 *Examples of communication*

(a) Suggest suitable methods of communication for each of the above cases.

Internal and external communication

Internal communication takes place inside a business between employees. Examples include:

- a manager giving a verbal warning to a subordinate for poor punctuality

- a board meeting where directors are discussing a possible merger.

External communication occurs when businesses exchange information with people and organisations outside the business. Examples include:

- a statement from a credit card company

- a focus group where people from the marketing department discuss a product with members of the public.

Methods of communication

Face-to-face communication

This takes place when spoken information is exchanged by people who can see each other. Face-to-face communication is effective. The advantages and disadvantages are shown in Figure 18.2. Some examples of face-to-face communication in business are given below.

- an interview where a candidate is being interviewed for a job

- at a training session where people are being taught new skills

- dealing with customers, either from behind a counter or in reception

- at a presentation to investors and the media reporting the financial progress of a company.

Advantages	Disadvantages
Allows immediate feedback.	Negative body language may create a barrier.
Encourages co-operation.	A record of the message may not be kept.
Allows new ideas to be generated.	Non-relevant information may be included.
Saves time.	In a meeting some people may not listen.

Figure 18.2 *Advantages and disadvantages of face-to-face communication*

Written communication

Businesses communicate written information using a variety of methods. Each of them has their own advantages and disadvantages.

- **Letters** are a common way to send written information. They are flexible because they can be sent to a variety of different people such as customers, employees and suppliers. The information in each letter can be expressed so that the recipient can understand it. Letters can also be used for confidential information and provide a record of the communication.

- **Reports** are used to communicate important information in a formal manner. They may be short, or complex and detailed. However, reports should be concise and carefully structured and presented. Reports can contain numerical data and graphics. The main disadvantage of reports is that they take time to research and write.

- **Memorandums (memos)** are used for internal communications only. They contain brief messages and are flexible. They are often used to remind people of events, confirm telephone conversations or pass on simple instructions.

- **Forms** are used to communicate routine information. Application forms are used to collect information for jobs, loans or licences. Claim forms for expenses and other entitlements, order forms and time sheets are all examples of different types of form.

- **Notice boards** are cheap to use and can pass on information to a large number of people. However, they can become untidy, are open to abuse and often overlooked.

QUESTION 1

TRM Finance Ltd
127 Bone St
London
WE4 5TY

9 April 2009

Dear Mrs Kumar,
RE: Loan No. FR266421H

Our records show that the last instalment for £132.65 was not paid by your bank on the 1 April 2009. If this is an oversight, please could you arrange for the payment to be made immediately.

If you are unable to make this payment, please telephone 0200 239 9987. May we remind you that according to the terms of the loan agreement an interest rate of 34.5% will be charged on late payments. This will be included in your next statement.

Yours sincerely
Alan Nutter (Senior Loan Controller)

Figure 18.3 *A letter sent by a finance company to a customer*

(a) Is the message in Figure 18.3 an example of internal or external communication?

(b) Outline the advantages of using a letter as a means of communication in this case.

Electronic communication

Nowadays, most businesses use electronic communications. It is possible to deliver messages instantly, all over the world and to a number of people at the same time using electronic methods.

- **Email:** Email is one of the most common methods of electronic communication. It allows businesses and individuals to communicate by sending text or images instantly via a computer. Email can be used to send letters, memos, reports, photographs, video, sound and any other image – even when people are not there to receive them.

- **Internet:** The internet can be used for internal and external communication. Many businesses use their own website to provide a wide range of information. The internet can be used to:

  - market products by displaying them on shopping sites

  - allow customers to buy products with credit and debit cards

  - provide general information about the history and nature of the business

  - advertise jobs to people inside and outside the business

  - obtain information about other companies and products for market research

  - obtain information about potential suppliers

  - deal with customer queries online.

- **Mobile phones:** These are a valuable method of communication for businesses. They are useful when employees work away from the office or move around frequently. Text messages can also be sent from a mobile phone. This is cheap and can be used for sending short memos. Modern mobile phones can be used to access the internet. This makes them even more useful.

- **Intranets:** An intranet is where all the computers in a particular department or organisation are linked together. This enables users to access common information. An advantage is that changes made to information such as timetables, staff diaries, stock lists, prices and company events can be updated instantly and be available to everyone.

- **Videoconferencing and teleconferencing:** Videoconferencing allows people in different locations to have face-to-face meetings. Individuals or groups of people in different parts of the world can be linked at the same time by using a system of cameras, computers and telephones. Teleconferencing is similar but the participants in the conference call are all linked by telephone. Each person can talk to all the others as though they were together.

- **Tannoy and public address (PA) systems:** These are often used in factories, hotels and large stores to pass on information to staff or customers. Messages are broadcast over the loudspeaker system for everyone to hear.

- **Electronic notice boards:** These perform a similar function to Tannoy and PA systems except that written messages, pictures, videos and sound are used. They communicate information to employees and visitors via visual display units located around the business, such as in reception. Other examples of electronic notice boards are departures and arrivals boards at train stations and airports.

Using communication methods appropriately

Quite often the same information can be sent using different methods of communication. A business must use the most appropriate method. Generally, methods should be used that minimise costs. For example, mobile telephones should not be used if a normal landline is available. A number of other issues are also important.

- Confidential information, such as people's personal details, should be communicated securely – using a letter for example.

- Sensitive information, such as a staff disciplinary matter, should be communicated face to face.

- Some communication, such as a job offer, must be supported by a document such as a letter.

- If immediate feedback is required, verbal communication will be needed.

- Standard information is best communicated using forms.

- Complex and detailed information is best communicated in a report.

Key fact

Online communication is not without problems:
- In some areas it is not possible to get a broadband connection.
- Connections can be lost when using the internet.
- Email inboxes get 'clogged up' with electronic junk mail called *spam*.
- Computer viruses can result in the loss of files.
- Computer hackers may get hold of sensitive and confidential information.

Key terms

External communication – communication between the business and those outside such as customers, investors or the authorities.

Internal communication – communication between people inside the business.

QUESTION 2

Li Shanshan is a finance manager for a Chinese toy manufacturer. When she arrived at the office one morning she identified a number of tasks for which she needed to use different methods of communication. She needed to:

● send a copy of the marketing budget to the marketing manager

● contact a sales rep in Japan to find out whether a large order had been secured

● interview two candidates for a job in the finance office

● explain to all staff in the department a new system for recording sales data.

For each of the above communication tasks:

(a) Suggest the most appropriate method of communication.

(b) Account for your answers in **(a)**.

Chapter review – Honda

Many businesses have their own website. These sites provide a wide range of information and some allow people to buy products online. The information on websites is available 24/7. It can be accessed from anywhere in the world and easily updated.

Visit www.honda.com and answer the following questions:

(a) Who is the sender in this communication? **(2 marks)**

(b) Suggest two stakeholders that might be interested in this website. **(2 marks)**

(c) State whether this is a formal or informal method of communication. **(2 marks)**

(d) Describe two pieces of information which can be obtained by receivers using this method of communication? **(4 marks)**

(e) Weigh up the advantages and disadvantages of the internet as a method of communication. **(10 marks)**

Chapter 19: Recruitment and selection

Getting started...

When businesses hire new employees they need to attract the best people – those with the right skills and experience. This is called recruitment and selection. There are several different stages in the recruitment process. Two of these are outlined in the examples below.

Rossmoor Ltd

Rossmoor Ltd provides sheltered and secure accommodation for the elderly. The company owns an apartment block. The advert in Figure 19.1 was placed in a local newspaper. The advert is designed to attract applicants for the post of Duty Manager.

Cosmos Electronics

Cosmos Electronics, a Japanese electrical engineering company, recruits a lot of its managers internally. This means they try to promote people who already work at the company. Suzi Kato, the human resources manager, said: 'We have recruited internally for many years. There are some clear advantages. For example, promoting from within is safer. We know what these people are like and what their potential is. They are proven workers. It is also cheaper and quicker to recruit in this way.'

(a) (i) What is the purpose of the Rossmoor advert?
 (ii) What sort of person is the business trying to attract?
 (iii) How much pay is Rossmoor Ltd offering the successful applicant?

(b) (i) How does Cosmos Electronics recruit many of its managers?
 (ii) State two advantages of recruiting managers in this way.

> **Rossmoor Ltd**
> Require a mature and confident
> ## DUTY MANAGER
> To work 19.6 hours a week on a 5 week rota basis to include some weekends and sleepovers. Excellent working conditions.
> Rate of pay £8.95 per hour plus holiday pay.
> Sleepover rate £27.35. Relevant N.V.Q. preferred but not essential as training will be provided. This post is subject to an enhanced C.R.B. clearance.
> **Closing date 30th October 2009**
> **Contact manager/Duty manager 00724 111222**

Figure 19.1 *Rossmoor Duty Manager advert*

Figure 19.2 *An electronics factory*

Recruitment

In a large business, the human resources department is responsible for employing staff. A business may need new staff because:

● the business is expanding and more labour is needed

● people are leaving and they need to be replaced

● positions have become vacant due to promotion

● people are required for a temporary period to cover staff absence due to maternity or paternity leave, for example.

Key fact

Recruitment is important because, if the wrong people are selected, it can be expensive. This is because, if new recruits leave, all the costs of advertising, interviewing, induction and training will have to be repeated.

Internal and external recruitment

One way of recruiting staff is to appoint someone who already works for the business. This is called **internal recruitment**. A business might do this by advertising the post internally or appointing someone who is thought to be suitable. The advantages of internal recruitment are that:

● it is cheaper because it saves on advertising

● internal recruits are familiar with company policy and working practices

● staff may be more motivated if they know there is a chance of promotion

● the ability, personality, attitude and potential of the person appointed will be more predictable.

All businesses have to use **external recruitment**. This is where new staff are recruited from outside the business. The advantages if this are that:

● a business will have a much larger pool of potential employees to choose from

● a new person may be very talented and have some have fresh ideas which could help the business become more competitive.

A number of different methods might be used to attract applicants from outside the business. Some of the main ones are shown in Figure 19.3.

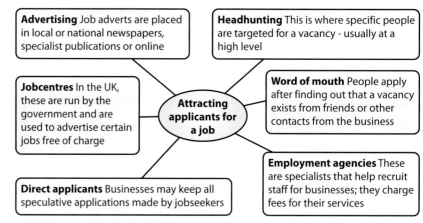

Figure 19.3 *Ways in which a business might attract applicants for a job*

Stages in the recruitment process

The recruitment process may be broken down into a number of stages. These are shown in Figure 19.4.

● The first stage is to identify the number and type of staff that need to be recruited. The overall business plan will help provide this information. For example, if the business is planning to expand larger numbers of applicants will need to be attracted. A business may also need to choose between full-time, part-time, temporary or permanent workers.

● The right people are more likely to be selected if a job description and person specification are drawn up. These are explained below.

● Advertising costs money so businesses must place job advertisements in places where they are likely to attract sufficient interest from the 'right' sort of applicants. For example, a hospital would not use a national newspaper to advertise jobs for porters. A local newspaper or a jobcentre would be more

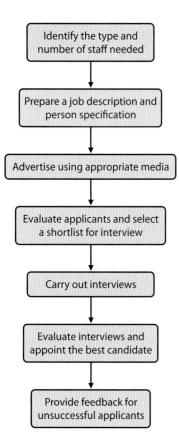

Figure 19.4 *Stages in the recruitment process*

suitable. On the other hand, a vacancy for a senior manager is an important position and a business would want to attract interest from a wide area. Therefore a national newspaper would be suitable.

- Job applications may be made on standard forms sent out to applicants who respond to an advert. Some applicants might write letters and include a **curriculum vitae (CV)**. This is a document which contains personal details, qualifications, experience, names of referees, hobbies and reasons why the person is suitable for the job. A business must sort through all the applications and draw up a shortlist. This is because it is not normally possible to interview every single applicant. Also, some applicants will be unsuitable.

- Shortlisted applicants will be invited for an interview. This is where interviewers can find out more about the applicants by asking questions. It also gives candidates the opportunity to provide more detailed information and to ask questions about the job and the business. Interviewing is often best done by people who are experienced or have been trained in interviewing. For many jobs interviews are carried out by more than one person. This provides an opportunity for a discussion about the performance of candidates in their interviews.

- After the interviews the interviewers must decide who to appoint. In many cases, candidates are told the outcome of the interview by post. This gives the business more time to evaluate the performance of the candidates. A business might also check references before making a final decision.

- The recruitment process ends when a job offer has been made and accepted. It is also courteous to provide feedback to the unsuccessful candidates.

QUESTION 1

Mirpur Garments Ltd, based in Dhaka, makes ladies wear for a number of European customers. The company is expanding fast and has been taking on new staff regularly during the last three years. The personnel manager has been instructed to recruit seven new machinists and a purchasing manager – all to start in 10 weeks' time. The machinists will be recruited externally but the purchasing manager will be recruited from the existing purchasing team. It is expected that three suitable people from the department will apply.

(a) Outline the advantages of recruiting internally for the job of Purchasing Manager.

(b) How might the vacancies for the machinists be advertised?

Job description

A **job description** states the title of the job and outlines the tasks, duties and responsibilities associated with that job. If a new job is created, a new job description may have to be prepared. If a business is replacing someone who is leaving, the job description may be the same. However, when the holder of the post leaves the job description may be updated.

The main purpose of a job description is to show clearly what is expected of an employee. Extracts from it are likely to be used in a job advert. It might also be used during appraisal to see how well an employee has performed in relation to what was expected of them. Figure 19.6 shows an example of a job description.

Figure 19.5 *A machinist in a clothing factory*

Person specification

A **person specification** provides details of the qualifications, experience, skills, attitudes and any other characteristics that would be expected of a person appointed to do a particular job. It is used to 'screen' applicants when sorting through the applications. Applications which do not match the person specification can be ignored. It is common to state on the specification whether a particular requirement is 'essential' or 'desirable'. An example of a person specification is shown in Figure 19.7. The styles of both job descriptions and person specifications are likely to vary between different businesses according to their specific needs.

Job title
Accounts Clerk

General role
To join the accounting team in the recording of financial transactions and the handling of financial information.

Responsibilities
• Matching, batching and coding invoices.
• Matching invoices to purchase orders.
• Arranging payments through cheques and BACS.
• Allocating items of expenditure to cost centres.
• Dealing with internal expense claims.

Salary
AED60,000–85,000 depending on experience.

Hours and conditions of work
• 40 hours per week (7.30 am–4.30 pm)
• 5 weeks' holiday a year

Figure 19.6 *A job description for an accounts clerk with Dubai Construction*

	Essential	Desirable
Qualifications and Education	3 A Levels GCSE Grade 1 Maths and English Full driving licence Design or web-related qualification	A Level IT A management qualification
Experience	Sound knowledge of HTML Skilled in the use of Adobe Photoshop Proficient in Microsoft Office Knowledge of current legislation	Awareness of dynamic languages
Communication skills	Excellent oral communication skills Report-writing skills Foreign language	Spanish
Other skills	Team player Ability to work flexibly Excellent organisational skills	Ability to negotiate
Personal attributes	Self-motivated Willing to travel abroad	Creative

Figure 19.7 *A person specification for a Web Production Manager for Scottish IT company*

QUESTION 2

Nujumba Cement is a large cement manufacturer based in Nagpur, India. The company needs to recruit seven new employees to work in production. The job, called Production Worker, involves heavy manual work and some knowledge of cement manufacturing. The workers will be expected to handle heavy machinery, drive a forklift truck, clean machinery and equipment, and work in a team. The job will involve heavy lifting in a harsh working environment. The wage is Rs400 per hour and the working week is 40 hours long. Workers will be entitled to 4 weeks' holiday, free protective clothing and free lunches.

(a) Draw up a job description for the Production Worker jobs at Nujumba Cement.

(b) Outline two reasons why a business draws up a job description.

Job advertisements

A perfect job advertisement would attract a small number of perfectly suitable candidates for the job. However, it is not always possible to design such perfect advertisements. Some of the important information which is likely to be included in a job advert is listed below.

- job title
- name, address, email and telephone number of employer
- brief details of the job description
- skills, qualifications and work experience required for the job
- salary and other benefits
- method of application.

Chapter review – Internet job advertisement

The job of Sales and Marketing Director for a travel tour operator was advertised on the internet by fish4jobs, a website that advertises many vacancies (Figure 19.8).

(a) Draw up a simple person specification for the job of Sales and Marketing Director. (You **do not** need to show whether details are essential or desirable). **(6 marks)**

(b) How might a business use the person specification? **(2 marks)**

(c) State four important details that should be included in any job advertisement. **(2 marks)**

Applicants for the job shown have to apply with a CV.

(d) What is a CV? **(2 marks)**

(e) Why do businesses draw up short-lists of candidates when interviewing? **(2 marks)**

(f) To what extent do you think the business was right to recruit externally for this post? **(6 marks)**

◀ Back to results   ✉ Email me jobs like these   ✉ Send to a friend   🖶 Print   🗇 Save

Sales and Marketing Director UK/Europe
Travel Tour Operator, Bromley Kent

Salary: Up to £60,000 + benefits

Working hours: Full-time

APPLY NOW

Job type: Permanent

Industry sector: Travel & Leisure, Catering & Hospitality

Successful candidates would consider these responsibilities achievable:
Develop and implement a strategic & tactical sales and marketing plan to drive business growth with a focus on creating and developing brand awareness.
Oversee all activities to fulfil strategic objectives to agreed budgets, sales volumes, values, product mix and timescales.
Carry out competitor analysis, market and customer research to analyse market trends to uncover new business and sales opportunities.
Monitor and provide monthly management reports on activities, analysing past performance and proposing future activities and direction.
Arrange and lead business meetings, delivering sales presentation and product launches in a polished, professional manner.
Lead, direct and motivate to build the overall strength and performance of the sales and marketing teams.

Successful candidates will possess:
Degree in appropriate field or equivalent industry qualifications
Min 5 years' experience in a similar role either within the travel industry or similar field
Strong presentation & analytical skills
Ability to develop team while maintaining focus and achieving the ultimate goal
Ability to travel regularly and be able to work in the UK

Figure 19.8 *A job advert on fish4jobs*

Chapter 20: Legislation and human resources

Getting started...

People at work often need protection. In some jobs the working environment can be dangerous and workers need protection from employers who do not provide sufficient safeguards against accidents. Workers also need protection from exploitation, discrimination and unfair dismissal. Look at the example below.

Amir

Amir is an international student from India who works part-time with a fast food company in Australia. Amir injured his arm one night at work. He claimed that his manager did not call a doctor for him and refused to pay his medical bills. Amir was sacked one week after the accident.

He contacted the Australian Human Rights Commission and they organised a conciliation meeting. While the company did not agree with everything that Amir said, they agreed to attend the meeting. At the meeting the company agreed to:

- reinstate Amir to a similar job at a different location
- help him make a worker's compensation claim
- pay him the wages he had lost.

Amir's previous manager also wrote him a letter of apology.

(a) How does this case illustrate the need for protection at work?

(b) What do you think is meant by a conciliation meeting?

(c) How did Amir benefit from the meeting?

Employment protection

Governments often pass legislation to protect people at work. Without such protection some businesses would exploit their workers. For example, they might pay low wages, make them work long hours, deny them employment rights, discriminate against certain groups and dismiss them unfairly. In addition to providing a healthy and safe working environment businesses have other legal obligations.

Contract of employment

Workers are entitled to a **contract of employment**. This is a legally binding agreement between the employer and the employee. It is likely to contain details such as the start date, terms of employment, job title and duties, place and hours of work, pay and holiday entitlement, pension and sickness absence, termination conditions and details relating to disciplinary, dismissal and grievance procedures.

Discrimination

Businesses have to make a choice when recruiting staff or selecting employees for promotion or training. Choosing one person rather than another is known as **discrimination.** If a business chooses a person because they are more experienced and better qualified than another, this would be legal. However, it is illegal in most countries to discriminate on grounds of gender, race, disability, sexual orientation or age. When employing and promoting people, employers must base their decisions on the ability of candidates, and not whether they are male or female, for example. Many countries have legislation to protect groups from discrimination. Some examples are shown in Figure 20.1.

Businesses can suffer if they are seen to discriminate. They may:

- be involved in expensive legal battles
- fail to recruit or promote the best staff for the post
- de-motivate certain sections of the workforce
- create unnecessary tension or conflict between employees.

Unfair dismissal

Sometimes workers are dismissed unfairly. For instance, if workers are dismissed for joining a trade union or because they are considered too old or because they try to exercise their legal rights, they may have grounds to claim **unfair dismissal**. If an **employment tribunal** finds that a worker has been unfairly dismissed, it has the power to reinstate that worker.

> The **Sex Discrimination Act 1975** states that a person must not be discriminated against because of their gender. For example, adverts for jobs and job titles must be 'genderless'. Recruitment and selection must not be biased in favour of a particular gender. People should be promoted on grounds of ability not gender.

> The **Race Relations Act 1976** makes it illegal to discriminate on grounds of race. This means that a business cannot appoint someone who is white in preference to someone who is from an ethnic minority.

> The **Disability Discrimination Act 1995** defines disability as a 'physical or mental impairment which has a substantial and long-term adverse affect on people's ability to carry out normal day-to-day activities'. The act makes it unlawful for a business to discriminate on grounds of disability.

> The **Equal Pay Act 1970** states that an employee doing the same or 'broadly similar' work as a member of staff of the opposite sex is entitled to equal rates of pay and working conditions.

Figure 20.1 *Examples of UK legislation to protect workers against discrimination*

QUESTION 1

Graham Watkins was recruited by Glenhawk Ltd, a market research agency. He was told that his salary would be $46,000 pa and the hours of work would be 36 per week. This was stated clearly in his contract of employment. However, after seven months Graham was told that he would have to work once a month on a Saturday morning for four hours due to pressure of work. However, Graham said that he always took his children swimming every Saturday morning and that he would not be able to break this commitment. He was then threatened with the sack 'if he didn't pull his weight for the good of the firm' by his senior manager.

(a) Examine whether Glenhawk has the right to sack Graham for refusing to work Saturday mornings in this case.

The pay and hours of work will be clarified in a contract of employment.

(b) What other details might be included?

Health and safety at work

In many occupations the workplace can be a dangerous environment. Because of the danger to employees in all businesses, governments aim to protect workers by passing legislation which forces businesses to provide a safe and healthy workplace. This might involve:

● providing and maintaining adequate safety equipment and protective clothing such as fire extinguishers, protective overalls, hard hats, ear plugs and safety goggles

● ensuring workers have enough space to do their jobs

● guaranteeing a hygienic environment with adequate toilet and washing facilities

● maintaining workplace temperatures and reasonable noise levels

● providing protection from hazardous substances

● providing protection from violence, bullying, threats and stress in the workplace

● providing adequate breaks for rest.

In many countries legislation exists to protect people at work. In the UK the **Health and Safety at Work Act** was passed in 1974. This requires businesses to prepare a written statement of their general policy on health and safety. Businesses also have to provide training, information, instruction and supervision to ensure the health and safety of workers. Many businesses also follow codes of practice to meet health and safety standards at work. Finally, health and safety inspectors have the right to enter business premises to ensure that health and safety measures are in place and are being carried out by businesses and employees.

Did you know?

In 2008/09 in the UK:
- In **agriculture** there were 26 fatal injuries, a rate of 5.7 deaths per 100,000 workers.
- In **construction** there were 53 fatal injuries, with a rate of 2.4 deaths per 100,000 workers. There is an overall downward trend in the rate of fatal injury to workers in this sector.
- In **manufacturing** there were 32 deaths and the rate of fatal injury was 1.1 per 100,000 workers.
- In the **services** sector there were 63 fatalities and the fatality rate was 0.3 per 100,000 workers.

QUESTION 2

In India, it is reckoned that nearly 50,000 people die from work-related accidents or illness every year. In New Delhi in July 2009, a partially constructed bridge on the flagship metro project collapsed and six people were killed and several others injured. It emerged later that more than 90 workers had died in accidents during the construction of the metro in the last 10 years.

There is legislation in India to regulate health and safety in mining, factories, construction and agriculture, but this is not always enforced. Existing laws are also out of date and the enforcement agencies do not have clearly defined areas of authority. This often leads to confusion and a lack of enforcement. To combat the problem, KC Gupta, the head of the National Safety Council of India (NSCI), said that there was a need for a comprehensive law like Britain's Health and Safety at Work Act, 1974. This covers everything from offices to building sites and gives enforcement officers powers of prosecution.

(a) What evidence is there to suggest that health and safety provision for workers in India is inadequate?

(b) Why is health and safety legislation not working in India?

Other legislation

A range of employment legislation gives workers other rights, some of which are outlined below.

- maternity and paternity leave when children are born

- sickness pay during illness

- a legal minimum wage

- the right to join a trade union

- a limit to the number of hours worked during a week

- an explanation of the rules of conduct and what will happen if they are broken.

In the UK, workers receive quite a lot of protection from EU legislation. For example, in 1998, the **European Working Time Directive** allowed workers to limit their working hours to a maximum of 48 hours per week.

Chapter review – Protection at work

Nearly one in five people of working age (7 million, or 18.6 per cent) in the UK have a disability. In the UK, there are currently 1.3 million registered disabled people who are available for and want to work. The employment statistics below show the imbalance between disabled and non-disabled people in employment.

- Only half of disabled people of working age are in work (50 per cent), compared with 80 per cent of non-disabled people.

- Employment rates vary greatly according to the type of impairment a person has; only 20 per cent of people with mental health problems are in employment.

- 23 per cent of disabled people have no qualifications compared to 9 per cent of non-disabled people.

- The average gross hourly pay for disabled employees is £11.08 compared to £12.30 for non-disabled employees.

(a) What is meant by discrimination in the workplace? **(2 marks)**

(b) What evidence is there in this case study to suggest that the disabled face discrimination in the workplace? **(4 marks)**

(c) How might businesses suffer if they discriminate in the workplace? **(4 marks)**

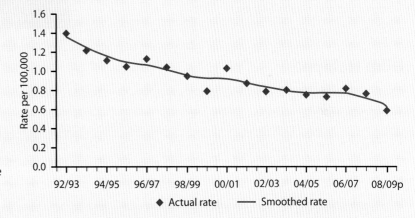

Figure 20.2 *Fatal injury rates to UK workers (1992/93 – 2008/09)*

(d) Outline two pieces of UK legislation designed to protect people from discrimination at work. **(4 marks)**

(e) (i) What does the graph in Figure 20.2 show? **(2 marks)**
(ii) What might account for the trend shown by the graph in Figure 20.2? **(4 marks)**

Chapter 21: Training

Getting started...

Most businesses have to train their workers. This means they have to be taught how to do their jobs. If workers are trained, they will be more productive. However, there are different ways in which workers can be trained. Look at the examples below.

Hemsley Fraser

Hemsley Fraser provides over 250 training courses and trains thousands of people each year. The company claims that 99.8 per cent of trainees say that given the opportunity they would like to attend another Hemsley Fraser course. Some of the courses offered cover:

- Management and leadership
- Secretarial and administration
- Customer services
- Sales
- Health & safety and first aid
- Information technology
- Marketing and public relations
- Many other subjects.

Figure 21.1 *People attending a course*

Dilip Halappa

Dilip Halappa spent five years training as a mechanic in Chennai. He worked for an Indian haulage company and spent one day a week at college. The rest of time was spent at work learning how to maintain and service lorries. He worked with a senior mechanic who was responsible for his development. Dilip had to pass some exams during the five years and at the end was awarded a recognised qualification as a motor mechanic. He is now a fully qualified motor mechanic and has worked for the same company for nine years. During his apprenticeship Dilip's employer paid all the course fees for his college tuition.

(a) Outline one advantage and one disadvantage of a large retailer using the services of Hemsley Fraser to train its staff in customer services.

(b) How did Dilip Halappa train to be a motor mechanic?

Training

It is unlikely that an employee would go through his or her working life without some form of **training**. Training involves increasing the knowledge and skills of workers so they can do their jobs more effectively. Some new employees need little training because they learnt skills at school, college or another business. However, others may need thorough training because they are young or new to the job. Training can be expensive and in some cases the cost discourages investment in training. This may result in lower productivity and a loss of competitiveness. It might also be a danger to workers. The need for training is discussed later in this chapter.

Induction training

When people start a new job they are likely to receive some **induction training**. This helps new recruits settle in and become familiar with their new surroundings. If firms fail to provide adequate induction training, staff may feel anxious. This might lead to poor productivity. At worst, staff may leave because they have not settled. The nature of induction training will vary between businesses but Figure 21.2 shows what it might involve.

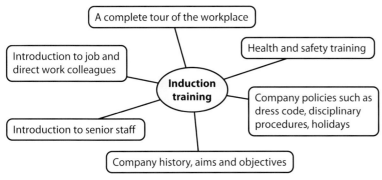

Figure 21.2 *Induction training*

QUESTION 1

Orange is one of the world's largest mobile communications companies. It recently ran an advertising campaign to tell customers about some new deals. These adverts generated a huge increase in customer calls at Orange's call centres. To cope with this increase, Orange recruited 1,000 new customer service workers.

Orange runs a three-week induction programme for new call centre staff. The training covers brand awareness, product and systems training, and customer service skills. 'We pride ourselves on our customer service,' said Lisa Blewitt, Orange's training manager. 'It is very important that each of our new employees receives a comprehensive induction, so that they can provide excellent service to customers.'

Figure 21.3 *A girl using a mobile phone*

(a) What is the purpose of induction training?

(b) What might new recruits learn during the induction programme?

(c) Why is induction training so important?

On-the-job training

One of the most common methods of training is **on-the-job training**. This means that workers are trained in the workplace while the job is being done. A number of different approaches might be used by a business.

- **Watching another worker:** On-the-job training by an existing member of staff is a common method. It involves a new recruit watching and copying the actions of an experienced and competent employee. This method can work well if the existing member of staff is a good and committed teacher. If not, the quality of training might be poor.

- **Mentoring:** This is where a trainee is paired with an experienced member of staff for a given period. The trainee is put to work without direct supervision but can call on the mentor for advice and guidance. Mentoring is used to help train teachers in the UK.

- **Job rotation:** This may involve a new recruit spending a period in different departments at a business. By working in a range of departments the employee will learn the different skills required and will gain a broad knowledge of how the business works. This approach will also improve the flexibility of the business.

The advantages and disadvantages of on-the-job training are summarised in Figure 21.4.

Advantages	Disadvantages
Output is being produced	Output may be lost if workers make mistakes
Relevant because trainees learn by actually doing the job	May be stressful for the worker – particularly if working with others
Cheaper than other forms of training	Staff may get frustrated if they are 'unpaid' trainers
Can be easy to organise	Could be a danger to others, e.g. surgeon or train driver

Figure 21.4 *Advantages and disadvantages of on-the-job training*

Off-the-job training

Some employees receive training away from the normal work area. This is called **off-the-job** training. For example, it might involve workers going to college once a week. Alternatively, it might involve a small group of managers travelling overseas to learn about a new management techniques. The advantages and disadvantages of off-the-job training are summarised in Figure 21.5.

The need for training

The main reason for training is to provide workers with the skills and knowledge needed to do their jobs effectively. As a result their productivity will increase. However, there are several other reasons.

Advantages	Disadvantages
Output is not affected if mistakes are made	No output because employees do not contribute to work
Learning cannot be distracted by work	Some off-the-job training is expensive if provided by specialists
Training could take place outside work hours if necessary	Some aspects of work cannot be taught off-the-job
Customers and others are not put at risk	It may take time to organise

Figure 21.5 *Advantages and disadvantages of off-the-job training*

- **Keeping workers up-to-date:** Workers will need training if there are changes which might affect their jobs. Some examples might include:

  - new health and safety procedures

  - new technology

  - after a takeover

  - new working practices

  - new legislation.

- **Improving labour flexibility:** Some businesses train their workers in a range of different jobs so that they are multi-skilled. This provides businesses with added flexibility.

- **Improving job satisfaction and motivation:** Workers will feel secure if they have been trained to do their job effectively. Not being able to do a job properly will be a source of frustration and dissatisfaction for workers. It is also argued that training can be used to motivate staff.

- **New jobs in the business:** Sometimes, due to expansion, new products or new technology, new jobs are created. This often means that some staff will need retraining.

- **Training for promotion:** Training is usually needed when workers are promoted. At each stage of the promotion process staff will need to learn new skills and methods. This allows them to handle the different duties and new responsibilities.

QUESTION 2

PricewaterhouseCoopers (PwC) is an international provider of professional services including accountancy, auditing, taxation and business advice. The company provides on-the-job and off-the-job training, particularly for new recruits. PwC provides opportunities for staff to learn and develop new skills. For example, if a new recruit opts for a commercial apprenticeship (auditing and accounting), they will spend three years working in different departments to get experience in the different aspects of the business. Employees will also attend internal and external training courses to prepare them for final exams. They will work in the following areas during their training:

- general operations (marketing, internal services, finance and human capital)
- specialist departments (tax and legal and auditing/assurance).

(a) Outline the difference between off-the-job and on-the-job training.

(b) How might PwC benefit from training its staff in different departments?

Government training schemes

It is common for governments to provide training. Most training initiatives are designed to equip people with the skills and knowledge required by employers. Some examples of the schemes available in the UK are outlined below.

- **Apprenticeships:** As employees, apprentices earn a wage and work alongside experienced staff to gain job-specific skills. Off the job, usually on a day-release basis, apprentices receive training to work towards nationally recognised qualifications. Anyone living in England, over 16 and not in full-time education can apply.

- **Flexible New Deal:** The Flexible New Deal is a programme of active labour market policies originally introduced by the government in the UK in 1998 as the New Deal. It was relaunched in 2010 as the Flexible New Deal. The purpose is to reduce unemployment by providing training, subsidised employment and voluntary work to the unemployed.

- **National Vocational Qualifications (NVQs):** The NVQ is a 'competence-based' qualification. This means people learn practical, work-related tasks designed to help develop the skills and knowledge required to do a job. NVQs are based on national standards for various occupations. The standards outline what a competent person in a job could be expected to do. They are awarded at different levels (1 to 5, with 5 being the highest). NVQs can be obtained in many business sectors such as administration, sales, marketing, health and social care, food, catering, leisure services, construction, manufacturing and engineering.

The benefits of training

Although it is expensive both managers and employees will benefit from training.

- **Managers:** Businesses will benefit from training if productivity is increased. This is because profit may rise if employees produce more. Managers will benefit because workers may be better motivated and more satisfied. This makes them more co-operative and easier to work with. Workers may also be more flexible, which will help managers in their organisation. Providing training may also improve the image of the business and make it easier to attract and retain high-quality staff.

- **Employees:** If workers have been trained, they will be able to do their jobs more effectively. This should reduce anxieties about their work and provide more job satisfaction. Employees may also feel valued if their employer is paying for their training. They may develop a range of skills which they can use in the future – to gain promotion or get a better job.

The costs of training

Some businesses are reluctant to invest heavily in training because of the costs. Some of the main ones are outlined below.

- **Training courses and other resources:** Training can be very expensive. Businesses will have to pay training providers if they use external training. Even internal training can be expensive if specialist training staff and equipment is needed.

- **Loss of output:** If workers are involved in off-the-job training they will not be producing anything. This will result in lower output levels. Even if workers are trained on the job there may be a loss of output due to mistakes and slow work associated with 'learners'.

- **Employees leaving:** Businesses are likely to get very frustrated if employees leave and join a rival company after they have invested in training them. Some businesses actually prefer to recruit workers that have already been trained by others to avoid such costs.

Chapter review – ME plc

ME is a growing electrical engineering company. It makes signalling equipment for the rail industry. The company is benefiting from the growth in rail travel and has recently invested in some computerised machinery. However, the introduction of the new technology has not been without problems. The conversation below took place between the production manager and the chief executive of ME plc.

CE: 'Another $120,000 on training is too much. It is double the annual training budget.'

PM: 'But without the training it will take at least another six months before the new system is up and running.'

CE: 'I know that training is necessary but it's so expensive. Plus, what happens when the trained workers leave and go and work for someone else?'

PM: 'I appreciate that, but **we** often get workers that have been trained elsewhere.'

CE: 'How many need to be trained?'

PM: 'About 15 – but if we trained all 30 staff we get more flexibility and won't have to spend on training again for quite a while.'

CE: 'Look – here's the deal. You can have $60,000 for on-the-job training. I don't want workers going off on one of these 'training holidays' for two weeks. We lose too much production and I would rather staff were trained on our system – not some simulator.'

(a) Why is training needed at ME plc? **(2 marks)**

(b) State two other reasons why a business might need to train its staff. **(2 marks)**

(c) Analyse two reasons why businesses may be reluctant to spend on training. **(4 marks)**

(d) Discuss the advantages and disadvantages of on-the-job training to ME plc. **(6 marks)**

(e) Analyse the benefits of training to employees and customers at ME plc. **(6 marks)**

Chapter 22: Motivation at work

Getting started...

Productivity can vary, which means that some workers produce more than others. There are several reasons for this. Some people are more capable, some are more experienced and others have received more training. However, another reason is that they are better motivated. They have drive and are more inclined to work harder. Look at the example below.

Brad Cummings and Alan Shumaker

Brad Cummings and Alan Shumaker both work for Silver City Chemicals, a chemical processing company based in Nevada, US. They are maintenance engineers and have been with the company for eight years. Brad is a highly motivated worker. He is punctual, reliable, supportive of his colleagues, enjoys solving problems and often gives up his own time to help new recruits. He enjoys his job and has recently been promoted. In contrast, Alan is poorly motivated. He is unreliable, lacks drive and is often late for work. He also has a reputation for being unco-operative and difficult to work with. He does not like his job and has received a written warning for poor attendance.

(a) State two possible reasons why Alan is poorly motivated.

(b) Outline why you think motivation is important to businesses.

What is meant by motivation?

Motivation is the desire to achieve a goal. Some people are self-motivated. This means they have the drive to achieve goals on their own. They do not need any encouragement. However, others need to be motivated. They need a push, pressure or incentives. For example, some students are self-motivated. They aim to achieve good results. They will attend all lessons, meet coursework deadlines and study hard. In contrast, some students lack the drive to achieve goals. These students will need encouragement such as rewards for good attendance or praise for missing deadlines.

Why is employee motivation important in business?

If a business has a well-motivated workforce, it will perform better. Labour productivity will be higher and therefore profits are likely to be higher. The main benefits are summarised in Figure 22.1.

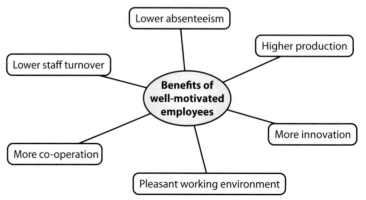

Figure 22.1 *The main benefits of having well-motivated employees*

- **Higher production:** Well-motivated employees will work harder. They are likely to take more pride in their work, complete tasks quickly and feel that their jobs are important. As a result, they will produce higher levels of output.

- **Lower staff turnover:** If workers are well motivated, they are less likely to leave their jobs. This means that staff turnover (the rate at which people leave a job) will be lower. This is good for a business because, if staff turnover is high, recruitment, selection and training costs will be higher.

- **Lower absenteeism:** Poorly motivated staff are more likely to take time off. They may also become depressed, use minor illness as an excuse for missing work or simply take time off. This is bad for business because production will be lost.

- **More co-operation:** Businesses need workers to co-operate. For example, more and more businesses organise their staff into teams. Therefore, if workers do not co-operate with each other teamwork will be disrupted. At worse, conflict might result if a team member is unco-operative. However, well-motivated employees are likely to be co-operative, so a good team spirit is likely to develop.

- **More innovation:** Businesses need to innovate by developing new products, new production processes and new systems to remain competitive. Well-motivated workers are more likely to be innovative than poorly motivated workers. This is because poorly-motivated workers 'don't really care'.

- **Pleasant working environment:** If workers are motivated, the working environment and atmosphere is likely to be pleasant. Workers are more likely to be cheerful, courteous, supportive and positive. This is important if workers have to deal with customers.

QUESTION 1

Red Star Holdings make automatic teller machines (ATMs) for the banking industry. Two years ago the company faced a staffing crisis because too many staff were leaving. The production manager had told the board repeatedly that worker morale was low and motivation poor. He thought the main reason for this was because the machinery was out of date and prone to breakdowns. As a result, earnings were being reduced due to so much 'downtime'. Eventually, in 2007, the board agreed to completely re-equip the factory.

(a) What is meant by a well-motivated employee?

(b) What evidence in Figure 22.2 suggests that workers were poorly motivated?

(c) What is likely to be the affect on the working environment if workers are not motivated?

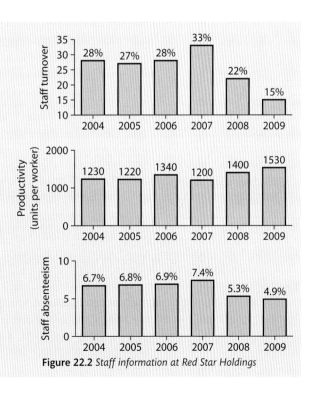

Figure 22.2 *Staff information at Red Star Holdings*

How can businesses influence motivation?

Businesses can change the motivation of workers because they can meet a number of human needs. These are outlined below.

- **Physiological needs:** Humans have some very basic needs which are called **physiological needs**. They include food, drink, shelter, warmth and rest. Humans also need protection from physical and physiological threats. If these needs are not met humans cannot survive. Work provides the means to satisfy these needs. By going to work people can earn money to buy food, clothes and safe shelter.

- **Social needs:** People are social animals. This means that they have **social needs**. People like to communicate and make friends. People also like to be cared for and belong to groups. Work can satisfy social needs. This is because people often work with others. This provides opportunities for people to meet and develop friendships and relationships.

- **Other needs:** In addition to physiological and social needs people also have higher needs. For example, most people want to be respected and recognised. They may also want to respect themselves. A lot of people want to develop skills and also develop as a person. Finally, many people want to reach their full potential. For example, they may want to create something or stand out in some way. Businesses can meet these needs by providing challenging and creative work and opportunities for promotion, for example.

Maslow's hierarchy of needs

A number of experts have developed theories which suggest ways in which workers can be motivated by satisfying the needs outlined above. Abraham Maslow recognised these needs but arranged them into a hierarchy showing that some needs are more important than others. **Maslow's hierarchy of needs** is usually presented in a pyramid and is shown in Figure 22.3.

- **Physiological needs:** These are at the bottom of the pyramid. They are the basic human needs. They include food, drink, shelter, warmth and rest. If these needs are not met humans cannot survive.

- **Safety and security:** People need protection from any form of danger and physical and psychological threats. They also need routine and familiarity.

- **Social needs:** People are social animals and need affection, trust, acceptance and to be cared for. They also want to belong to a recognised group.

- **Esteem needs:** People need to be recognised and respected and their achievements praised. They also want self-respect and self-esteem.

- **Self-actualisation:** This means that people need to reach their full potential and feel some fulfilment in what they do. These needs are at the top of the pyramid. Figure 22.4 shows how the needs in the hierarchy can be satisfied at work.

Did you know?

Businesses often organise their workers into teams. This is because teams of workers are more productive. It also helps to satisfy social needs because people are given the chance to form closer ties with people who have a common aim. Belonging to a team gives people a sense of identity and they may feel more secure.

Figure 22.3 *Maslow's hierarchy of needs*

Need	Work can provide
Physiological	Adequate pay – subsidised meals and accommodation
Safety and security	Job security and safe working conditions
Love and belonging	Teamworking, good communication systems and social facilities
Esteem	Praise for doing a good job; awards and rewards for achievement
Self-actualisation	Opportunities to be challenged, creative, solve problems and make decisions

Figure 22.4 *How work can satisfy people's needs*

Maslow also said that when businesses try to motivate workers by satisfying their needs, they need to recognise the following:

● Once one set of needs have been satisfied they are no longer a motivator. Workers can only be motivated by achieving the next set of needs in the hierarchy. Therefore if a worker has enough pay and feels secure at work, raising pay levels would not motivate that worker. A business would have to find ways of satisfying higher needs.

● If lower needs are not met, workers cannot be motivated if a business tries to meet higher needs. For example, if pay was inadequate, workers would not be motivated if a business was giving workers the chance to be creative.

● If a business fails to meet a particular need, workers are not likely to be motivated. For example, if a worker is overlooked for promotion, that worker may start to slack or look for another job.

Herzberg two-factor theory

Frederick Herzberg discovered that certain factors at work would help to give employees **job satisfaction**. He called these **motivators**. He also found that other factors can leave workers dissatisfied. He called these **hygiene factors**. Examples of these are shown in Figure 22.5.

Motivators	Hygiene factors
Achieving aims	Pay
Chance of promotion	Working conditions
Responsibility	Job security
Interesting work	Quality of supervision
Recognition	Staff relationships
Personal development	Company policy

Figure 22.5 *Herzberg's motivators and hygiene factors*

Herzberg said businesses must find ways of giving workers job satisfaction to motivate them. For example, they would have to ensure that jobs were interesting and that worker's achievements were recognised. Workers must also be given the chance to excel and win promotion. As a result, job enrichment could be used to motivate workers. However, Herzberg also said that hygiene factors would not motivate workers. But if hygiene factors such as pay, working conditions and the quality of supervision were inadequate, workers would not be motivated.

QUESTION 2

Mothercare is a retailer of products for expectant mothers and children up to eight years old. It employs over 7,000 staff in 428 stores and online sales.

There is a feel-good factor at Mothercare that makes employees feel part of one big happy family. Employees feel a strong sense of family in their team and go out of their way to help each other. Two-thirds of employees earn £7,500 or less and this suggests that job satisfaction is more about the working environment and colleagues than money.

Figure 22.6 *Mother and baby*

Mothercare gives monthly awards for outstanding contributions from staff. They might receive gifts of flowers, dinner or hotel vouchers. Also, senior managers recognise exceptional effort at company meetings, road shows and in personal telephone calls. The firm identifies those with potential and offers sponsorship for professional qualifications, job swaps, coaching and training courses. Staff say that managers talk honestly and openly with them, are supportive and motivate them to give their best every day.

(a) Do you think Mothercare satisfies Maslow's social needs?

(b) Analyse the difference between Herzberg's motivators and hygiene factors.

(c) How does Mothercare recognise staff achievements?

Key terms

Hygiene factors (Herzberg's) – things at work that result in dissatisfaction.

Job satisfaction – the pleasure, enjoyment or sense of achievement that employees get from their work.

Maslow's hierarchy of needs – the order of people's needs starting with basic human needs.

Motivation – the desire to achieve a goal.

Motivators (Herzberg's) – things at work that result in satisfaction.

Physiological needs – the basic needs of humans for their survival.

Social needs – the need of humans to communicate, develop friendships and belong.

Chapter review – Data Connection

Data Connection is a communications technology company. Founded in 1981, Microsoft, Cisco and Juniper are among its clients. The company is progressive in how it treats and trains its personnel. It gives all its 314 employees the chance to take a new direction. Employees say work is an important part of their lives. They feel they can make a valuable contribution to the success of the business and are proud to work for it.

Chief executive John Lazar joined the firm 22 years ago as a software engineer and worked his way up. This is quite common. Many of the managers have worked their way through the company to the top.

Employees say managers care about them as individuals. They feel supported by them and think they talk openly and honestly with them. New employees are assigned a mentor who, along with managers, sets aside 50 days of their time to train a new employee in their first year. Every employee has an individual development plan that is updated every three months. 'Managing people here is about nurturing and getting the best out of them,' says recruitment manager Alison Jackson.

A flexible benefits package includes free private healthcare for employees and their dependents, critical illness cover, life assurance and profit-related pay.

(a) Why do people need to work? **(2 marks)**

(b) Identify two examples that show that employees at Data Connection are well motivated. **(2 marks)**

(c) State four reasons why staff motivation is important to businesses. **(4 marks)**

(d) Give two examples of Herzberg's hygiene factors as used at Data Connection. **(2 marks)**

(e) To what extent does Data Connection satisfy the needs outlined by Maslow's hierarchy? **(10 marks)**

Chapter 23: Financial rewards

Getting started...

Most people go to work to earn money. However, businesses may use different payment systems to reward their staff. For example, factory workers might be paid an hourly rate which means they get paid so much per hour for every hour they work. Each system has advantages and disadvantages. Look at the examples below.

GVS Life Assurance

Nasir Gul works for GVS Life Assurance. He sells life assurance policies. He earns a basic salary of $400 per month. However, for every policy he sells he gets another $200. Nasir is well motivated and hard working. He is happy with the payment method and can earn up to $3,500 a month. Some of his colleagues are less happy. They lack Nasir's charm and skills and are often under a great deal of stress trying to earn a living.

Gazzetta di Brescia

Edmundo Canonica is a reporter for the Gazzetta di Brescia, a newspaper published in Brescia, Italy. He is paid €24,000 per annum. His work involves digging out local stories and editing the reports of junior staff. Edmundo's working hours vary a lot. If he is chasing a big story, he might work more than 12 hours a day – even at weekends. However, when it is quiet he may only work 6 hours a day. Most of the staff working for the newspaper are paid annual salaries.

(a) (i) How much would Nasir earn if he sold 11 insurance policies during a month?
    (ii) State one advantage and one disadvantage of the payment system used by GVS Life Assurance.

(b) (i) What system of payment is used for most of the employees at Gazzetta di Brescia?
    (ii) What might be a disadvantage of this method for the employer?

Time rates

Many workers are paid according to the amount of time they spend at work. This payment system is called a **time rate**. It is a common system and involves paying workers so much per hour or per week. Therefore, someone who earns $8.50 an hour and works 37 hours a week will receive $314.50 ($8.50 × 37). This is **gross pay**, i.e. pay before deductions. A worker's **net pay** is what they take home. It is gross pay minus deductions such as:

● income tax

● national insurance contributions

● pension contributions

● contributions to an employer savings scheme

● trade union membership fees.

Workers may be paid **overtime**. This means they get a higher hourly rate for working extra hours. For example, workers might get paid time and a half for working after the normal working day, at weekends or during public holidays. Therefore, if the hourly rate is $8.50 an hour, the overtime rate at time and a half would be $12.75 ($8.50 × 1.5).

Key fact

Time rates are a suitable method of payment when it is difficult to measure the output of workers. They are also appropriate if the work involves a high degree of skill, care or precision. Rushing such work may be dangerous or result in costly errors. However, one problem with time rates is that productivity is not rewarded. With time rates people are paid for their attendance at work. Conscientious and productive workers get the same as those who try to avoid work.

Some employees are paid a **salary** which is expressed in annual terms and paid monthly. Salaries are usually paid to *non-manual* workers. In the 'Getting started' example, Edmundo Canonica's salary was €24,000 per annum. His monthly gross pay would have been €2,000 (€24,000 ÷ 12). Salaried workers are not always paid overtime. For example, teachers receive a salary and are expected to work as long as it takes to do their jobs.

QUESTION 1

West Park Motor Services carry out maintenance, servicing and repair work on motor cars. The company employs one manager, nine mechanics, one labourer and a receptionist. The mechanics are paid $9 per hour and time and a half for every hour they work over 38 hours during a week. The manager is paid a salary of $32,000 per annum with no overtime payments.

Figure 23.1 *A car workshop*

One of the mechanics worked 53 hours during a busy week in September.

(a) Calculate the gross pay earned by this mechanic.

(b) What is the difference between gross and net pay?

(c) What is meant by a salary?

Piece rates

Some workers are paid according to how much they produce. This system is called **piece rate**. An example would be an employee picking grapes in a vineyard being paid 50 cents a kilo. The main benefit of this system for businesses is that it rewards productive workers. Workers who are lazy or slow will not earn as much as those who are conscientious and productive. This system helps to motivate workers and businesses are likely to 'get more' out of their employees. However, piece rates do have problems.

● Piece rates cannot be used if work cannot be measured. For example, it is very difficult to measure the output of a hotel receptionist or a research scientist.

● The quality of output may suffer if people work too fast. They may take short cuts and make mistakes. In the above example, a labourer picking grapes may damage some of the fruit when picking too quickly.

● Workers might use dangerous practices trying to work too fast. For example, machinists may remove protective guards to speed up production and therefore risk injury.

Commission

Commission, like piece rates, is payment for reaching a target. This method is often used to reward sales staff. A salesperson may be paid entirely on the basis of their sales record. This means that income is zero if no sales are made. However, a more common approach is to pay a salesperson a relatively low basic salary and top it up with commission payments. This is the method used by GVS Life Assurance in 'Getting started' at the beginning of this chapter.

Bonus payments

Some firms make **bonus payments** to workers. Bonuses are paid in addition to the basic wage or salary. They are usually paid if targets are met. For example, machinists may be paid a bonus if they reach a weekly production target. Bonuses can also be paid to groups of workers. For example, a sales team may get a bonus if the whole team meets a sales target. The main advantage to businesses of bonus payments is that they are only paid if targets are met. This means that money is only paid if it has been earned. Bonus payments may help to motivate workers as they strive to reach a target to earn their bonus.

Performance-related pay

Performance-related pay (PRP) is used to motivate non-manual workers. PRP is designed specifically to reward workers whose output is difficult to measure. It was popular in financial services and the public sector in the 1990s in the UK. PRP works best if businesses use an *appraisal* system to evaluate staff performance. This involves meeting with individual workers every year to:

- discuss progress at work
- assess whether targets have been met
- set new targets for the next year.

If targets have been met or exceeded, workers would get paid more. Businesses like PRP because it links pay to performance and only workers who perform well will be paid more. However, the system does have problems.

- Some workers feel that it is unfair because appraisers may be inconsistent. For example, pay awards may be given to certain workers out of favouritism. This may demotivate staff and cause conflict.
- The financial incentives may not be high enough to motivate workers to improve their performance.
- Some workers may feel that the performance targets set are too demanding.
- Some workers may blame other factors if targets are missed. For example, there may have been problems with computer systems which affected performance.

Profit sharing

One way to reward staff is to give them a share of the profit. This is called **profit sharing**. One approach is to give workers a share of the profit as a bonus or an extra payment on top of their basic pay. The advantages of profit sharing are:

- It should help to motivate workers. This is because if they produce more, the business is likely to make more profit. This means their share of the profit will be higher.
- It might help to unite workers and shareholders. They will have the same goal because both stakeholders will benefit from higher profits.
- All employees can be involved whether they are production workers or administrative workers.

Did you know?

Some businesses pay their staff *loyalty bonuses*. These are usually paid annually. Such bonuses are not necessarily linked to productivity. They are designed to reward workers for their loyalty.

Key terms

Bonus systems – a payment in addition to the basic wage for reaching targets or in recognition for service.

Commission – a payment based on the value of sales, usually a percentage of sales made.

Gross pay – pay before deductions.

Net pay – an employee's take home pay, i.e. pay after deductions such as income tax and pension contributions.

Overtime – a rate of pay above the normal rate to compensate employees for working extra hours.

Performance related pay – a payment system designed for non-manual workers where pay increases are given if performance targets are met.

Piece rate – a payment system where workers receive an amount of money for each unit produced.

Profit sharing – where workers are given a share of the profits, usually as part of their pay.

Salary – pay, usually to non-manual workers, expressed as a yearly figure but paid monthly.

Time rate – a payment system based on the amount of time employees spend at work.

- It can be used to show workers that they are appreciated. Giving workers a share of their profit suggests that they are valued by the owners.

The main disadvantage of profit sharing is that profit is determined by many factors. Some of these are beyond the control of individual workers. For example, employees may work very hard during the year only to find that the business has made a loss because a new competitor has entered the market. Also, profit sharing is not likely to motivate workers if the amount received is small.

QUESTION 2

Benson Industries is a large engineering company. It makes electronic mechanisms, switching gear, computer components and panel instruments. Benson employs 7,560 workers and has operations in Europe and Asia. The workers have a wide range of skills and are employed in many different jobs. Two years ago the company introduced a profit sharing scheme. At Christmas employees share 15 per cent of the profit made by the business.

(a) Calculate the amount each worker will receive if the business makes a profit of $81.65m.

(b) Outline three advantages of profit sharing to Benson Industries.

Share ownership

Some businesses give employees shares in the company. This means they are entitled to a dividend and therefore a share in the profits. The advantages and disadvantages of this method are very similar to those of profit sharing outlined above. The only real difference is that employees are also part owners of the business. They might also be able to sell their shares at a profit if the share price rises. However, employees often have to hold on to the shares for a period of time before they can be sold.

Chapter review – Zeal Mining Co

Zeal Mining Co is a copper mining company based in Zambia. In 2007, it introduced a new payment system for production workers. The old time rate system was considered inappropriate. Productivity in most of the company's mines had been flat for 10 years. The new system was a piece rate system. It involved paying teams of miners according to their weekly output. There was resistance to the new system when it was first introduced. This was because workers were unable to work when machinery broke down. However, this problem was solved when the company bought new machinery.

Six months after the piece rate system was introduced labour productivity improved by 18 per cent. However, accidents in the mine rose by 32 per cent. Workers had found ways of working faster by neglecting health and safety procedures. Another problem was that administration staff were complaining. They said that because productivity had increased, their workload had risen. However, the new piece rates did not apply to them.

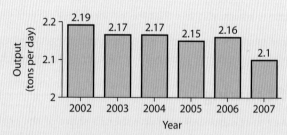

Figure 23.3 *Labour productivity at Zeal Mining Co*

(a) What evidence is there to suggest that workers at Zeal Mining Co need motivating? **(2 marks)**

(b) How does this case study highlight the main disadvantage of time rates as a method of payment? **(2 marks)**

(c) Analyse the advantages and disadvantages in this case study of piece rate as a system of payment. **(8 marks)**

The Human Resources manager at Zeal Mining Co has suggested using PRP to reward the administration workers.

(d) To what extent do you agree with this suggestion? **(8 marks)**

Figure 23.2 *A copper mine in Zambia*

Chapter 24: Non-financial rewards

Getting started...

All businesses pay workers money for their services. However, some businesses use other ways of rewarding workers. For example, some employees may be given a company car which can be driven for both business and personal use. Limited companies often give senior employees free shares. Alternatively, some businesses find ways of making work more interesting or fulfilling for their staff. Look at the examples below.

Oil & Gas Development Company (Pakistan)

The Pakistan government plans to give employees a 12 per cent stake in the state-owned Oil & Gas Development Company Ltd (OGDCL). The 438 million shares will be given free to the 10,576 employees in lots of 3,000 shares each. Workers will receive between one and 20 lots each, depending on their length of service. However, they will only be entitled to shares if they have been employed by the company for five years. They will get dividends while in employment. It is hoped that the scheme would create a sense of ownership among the workers, and that they would put more effort into their work.

Vodafone

Figure 24.1 *Formula One racing*

Valuing and rewarding staff is important at Vodafone. Staff get exciting opportunities, such as meeting Lewis Hamilton through its sponsorship of Formula One, or developing their skills by working abroad. Managers, who care about worker satisfaction, set workers challenging goals. These include gaining qualifications in finance, marketing, team leadership, customer service and IT. Vodafone matches funds raised by employees for charities. It also allows them to use 24 hours of work time each year to carry out volunteer work. Other benefits include a well-being centre with a gym, childcare vouchers and extra holidays.

(a) (i) How is the Pakistan government allocating shares to the employees of OGDCL?
   (ii) How might the business benefit from employees holding shares?

(b) Describe three non-financial benefits used to reward staff at Vodafone.

Non-financial rewards

Businesses use non-financial rewards for a number of reasons.

● Some people are not motivated by money.

● Some workers attach more importance to non-financial rewards.

● Financial incentive schemes are not always appropriate for many workers.

● Since more and more people work in teams, individual financial rewards are less appropriate.

Some non-financial rewards can satisfy workers' needs better than money. Examples of non-financial rewards include: **fringe benefits**; interesting work; opportunities to solve problems and make decisions; a sense of achievement; holidays and breaks; recognition and praise and a chance of promotion. Some of these are discussed in detail overleaf.

Fringe benefits

Some employees receive fringe benefits in addition to their normal pay. They are often described as the 'perks' of the job. Examples of fringe benefits are shown in Figure 24.2.

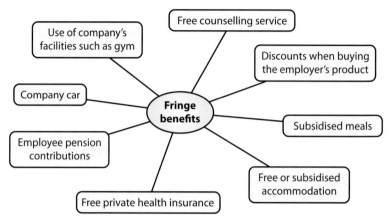

Figure 24.2 *Examples of fringe benefits*

Why might fringe benefits be used?

There are some good reasons for rewarding workers with fringe benefits.

- It may be cheaper to give employees $2,000 of fringe benefits than $2,000 in cash. Employees **may** also pay less tax if they take fringe benefits instead of cash.

- Productivity may improve because there is less staff absence. Workers may be healthier due to private healthcare and using the company gym, sports facilities and counselling services.

- Some benefits help to attract and retain better qualified employees for a business.

- Many benefits provide protection and security for workers and their families. This might help to improve worker satisfaction, such as free private health insurance.

- Some fringe benefits are performance related. This will help to motivate staff. Also, some fringe benefits are only available to senior staff. This might encourage employees to aim for promotion.

QUESTION 1

Morgan Stanley is a global financial services provider based in New York, US. Many employees earn over $50,000 pa. Morgan Stanley also provides free private healthcare for the whole family, child care, dental insurance, life assurance, performance-related pay and a share option scheme. An employee assistance programme helps staff outside of work. It includes a legal helpline and one-to-one counselling. Other benefits include a health and well-being programme and a free gym. Staff can also use an on-site medical centre, massage therapist, physiotherapist, and acupuncturist.

(a) What is meant by fringe benefits? (Use examples from the case study.)

(b) Outline two possible advantages of fringe benefits to Morgan Stanley.

Other non-financial rewards

Some businesses try to reward employees by making their working life more satisfying and challenging. Here are some of the methods that might be used.

- **Job enrichment:** Jobs can be made more challenging and rewarding if tasks require more responsibility and creativity. This is called **job enrichment**. Employees may be given the opportunity to develop unused skills. Developing such skills and taking on more challenging tasks should make work more interesting. It might also encourage staff to aim for promotion and they may feel valued.

- **Job rotation:** One way to make work more interesting is to allow employees to change jobs from time to time. This will give workers more variety and help to avoid boredom. This is called **job rotation**.

- **Teamworking:** This involves dividing the workforce into small groups. Each team will focus on a particular area of production and team members will have the same common aims. This can be rewarding for workers because they can form bonds and develop friendships more easily. Workers may develop a 'team spirit', which can improve motivation and productivity. They will also have a greater sense of belonging.

- **Recognition and praise:** If someone has done a good job it is important to show appreciation and praise them. It costs nothing to say 'Thank you and well done!'. If said sincerely, this can be uplifting for an employee.

- **Promotion:** Many people want to develop a career at work. This means they want to improve their skills, learn new ones and try to get promotion. A business can reward workers if there is a clear route to the top. The chance of promotion at work will help to motivate workers. Therefore businesses must use internal recruitment.

Did you know?

In a supermarket, job rotation might mean that staff switch between shelf-filling, trolley collection, customer services and the checkout. Job rotation should help motivate workers and provide a business with more flexibility.

Did you know?

Some businesses reward their employees by giving them awards and prizes as a means of showing recognition. Others offer training. This shows that a business is prepared to invest in workers.

QUESTION 2

Telefonica O2, the communications company, offers its 13,142 staff attractive rewards and benefits. It provides training and career opportunities in a friendly working environment. Managers have regular career conversations with staff to discuss how they can help them learn new skills. Each employee has a personal development plan.

A range of incentive and recognition schemes keeps employees feeling valued. They include the Spirit of O2 awards. This involves giving staff vouchers if they have gone the extra mile during the year. O2 also gives prizes for top performers such as concert tickets or the chance to see Arsenal play or an England rugby match. Staff are encouraged to present new ideas to the management. These help employees' ideas to get recognised. Managers, who care about staff as individuals, show their appreciation when people have done a good job.

Figure 24.3 *A music concert*

(a) How does Telefonica O2 help staff develop a career?

(b) How does Telefonica O2 show recognition to its workforce?

Drawbacks of non-financial rewards

Some of the drawbacks of non-financial rewards are outlined below.

- Some methods, such as job enrichment and job rotation, may mean changing working practices. Some workers may object to this because they are content with current methods. This change may cause conflict between managers and workers.

- Some methods may be expensive to introduce. Introducing job enrichment and job rotation will mean training for employees. There may also be some disruption and loss of production while training takes place.

- Employees may be unhappy if they think managers are using these methods just to get more work out of them for the same pay. Therefore it may be necessary to increase pay.

- For some workers it is not possible to make their jobs more satisfying. These tend to be unskilled jobs such as assembly work where one tedious assembly job is much the same as another.

Key terms

Fringe benefits – 'perks' over and above the normal wage or salary.

Job enrichment – making workers' jobs more challenging by giving them opportunities to be creative and take on responsibility.

Job rotation – allowing workers to change jobs from time to time.

Chapter review – Microsoft

Microsoft wants its people to realise their full potential. The company recruits about 25 graduates every year in the UK and they immediately go on a training course. The Microsoft Academy for College Hires is a two-year programme that helps new recruits adapt to the world of work. Over 80 per cent of the staff think the job is good for their personal development. A mentoring scheme ensures new graduates are supported by a colleague who has undergone the same induction. A $1,500 bonus also welcomes new graduates when they join Microsoft. Graduates are also given training specific to their role and get support if they want to obtain professional qualifications.

Workers are organised into teams. Employees say they also have fun. Regular events at team, department and company level ensure success is celebrated and staff remain engaged. Managers have morale budgets which are used to keep teams happy and motivated. One new Microsoft building provides a light, open and airy working environment. It has informal areas to encourage creative and relaxed thinking. Other benefits at Microsoft include a share option scheme, a gym, childcare facilities, private health insurance, generous maternity and paternity leave and good holidays.

(a) What is meant by non-financial rewards? (Use examples from this case study.) **(2 marks)**

(b) Why do businesses such as Microsoft use non-financial rewards? **(2 marks)**

(c) State two fringe benefits enjoyed by workers at Microsoft. **(2 marks)**

(d) Why do you think praise is important at work? **(2 marks)**

(e) How important do you think training is at Microsoft? **(4 marks)**

(f) How effective do you think team working is at Microsoft? **(4 marks)**

(g) Outline two possible disadvantages of non-financial rewards. **(4 marks)**

Section 3: Accounting and finance

Chapter 25: Sources of finance – short-term

Getting started...

No business can get started or survive without adequate finance. This means that money is needed to set up a business and to keep it running. Finance is also needed to help a business expand. Look at the examples below.

Emily Robinson

Emily Robinson received $40,000 in redundancy pay when she lost her job as an investment banker in Chicago. She now plans to set up an employment agency to supply staff in the financial services sector. She believes that when the economy picks up this sector will recover quickly. Therefore financial institutions will need to recruit staff again. However, she needs an office, desks, filing cabinets and computers. She also plans to spend a lot on advertising to establish her business. Emily reckons this will all cost $70,000 in total. She needs to find another $30,000 to set up the agency.

Dabengwa Crafted Furniture Ltd

Henry Dabengwa runs a small business making furniture and other wooden products. He rents a workshop in Harare, Zimbabwe, and specialises in teak products such as doors, chairs, bar stools, staircases and window frames. He employs four people and sells to both business and residential customers. Henry has just received a big order from a hotel in Harare. The hotel wants Henry to make some furniture to help refurbish all the rooms. To complete the order Henry needs $5,000 to pay for raw materials.

(a) Why is finance needed in the above examples?

(b) How might finance be raised by Emily Robinson and Henry Dabengwa?

Figure 25.1 *Henry Dabengwa specialises in teak products such as staircases*

The need for funds

- **Start-up capital:** Funds are most needed when first setting up a business. This is because a lot of resources are needed before trading can begin. Some of these resources are 'one-off' items. For example, a new restaurant would need to buy cookers, refrigerators, utensils, furniture, glassware, cutlery, crockery and other equipment. Once these 'one-off' costs have been met, they may not be repeated for many years. Other start-up costs might include research, converting premises, legal fees, website design and marketing.

- **Working capital:** Once a business starts trading it will earn revenue. This money can be used to meet the day-to-day running costs of the business such as wages, raw materials, components and utility bills. However, sometimes the revenue from sales may not cover all expenditure. This is when a business will need to borrow money. The money needed to fund day-to-day expenditure is called *working capital*. This is discussed in Chapter 27.

- **Expansion:** Once a business is established the owners often want to expand. They may want to:

  - expand capacity to meet growing orders

  - develop new products

Key fact

Most entrepreneurs risk their own money when starting a business. However, this money is rarely enough. They need to find finance from other sources. Also, businesses often struggle to find start-up capital and may start trading with insufficient funds.

- branch into overseas markets
- diversify.

These activities often require large amounts of money. Most businesses have to find extra funding to expand. This is because internal sources of finance, such as profit, are not adequate.

- **Emergency funding:** Businesses often get unexpected bills – a tax demand perhaps. If the business does not have enough money it will need to get some very quickly. Businesses have to manage their *cash flow* (see Chapter 29) carefully. If businesses run out of cash, they will not be able to continue trading. Consequently, businesses are often forced to raise money quickly when cash runs short.

Figure 25.2 *A common pest*

QUESTION 1

Al-Sayed Raouf wants to set up a pest control business in Giza, Egypt. He plans to help hotels and restaurants in Giza deal with pest control problems such as rats and cockroaches. He has found some premises and has produced a list of resources that will be needed to start the business. This is shown in Figure 25.3.

(a) (i) Calculate the total amount of start-up capital that the business will need in this case study.
(ii) Al-Sayed Raouf has EGP500 of his own money. How much more will he need to raise in start-up capital?

(b) Why is the need for funds probably at its greatest when businesses are first set up?

(c) Why will Al-Sayed Raouf need working capital?

Start-up costs	EGP
Van	320
Mobile phone	25
Lease on premises	400
Pest control manual	80
Rat traps	200
Cockroach traps	300
Safety boots	25
Disposable gloves	40
Bait gun	25
Sewer bait depositor	150
Pesticides	200
Pesticide storage locker	95
Rechargeable hand lamp	40
Other equipment	200
Other set-up costs	300

Figure 25.3 *Start-up costs for Al-Sayed Raouf's pest control business*

Internal and external finance

Sources of finance may be internal or external. External sources are those which come from outside the business. Examples might be the sale of shares, bank loans, overdrafts or trade credit. These are discussed later in the chapter. Internal sources come from inside the business and can only be used when the business is established. This is because new businesses, are usually short of finance. There are three main internal sources of finance.

- **Retained profit:** Retained profit is profit that has not been returned to the owners. It is retained by the business. It is the most important source of finance for a business because it is cheap. There are no charges such as interest, dividends or administration. However, if profit is used by the business, it cannot be returned to the owners. Some owners might object to this.

- **Working capital:** It may be possible to use some working capital to provide extra finance for the business. This can be done by:

  - reducing the trade credit period, say from 90 to 60 days. This means that customers have to pay for their goods sooner.

- reducing the amount of stocks held. This means money is released and can be used to boost cash reserves.

- delaying payments to suppliers so that the business holds on to its cash for longer.

- **Sale of assets:** An established business may be able to sell some unwanted *assets* to raise finance. For example, machinery, land and buildings that are no longer required could be sold off. Large companies can sell off parts of their organisation to raise finance.

Short-term sources of finance

Businesses often need to borrow money for a short period. This is called **short-term finance** and is money borrowed for *one year* or less. Short-term finance is often used to boost working capital. Here are some examples.

- Some businesses have seasonal trade. A farmer, for example, may need to borrow money for a few months until revenue comes in from selling the harvest.

- A textiles manufacturer may need short-term finance to pay for raw materials and wages to meet a large order.

- A firm might need a short-term loan because it is waiting for a customer to pay.

Short-term finance is also likely to be needed to meet emergency expenditure. For example, if a machine breaks down unexpectedly, the repair costs might have to be met by a short-term loan. The main sources of short-term finance are outlined below.

- **Bank overdraft:** This is a common source of finance for most businesses. A bank overdraft means a business can spend more money than it has in its account. In other words, they go *overdrawn*. An overdraft limit will be set by the bank and interest is only charged when the account is overdrawn. Bank overdrafts are simple and flexible. However, the bank has the right to call in the money owed at any time. It may do this if it thinks the business is struggling.

- **Bank loan (unsecured):** A loan is a fixed agreement between a business and the bank. The amount borrowed, and interest, must be repaid in regular instalments over a fixed period. Bank loans can be short-term or long-term sources of finance. The main advantage of a bank loan is that a business will know exactly what it has to pay every month.

- **Hire purchase:** Small businesses often use **hire purchase** (HP) to buy tools, equipment, vehicles and machinery. What are the features of a HP agreement?

  - A business usually makes a down payment.

  - The remainder is paid in monthly instalments.

  - The goods bought do not legally belong to the buyer until the very last instalment has been paid.

  - If the buyer falls behind with the repayments, the goods can be repossessed.

  - HP agreements can be short-term and long-term.

The main problem with HP is that it is usually more expensive than a bank loan. This is because lenders are not as strict when checking the creditworthiness of borrowers.

- **Leasing:** A **lease** is a contract which allows businesses to use resources such as property, machinery or equipment in return for regular payments. Leasing is like renting or hiring really. For example, a farmer might lease a combine harvester for six weeks during the harvest period. The farmer will probably pay a daily or weekly rate for the term of the lease. Leasing may be long-term or short-term. There are some advantages of leasing.

  - A business can use expensive equipment without having to buy it outright.

  - Maintenance and repair costs are not the responsibility of the user.

  - Hire companies can offer the most up-to-date equipment.

  - Leasing is useful when equipment is only required occasionally.

  - A leasing agreement is easier for a new business to obtain than other forms of loan finance. This is because the leasing company is only hiring out equipment.

  However, the main disadvantage with leasing is that over a long period it is dearer than buying plant and machinery outright.

- **Trade credit:** Businesses often buy resources and pay for them at a later date, usually within 30–90 days. This is called *trade credit* and is a cheap way of raising finance. It means a business holds on to its cash for longer. However:

  - many suppliers encourage early payment by offering discounts

  - the cost of goods is often higher if firms buy on credit

  - delaying payment may result in problems with suppliers.

- **Credit cards:** Credit cards are popular because they are convenient, flexible and avoid interest charges if accounts are settled within the credit period. They can be used by executives to meet expenses when travelling on company business. Small businesses use credit cards to buy materials from suppliers. However, interest rates on credit cards are very high if accounts are not settled within the credit period, usually 56 days.

Key terms

Hire purchase – buying specific goods with a loan, often provided by a finance house.

Leasing – renting or hiring equipment or property.

Retained profit – the profit held by a business rather than returning it to the owners.

Short-term finance – money borrowed for one year or less.

Chapter review – Propshore Ltd

Propshore Ltd is a boat manufacturer. In 2008, the business made a profit of $2.1m but in 2009 lost $79,000 due to the global recession. Wally Spencer, the main shareholder in the business, said: 'Trading conditions are very difficult now and will be for at least the next 18 months. Fortunately, we have been cautious in the past and retained quite a lot of profit ... this will hold us in good stead.'

Propshore need to replace some computer equipment which is now out of date. Wally is not sure whether he should lease the equipment or take out a $10,000 bank loan. He is concerned that computers go out of date very quickly. However, leasing is usually more expensive than buying equipment.

(a) What is meant by short-term finance? **(2 marks)**

(b) Why is retained profit an internal source of finance? **(2 marks)**

Propshore Ltd often uses retained profit to fund business activity.

(c) What is the main reason for using this method of financing? **(2 marks)**

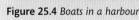

Figure 25.4 *Boats in a harbour*

Propshore uses trade credit to buy raw materials.

(d) Analyse one advantage and one disadvantage of trade credit as a source of finance. **(4 marks)**

(e) Discuss whether Propshore should lease the computer equipment or buy it with a short-term bank loan. **(8 marks)**

Chapter 26: Sources of finance – long-term

Getting started...

Businesses have to decide which source of funds is best for their needs. They often have to choose between long-term and short-term sources and may be faced with a choice between alternative sources of finance. Most businesses are likely to use several different sources. Look at the example below.

Yanbu Cement Company

The Yanbu Cement Company (YCC) is one of Saudi Arabia's biggest cement companies. It recently built a new production line at the Yanbu Site and new HQ offices in Jeddah.

Demand for cement is expected to rise because the Saudi government is developing some new cities. A number of commercial and residential construction projects are planned along with some infrastructure developments. As a result, Yanbu said it would spend SAR1.5bn to raise capacity by 48 per cent. YCC will fund the expansion through internal sources and a loan from the National Commercial Bank.

The company has issued share capital of SAR1,050m. At the end of June 2009, YCC had a bank overdraft of SAR2.94m, owed SAR8.03m to suppliers and owed SAR7.4m in other bank loans.

(a) How did the Yanbu Cement Company raise its capital?

Yanbu Cement Company is going to raise SAR1.5bn to expand capacity.

(b) (i) What source of finance is the business going to use?
(ii) Identify other sources of funds used by the company.

Figure 26.1 *Industrial cement mixing*

Long-term sources of finance

Long-term finance is money borrowed for more than one year. External long-term funds can be in the form of capital or loans. Capital is the money put in by the owners and loans are borrowed money. The main sources of long-term finance are outlined below.

- **Owner's capital:** Small businesses are often set up using money belonging to the owner. For example, entrepreneurs may put their savings or money raised from friends and relatives into a business. This is a cheap source of finance because there is no interest to pay. However, the owner's capital is rarely enough to start a business. Also, once this money is put into the business it is not likely to be taken out.

- **Share capital:** For limited companies **share capital** is an important source of external finance. The sale of shares can raise very large amounts of money. When limited companies are formed, shares are issued to raise start-up capital. However, limited companies can raise more money by selling more shares in the future. The main advantage of selling shares to raise capital is that interest payments are avoided. However, shareholders will expect to be paid dividends if the business is successful.

Key fact

Share capital is *permanent* capital. This means that it is not repaid (as long as the company is still trading).

- **Loan capital:** Loan capital is money that is borrowed, usually from banks and other financial institutions. It may come from a number of sources.

  - **Debenture** holders are creditors of a company, not owners. Debenture holders are entitled to a fixed rate of return, but have no voting rights. They must also be repaid on a set date – when the debenture matures. Public limited companies (plcs) use this long-term source of finance.

  - **Mortgages** are long-term loans and the borrower must use land or property as security. This means that if the borrower fails to make the repayments, the lender can repossess the property. Mortgages are popular because the interest rates are much lower than those on unsecured bank loans. Mortgages may be taken out for up to 25 years.

  - **Venture capitalists** provide funds for companies that have some potential, but are considered too risky by other investors. Venture capitalists often use their own funds, but also attract money from other lenders. They usually take a stake in the business which means they can influence decision making. They are often keen to sell their stakes at a profit after about five years.

Government finance

In many countries governments give financial help to businesses. Governments prefer to give money to businesses that set up in regions where there is heavy unemployment. Small businesses are also favoured, as are start-ups. The government may give a business a grant which does not have to be repaid. Alternatively, it may lend businesses money at low rates of interest. Another option is to provide a guarantee scheme where the government promises to repay a business loan to a lender if the business fails. Some examples of UK government finance schemes are outlined below.

- **Enterprise Finance Guarantee (EFG):** is for businesses with a turnover of up to £25 million who cannot get the finance they need. This will enable businesses to get loans of between £1,000 and £1million.

- **Working Capital Scheme (WCS):** involves government guarantees to banks of up to £10 billion, which will support bank lending of up to £20 billion.

- **Capital for Enterprise fund (CFE):** this allows companies to fund business development by selling debt in exchange for an equity stake in their business.

- **Enterprise Capital Funds (ECFs):** this fund offers up to £2 million to businesses that cannot raise funds from venture capitalists.

Did you know?

In India, the public sector banks are the major source of financial assistance to businesses. They extend credit support to the firms in the form of loans, advances, project financing, loans and export finance. For example the State Bank of India (SBI) provides a wide range of financial products and services that can cater for any business or market requirement.

QUESTION 1

Tune Hotels is a budget hotel chain with five hotels in Malaysia. It claims to offer a Five-Star service at One-Star prices. It now wants to set up a franchising operation and develop more hotels in other Asian countries. Tune Hotel's CEO Mark Lankester said: 'We are looking at 20 franchised hotels in India, 20 in Indonesia, Singapore and Malaysia and possibly 20 more in Thailand.' The company is considering raising $25m by issuing shares.

(a) Why is Tune Hotels planning to raise $25m?

(b) Using this case study as an example, state what is meant by a long-term source of capital.

(c) Outline one advantage of raising capital by selling shares.

Choosing sources of finance

Businesses have to decide how to raise finance. Generally, businesses need to decide what sources are available, which is the most suitable and which is the cheapest. The following factors are likely to affect the choice of finance.

● **Cost:** Businesses obviously prefer the cheapest sources of finance. They have to consider both the interest payments and administration costs. For example, share issues can carry high administration costs while the interest payments on bank overdrafts tend to be relatively low. Interest rates on mortgages are also competitive. Other costs also have to be taken into account. For example, if venture capitalists provide funding, they usually want a stake in the business. This means that the owners will lose some control.

● **Use of funds:** When a company undertakes heavy capital expenditure, it is usually funded by long-term sources. For example, the building of a new plant may be financed by a share issue or a mortgage. Money needed for working capital is usually financed by short-term sources. For example, the purchase of a large amount of raw materials may be funded by trade credit or a bank overdraft.

● **Status and size:** Sole traders, which tend to be small, are limited in their choices of finance. For example, long-term sources may be mortgages and perhaps the introduction of some personal capital. Public and private limited companies can usually obtain finance from many different sources. In addition, due to their size and added security, they can often demand lower interest rates from lenders.

● **Financial situation:** The financial situation of businesses is likely to change. When a business is in a poor financial situation, it is difficult to raise finance. At the same time, the cost of borrowing rises. Financial institutions are more willing to lend to secure businesses which have *collateral* (assets which provide security for loans).

● **Risk:** Companies sometimes have to choose between selling shares or taking out loans when raising finance. Taking out a loan may be more risky because interest has to be paid. One way of measuring the risk is to look at the **gearing** of the company. This is the relationship between the loan capital and share capital. A company is said to be *high geared* if it has a lot of loan capital relative to share capital. A *low geared* company has a relatively small amount of loan capital. The gearing of a company might influence its choice of finance. If a business is high geared, it may be reluctant to raise even more finance by borrowing. It may choose to issue more shares instead, rather than increasing the interest to be paid on loans. Figure 26.2 shows the advantages and disadvantages of being low or high geared.

	Advantages
Low geared	The burden of loan repayments is reduced The need for interest payments is reduced Volatile interest rates are less of a threat
High geared	Interest can be offset against tax Ownership is not diluted Debt is reduced once loans are repaid
	Disadvantages
Low geared	Dividend are paid indefinitely Company ownership is diluted Dividends are paid after tax
High geared	Interest payments must be met Changes in interest rates cause uncertainty Loans have to be repaid

Figure 26.2 *Advantages and disadvantages of being high geared and low geared*

QUESTION 2

D'Souza Ltd, a private limited company owned by Felix and Tariq D'Souza, is a food wholesaler based in Ahmadabad, India. It supplies more than 400 stores, some of which it also owns. Its wholesale arm supplies fresh and frozen food from a warehouse in Ahmadabad. Other operations include the D'Souza corner shop chain and shop developer D'Souza Group Property. Sales in 2008 reached Rs27.8bn, when the group opened 27 new stores. A further 28 are planned for this year. D'Souza employs 1,847 staff and made a profit of Rs755m in 2008.

Key terms

Debenture – a long-term loan to a business.

Gearing – the amount of capital raised from loans in relation to the amount raised from the sales of shares.

Long-term finance – money borrowed for more than one year.

Mortgage – long-term loan secured with property.

Share capital – money raised from the sale of shares in a limited company.

Venture capitalists – specialists (individuals or financial institutions) which provide funds for businesses, usually in exchange for an equity stake.

(a) State whether the following expenditure by D'Souza Ltd would require long-term or short-term funding:

  (i) buying land for new stores
  (ii) paying wages
  (iii) buying food from farmers and other suppliers
  (iv) buying new lorries for distribution.

D'Souza Ltd could not sell shares on the stock market to raise finance.

(b) What is the reason for this?

(c) What sources of finance might be suitable to fund the building of a Rs350m warehouse for D'Souza Ltd?

Figure 26.3 *Interior of an Indian food store*

Availability of finance

Some sources of funds are not available to all businesses. For example, sole traders and partnerships cannot sell shares or debentures. Small businesses may be refused finance because they are too risky. Also, during 2008 and 2009 there was a global recession. This was caused by a banking crisis and resulted in a 'credit crunch'. This meant that the availability of funds was very limited. Financial institutions were reluctant to lend because they feared risk.

Chapter review – Gulf Oil Supplies

Gulf Oil Supplies makes drilling and engineering equipment for the UAE's oil industry. It was set up in 1999 with AED1,000,000 of share capital, owned equally between Ali Ibrahim and Yousef Maaded, a AED250,000 bank loan and a AED50,000 government grant. Yousef, who studied Business Management at UAE University, insisted that the business should be properly funded at the start. He knew that small businesses that lacked funding in the initial stages would struggle. The company rents a factory unit and leases about 80 per cent of its plant, machinery and equipment.

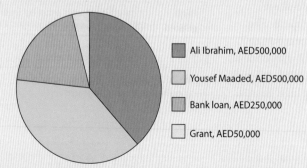

- Ali Ibrahim, AED500,000
- Yousef Maaded, AED500,000
- Bank loan, AED250,000
- Grant, AED50,000

Figure 26.4 *Gulf Oil Supplies start-up capital*

The company has done well since starting up, helped by the rising oil price. Most of the company's growth has been funded from retained profit. Ali and Yousef have been happy to retain around 90 per cent of the profit for investment purposes. This has avoided the need to borrow large amounts of money. However, in 2006, Ali and Yousef decided it was time to move to a larger factory. They calculated that they would need to raise AED1,200,000 to move and update their technology. Half of the money would come from retained profit but the rest would have to come from other sources.

Figure 26.5 *Oil drilling equipment*

(a) Examine how Gulf Oil supplies raised its start-up capital. **(2 marks)**

(b) What is the main advantage of using a government grant as a source of finance? **(2 marks)**

Many new businesses struggle because they do not have enough capital when they start up.

(c) How did Gulf Oil Supplies avoid this problem? **(4 marks)**

(d) **(i)** What is meant by gearing? **(2 marks)**
  (ii) What has happened to the gearing as a result of the expansion? **(2 marks)**
  (iii) State two disadvantages of being highly geared. **(2 marks)**

(e) Discuss how Ali and Yousef should raise the rest of the money for the new technology. **(6 marks)**

Chapter 27: Working capital

Getting started...

Businesses need money to meet the costs of day-to-day trading. For example, an airline company such as Emirates will need money to pay for aviation fuel, airline meals, airport services, wages, and so on. If it does not have enough money to meet these costs, it will not be able to trade. Look at the example below.

ELCO

On 23 July 2009, Felipe Passarella, the managing director of ELCO, was a worried man. The electrical engineering company was running out of cash. He had just heard that a customer had gone bankrupt owing ELCO a lot of money. This money was needed to help buy some materials for a big order. Staff wages of $12,700 were also due to be paid on 30 July and ELCO was $12,300 overdrawn at the bank. The overdraft limit was $20,000. The profit on the big order would be $48,000, but this would not be received until the order had been completed and delivered.

Figure 27.1 *A frantic MD!*

(a) How much money does ELCO need to pay the wages on 30 July 2009 (assume no other income or expenses)?

(b) How might Felipe deal with the problem?

(c) What might happen to the business if Felipe cannot get enough cash to pay the wages on 30 July 2009?

What is working capital?

Working capital is the amount of money needed to pay for day-to-day trading. It is used to buy resources and pay bills such as wages, insurance and advertising. Working capital is the difference between the liquid assets of a business, such as cash and stocks, and the money owed by a business which must be repaid within a year. Working capital is shown in the balance sheet and is calculated by subtracting current liabilities from current assets:

$$\text{Working capital} = \text{current assets} - \text{current liabilities}$$

If a business has current assets of $675,600 and current liabilities of $435,200, the value of working capital is $240,400. This means that the business has $240,400 to meet its immediate expenses.

The amount of working capital a business has is important. It can show how well a business is performing.

The working capital cycle

The **working capital cycle** in Figure 27.2 shows the movement of cash and other liquid resources into and out of a business. It helps to illustrate the time intervals between payments made by a business and the receipt of cash.

Did you know?

A business that is struggling is likely to have less working capital. Consequently, if a balance sheet shows a low level of working capital, this suggests that the business may be in trouble.

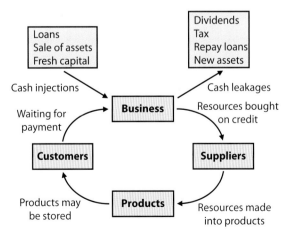

Figure 27.2 *The working capital cycle*

What does the working capital cycle show?

- Businesses often purchase resources on credit. This means that a business can obtain resources without having to pay for them immediately.

- A second interval exists while resources are made into goods or services. The length of this interval depends on the nature of the business. Other costs such as wages are incurred during this time.

- When production is complete goods may be stored before they are sold. This enables a business to cope with unexpected increases in demand. When goods are distributed there will be transport and handling costs.

- A final interval occurs when goods have been sold. If trade credit is given to customers it might be 30–90 days before payment is received. Once cash has been collected much of it is used to keep the process going – buying more materials and paying wages, for example.

- A business may get injections of cash from loans, asset sales and fresh capital. However, there will also be cash drains. Cash will leak from the cycle to pay dividends, tax, repay loans or buy new fixed assets.

	2009
Current assets	(NAD)
Stocks	4,500
Debtors	230
Cash	6,700
Current liabilities	
Trade creditors	1,200
Leasing charges	500
Other creditors	2,100

Figure 27.3 *Current assets and current liabilities for the Angula family's gift shop*

QUESTION 1

The Angula family run a gift shop in Windhoek, Namibia. The shop is busy during the tourist season but can struggle during the low season. Figure 27.3 shows the current assets and current liabilities for the business at the end of the busy season in 2009.

Businesses such as the Angula's gift shop need working capital.

(a) Outline the main reason for working capital.

(b) How much working capital does the gift shop have?

(c) What is likely to happen to working capital during the low season?

Figure 27.4 *A gift shop in Africa*

Managing working capital

The time intervals outlined above are important when managing working capital. Businesses can improve their working capital by:

- delaying payments to suppliers

- reducing production time so that goods can be sold more quickly

- reducing the time goods are stored before they are delivered to customers

- reducing the time it takes for customers to settle their bills.

How much working capital does a business need?

Different businesses may need different amounts of working capital. For example, firms that sell goods for cash, such as retailers, can operate with less working capital. However, it is often said that if the value of current assets is between one and a half or two times bigger than current liabilities, a business will have enough working capital. The *current ratio* and the *acid test ratio* can be used to monitor the size of working capital. This is discussed in Chapter 35.

Working capital problems

A business may run short of working capital for many reasons. Here are some examples.

- **Buying too many fixed assets:** When a business first starts trading money is short. Buying expensive assets such as equipment and vehicles uses up cash. It may be better to lease some of these to save working capital.

- **Unexpected expenditure:** Businesses may have to meet some unforeseen expenditure. Equipment breakdowns, tax demands and strikes are common examples.

- **Unexpected fall in demand:** Working capital may dwindle if sales start to fall due to an unexpected fall in demand. This might be caused by a sudden change in fashion, a new competitor entering the market or a decline in trading conditions.

- **Seasonal factors:** Sometimes trade fluctuates for seasonal reasons. For example, farmers have a large cash inflow when their harvest is sold. For much of the year, though, they have to pay expenses with no cash flowing in.

Methods of improving working capital

Cash flow problems might be avoided by controlling working capital. The use of budgets and cash flow forecasts will improve the financial management of the business. However, firms may still run short of working capital. A few examples of measures that a business might take are outlined below.

- **Get an overdraft or a short-term loan:** One way to boost working capital is to borrow some money. Most businesses can use overdrafts (See Chapter 25) when cash is short. It may also be possible to get a short-term loan if working capital is low.

- **Get some fresh capital:** Owners may be able to put some new capital into the business. For example, small business owners may be able to use savings or take out loans. They may use personal possessions as security. Limited companies may be able to sell shares to raise fresh capital.

- **Sell goods for cash:** Some businesses can boost working capital by offering discounts for cash sales. Customers may be keen to pay cash if discounts are attractive.

- **Delay payments:** A business may be able to delay payments to suppliers. This will help to save cash for a while.

QUESTION 2

Urals Energy is a Russian oil company. In January 2009, it managed to borrow some money to keep production going, and to meet some other debts. The company, which is heavily in debt, also said it was selling its shares in two important businesses. The money raised will be used to pay off debt. On 6 January, the company said it would get a small loan to maintain liquidity until the share deal had been finalised. Urals Energy owed money to contractors and suppliers which had to be paid by the end of January. News of the new funding sent Urals Energy's shares up 13 per cent at 3.25 cents.

It is suggested that Urals Energy was short of working capital.

(a) What evidence is there to support this view?

Just after the new funding was announced, the share price for Urals Energy increased.

(b) What might account for this?

Key terms

Working capital – the funds left over to meet day-to-day expenses after current debts have been paid. It is calculated by current assets minus current liabilities.

Working capital cycle – the flow of liquid resources into and out of a business.

Chapter review – Canton Metals

Canton Metals make metal components for car engines. It has a factory in Guangzhou and employs more than 50 staff. In 2008, the company experienced a 40 per cent fall in demand due to the global recession. This meant that the cash coming into the business fell sharply. Another problem was the 90-day credit terms agreed with customers. This meant that the business had to wait over three months to receive payment from customers. Some customers were also very slow to pay. An emergency board meeting was held to discuss working capital problems. Canton Metals was about to exceed its $2,500,000 overdraft limit and would run out of cash within two weeks. As a result, an emergency board meeting was held and the following measures were agreed.

● Obtain an unsecured loan from the bank (if possible).

● Reduce the trade credit period to 30 days.

Figure 27.5 shows the current assets and current liabilities for Canton Metals in 2008 and 2007.

	2008	2007
	$000	$000
Current assets		
Stocks	1,229	1,001
Work-in-progress	3,445	1,765
Debtors	2,189	1,778
Cash at bank	0	1,239
Current liabilities		
Trade creditors	3,112	2,311
Taxation	1,299	1,365
Other creditors	2,100	1,765
Bank overdraft	2,460	0

Figure 27.5 *Current assets and current liabilities for Canton Metals*

(a) Define the term working capital. **(2 marks)**

(b) (i) Calculate the working capital for Canton Metals in 2007 and 2008. **(4 marks)**
   (ii) Do the answers in **(i)** support the view that Canton Metals has a shortage of working capital? **(2 marks)**

(c) How might Canton Metals encourage customers to pay immediately for their goods? **(2 marks)**

(d) Analyse how the measures agreed by the board will improve Canton Metals' working capital position. **(4 marks)**

(e) Discuss whether Canton Metals is in danger of going out of business. **(6 marks)**

Chapter 28: Budgets

Getting started...

To run a successful business it is important to plan ahead. Business planning often involves forecasting future income and expenditure. These forecasts are presented in a budget and can help a business achieve its financial aims. Look at the example below.

Gethin Foods

Gethin Foods is a large food processing company and makes ready-made meals for supermarkets. Every four months the production manager prepares a production cost budget. It shows the costs of producing the planned output for the next four-month period. This helps to keep production costs under control. It also helps the purchasing department to plan orders for materials and the finance department to plan payments to suppliers. Figure 28.1 shows a production cost budget for Gethin Foods.

(a) What does the budget in Figure 28.1 show?

(b) How does Gethin Foods use their production cost budget?

					($m)
	Jul	**Aug**	**Sep**	**Oct**	**Total**
Food products	11.5	11.7	11.9	12.1	47.2
Other raw materials	2.6	2.7	2.8	3	11.1
Factory wages	9.5	10	10	10.2	39.7
Factory overheads	4.6	4.6	4.6	4.6	18.4
Total	28.2	29	29.3	29.9	116.4

Figure 28.1 *Production cost budget for Gethin Foods*

What is a budget?

Larger businesses are more difficult to control than smaller ones. A small business can be run informally. The owner will know everyone, be aware of what is going on and will make all decisions. In larger businesses work and responsibility are delegated to managers. This makes informal control ineffective. Budgeting will help to improve control.

A **budget** is a plan. It shows how much money a business, or a department, plans to spend or receive in the future. Budgets are normally presented in a table using a spreadsheet. Each column represents monthly expenditure or income plans. Figure 28.2 shows a six-month overheads budget for Harry Enser Ltd, a producer of leather goods.

> Rent and rates are constant throughout the whole period

> Electricity charges are expected to rise sharply in April

> A one-off insurance premium has to be paid in April. This will increase overheads sharply in that month

	Jan	Feb	Mar	Apr	May	Jun	Total
Rent and rates	1,100	1,100	1,100	1,100	1,100	1,100	6,600
Electricity	1,500	1,600	1,550	1,900	1,950	2,000	10,500
Insurance				1,200			1,200
Administration expenses	850	900	950	950	970	990	5,610
Other overheads	1,800	1,750	1,850	1,750	1,800	1,400	10,350
Total overheads	5,250	5,350	5,450	6,900	5,820	5,490	34,260

> Administration expenses rise slowly but consistently over the time period

> Total overheads for the period are €34,260

Figure 28.2 *Overheads budget for Harry Enser Ltd*

Sales budgets

Sales budgets usually show the planned income from sales. They are important because they affect all other budgets in the business. For example, if a business plans to increase sales, it will also have to increase production. A sales budget can show the quantities of output a business plans to sell or the sales revenue.

Figure 28.3 shows a sales budget for CleanCo, a producer of cleaning products.

							(units)
	Jan	Feb	Mar	Apr	May	Jun	Total
Floor cleaner	50,000	50,000	51,000	52,000	52,000	53,000	308,000
Bathroom cleaner	34,000	35,000	35,000	36,000	36,000	36,000	212,000
All purpose cleaner	102,000	104,000	105,000	107,000	109,000	110,000	637,000
Window cleaner*	3,000	5,000	7,000	10,000	15,000	20,000	60,000
* Window cleaner is to be launched in January 2009							

Figure 28.3 *Sales budget for CleanCo – 2009*

QUESTION 1

Pablos is a department store located in the centre of Malaga, Spain. It attracts a lot of English shoppers because its layout and product range is similar to some UK department stores. Figure 28.4 shows the six-month sales budget for the store. It is used by the manager to help forecast the sales revenue for the six-month period.

							(€)
	Jan	Feb	Mar	Apr	May	Jun	Total
Foodhall	24,500	25,800	26,500	26,500	27,000	27,500	157,800
Ladieswear	45,000	46,000	46,000	47,000	50,000	52,000	286,000
Menswear	31,000	31,500	31,500	32,000	34,000	34,500	194,500
Childrenswear	36,000	36,000	37,000	38,000	38,000	39,000	224,000
Total	136,500	139,300	141,000	143,500	149,000	153,000	862,300

Figure 28.4 *Sales budget for Pablos department store (€)*

(a) Why is a sales budget so important?

(b) What is the total planned sales revenue for the six-month period at Pablos?

(c) What is expected to happen to monthly revenue at Pablos over the time period?

Production budgets

Production budgets are used to plan production levels for a specified future period. They may show output levels or production costs. They are influenced by the sales budget. Figure 28.5 shows the production budget for CleanCo. Monthly production levels are influenced by the sales budget in Figure 28.3.

	Jan	Feb	Mar	Apr	May	Jun	Total (units)
Floor cleaner	51,500	51,500	51,500	51,500	51,500	51,500	309,000
Bathroom cleaner	35,000	35,000	35,000	35,000	35,000	35,000	210,000
All purpose cleaner	107,000	107,000	107,000	107,000	107,000	107,000	642,000
Window cleaner*	10,000	10,000	10,000	10,000	10,000	10,000	60,000

Figure 28.5 *Production budget for Clean Co – 2009 (units)*

Marketing budgets

A marketing budget is often used to help control costs in the marketing department. It may show how the money allocated to the marketing department is spent. The marketing budget in Figure 28.6 shows how the marketing department for a business plans to spend money on staff, advertising, the company website and other marketing expenses. The budget shows that:

- the business plans to increase expenditure on internet advertising at the expense of newspaper advertising

- a big expense is to be incurred in March where other marketing expenses rise from the usual $2,000 to $9,000. This might be a one-off PR or exhibition expense.

- the marketing department plans to spend a total of $109,000 in the time period.

	Jan	Feb	Mar	Apr	May	Jun	Total ($)
Wages	5,000	5,000	5,000	5,000	5,000	5,000	30,000
Internet advertising	3,000	4,000	5,000	6,000	7,000	8,000	33,000
Newspaper advertising	4,000	4,000	3,500	3,500	3,000	3,000	21,000
Website	1,000	1,000	1,000	1,000	1,000	1,000	6,000
Other marketing expenses	2,000	2,000	9,000	2,000	2,000	2,000	19,000
Total expenses	15,000	16,000	23,500	17,500	18,000	19,000	109,000

Figure 28.6 *An example of a marketing budget*

The advantages of budgets

Some of the key advantages of budgets are outlined below.

- **Control and monitoring:** Managers can keep control of a business by setting objectives and targets. These are represented by budgets. Success in achieving those targets can be found by comparing the actual results with the budget. If there are big differences between the two, a business will need to find out the reasons why and take action.

- **Reduce fraud:** Budgets can help to reduce fraud in a business. All spending in a business has to be authorised by budget holders. This means that no one else can spend money without the budget holder's permission. This stops staff from spending money fraudulently, such as buying things for themselves.

- **Planning:** Budgeting forces management to think ahead. Without budgeting, too many managers would work on a day-to-day basis, only dealing with opportunities and problems as they arise. Budgets help to anticipate problems and develop solutions in advance.

- **Efficiency:** One of the main reasons why budgets are used is to keep costs down. Budgets often mean that budget holders have to justify expenditure. If they cannot do this, money will not be given. This means that money is not wasted and efficiency improves.

- **Motivation:** Budgeting should act as a motivator to the workforce. It provides workers with targets and standards. Improving on the budget position is an indication of success. Fear of failing to reach budgeted targets may make staff work harder.

Key terms

Budget – a plan that shows how much money a business expects to spend or receive in a specified period.

Chapter review - Kosovo Mining Corporation

Kosovo Mining Corporation operates several coal mines in Kosovo. In the last six months of 2008, the company was confident that its coal would sell for €60 a tonne. Based on this price a sales revenue budget was drawn up for this period. It is shown in Figure 28.7. A production cost budget for the mining company is shown in Figure 28.8.

	Jul	Aug	Sep	Oct	Nov	Dec
Output (tonnes)	100,000	110,000	110,000	130,000	140,000	150,000
Revenue (€000)	6,000	6,600	6,600	7,800	8,400	9,000

Figure 28.7 *Sales budget for Kosovo Mining Corporation - 2008*

						(€000)
	Jul	Aug	Sep	Oct	Nov	Dec
Wages	1,100	1,200	1,200	1,400	1,600	1,700
Electricity	270	280	280	290	300	310
Transport	900	990	990	1,100	1,200	1,400
Production overheads	2,300	2,300	2,400	2,500	2,500	2,600

Figure 28.8 *Production cost budget for Kosovo Mining Corporation*

Figure 28.9 *Open-cast coal mining*

(a) Calculate the planned sales revenue for Kosovo Mining Corporation for the whole six-month period. **(2 marks)**

(b) Calculate the monthly and total production costs for the six-month period. **(4 marks)**

(c) Account for the pattern of costs over the time period. **(2 marks)**

(d) Analyse the possible advantages to Kosovo Mining Corporation of preparing budgets. **(12 marks)**

Chapter 29: Cash flow forecasts

Getting started...

*The flow of money into and out of a business is called **cash flow**. Cash flows out of a business when payments are made for resources such as materials and labour. Cash flows into a business when customers pay for goods and services. Cash also flows in when other income is received, such as interest. Look at the cash flows in the examples below.*

NK's Galle Bus Service

Nadeeka Karunaratne runs a bus service along the busy Galle Road transporting passengers between Colombo, the capital of Sri Lanka, and the coastal town of Galle. During May in 2009 Nadeeka paid out Rs3,200 for diesel, Rs3,500 for repairs to a bus, Rs2,000 in wages and Rs500 in other running costs. During the month Nadeeka's bus service collected a total of Rs9,300 in bus fares.

Northbridge Engineering

Northbridge Engineering make concrete products such as chimney copings, concrete slabs, lintels, sills and door thresholds for the building industry in Western Australia. In June 2009 the business paid $45,600 to its workers, $145,000 for raw materials, $31,890 in bills for rent, utilities and other expenses and $12,300 to the tax authorities. During the same month the company received payments of $311,800 from customers, $1,400 interest and $50,000 from a bank loan to help pay for some new machinery.

(a) Identify ways in which cash is flowing into and out of the above businesses.

(b) (i) Calculate the net cash flow (cash inflows – cash outflows) for NK's Galle Bus service.

　　(ii) What does the answer in **(i)** show?

The importance of cash

Cash is the most **liquid** of all business assets. Cash is the notes and coins a business keeps on the premises and any money it has in the bank. Without cash a business cannot trade. It is reckoned that about 20 per cent of business failures are due to poor cash flow. Even when trading conditions are good, businesses can fail. If a business does not have enough cash to pay its immediate bills it cannot trade.

Controlling cash flow

It is important that a business continually monitors and controls its cash flow. It must ensure that it has enough cash to pay staff wages and bills when they are due. A business will have better control over its cash flow if it:

● keeps up to date business and financial records

● always plans ahead by producing accurate cash flow forecasts

● operates an efficient credit control system which prevents slow or late payment.

Cash inflows and outflows

● **Cash inflows:** The money coming into a business is called a **cash inflow**. Cash flows into a business when income is received. Examples of cash inflows are sales revenue, loans, fresh capital from the owners, interest and the sale of assets. The expected cash inflows for Kamal Motor Services (Cairo) in June 2009 are shown in Figure 29.1.

● **Cash outflows:** The money going out of a business is called a **cash outflow**. Cash flows out of a business when payments are made. This might include wages, materials, utilities, machinery, rent and tax. Expected cash payments for Kamal Motor Services in June 2009 are shown in Figure 29.1.

● **Net cash flow:** The difference between cash inflows and cash outflows is called the **net cash flow**. A business will hope that for most of the time the net cash flow is positive. This means that more cash flows in than flows out. However, there will be times when the net cash flow is negative. This means that a business may have to borrow some money. The net cash flow for Kamal Motor Services in June 2009 is E£1,450 (E£8,950−E£7,500).

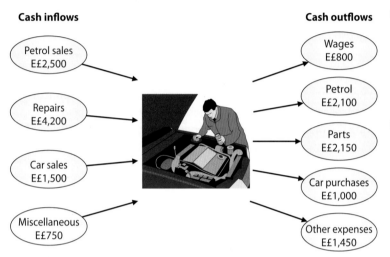

Figure 29.1 *Forecast cash inflows and outflows for Kamal Motor Services*

Cash flow forecasts

Most businesses produce a regular **cash flow forecast**. This is a financial document and shows the expected *cash inflows* and *cash outflows* over a future period. All the figures in the forecast are estimated because they are in the future.

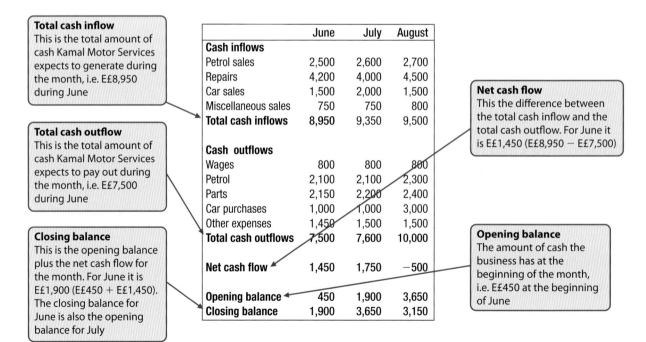

Total cash inflow
This is the total amount of cash Kamal Motor Services expects to generate during the month, i.e. E£8,950 during June

Total cash outflow
This is the total amount of cash Kamal Motor Services expects to pay out during the month, i.e. E£7,500 during June

Closing balance
This is the opening balance plus the net cash flow for the month. For June it is E£1,900 (E£450 + E£1,450). The closing balance for June is also the opening balance for July

Net cash flow
This the difference between the total cash inflow and the total cash outflow. For June it is E£1,450 (E£8,950 − E£7,500)

Opening balance
The amount of cash the business has at the beginning of the month, i.e. E£450 at the beginning of June

	June	July	August
Cash inflows			
Petrol sales	2,500	2,600	2,700
Repairs	4,200	4,000	4,500
Car sales	1,500	2,000	1,500
Miscellaneous sales	750	750	800
Total cash inflows	8,950	9,350	9,500
Cash outflows			
Wages	800	800	800
Petrol	2,100	2,100	2,300
Parts	2,150	2,200	2,400
Car purchases	1,000	1,000	3,000
Other expenses	1,450	1,500	1,500
Total cash outflows	7,500	7,600	10,000
Net cash flow	1,450	1,750	−500
Opening balance	450	1,900	3,650
Closing balance	1,900	3,650	3,150

Figure 29.2 *Cash flow forecast for Kamal Motor Services*

The forecast shows the planned cash flow of the business month by month. A cash flow forecast is shown for Kamal Motor Services in Figure 29.4. It is a three-month forecast drawn up in May.

The forecast shows that the cash position is expected to improve over the three months. At the end of June the business expects to have a closing cash balance of $1,900. By the end of August the cash balance is expected to be $3,150. However, there is a negative net cash flow in August. This is due to the extra money the business plans to spend buying cars for resale.

QUESTION 1

Yosuke Makino owns a bookshop near the University of Osaka, Japan. He sells educational books to students but also has a large stock of fiction books. Unfortunately the business has been struggling in recent months. He thinks that many students are sharing books and therefore his sales are suffering. Figure 29.3 shows a cash flow forecast for the bookshop at the beginning of 2009. It is incomplete.

	Jan	Feb	Mar
Cash inflows			
Book sales	3,000	3,500	3,100
Fresh capital			2,000
Interest		150	
Total cash inflows	**3,000**	**3,650**	**5,100**
Cash outflows			
Stock	1,700	1,790	1,900
Casual labour	500	500	500
Rent	1,000	1,000	1,000
Other expenses	230	240	230
Total cash outflows	**?**	**?**	**?**
Net cash flow	**?**	**?**	**?**
Opening balance	**230**	**?**	**?**
Closing balance	**?**	**?**	**?**

Figure 29.3 *Cash flow forecast for Yosuke Makino's bookshop*

(a) What is the difference between cash inflows and cash out flows? (Use an example from this case study.)

(b) Complete the cash flow forecast for Yosuke Makino's bookshop to show:

    (i) the total cash outflows for each month;
    (ii) the net cash flows for each month;
    (iii) the closing balance for each month;
    (iv) the opening balance for February and March.

It is suggested that Yosuke Makino's bookshop is struggling.

(c) What evidence is there in the forecast to support this view?

Key terms

Cash flow – the flow of money into and out of a business.

Cash flow forecast – the prediction of all expected receipts and expenses of a business over a future time period which shows the expected cash balance at the end of each month.

Cash inflows – the flow of money into a business.

Cash outflows – the flow of money out of a business.

Liquid asset – an asset which is easily changed into cash.

Net cash flow – the difference between the cash flowing in and the cash flowing out of a business in a given time period.

Why are cash flow forecasts important?

Businesses draw up cash flow forecasts to help control and monitor cash flow. What are the advantages?

- **Identifying cash shortages:** A forecast can help to identify in advance when a business might need to borrow cash. The forecast clearly shows how much cash is left at the end of each month. This will help to identify when, or if, a bank overdraft will be needed.

- **Supporting applications for funding:** When trying to raise finance, lenders often insist that businesses support their applications with a cash flow forecast. This will help to show the future outlook for the business.

- **Help when planning the business:** Careful planning in business is important. It helps to clarify aims and improve performance. Producing a cash flow forecast is a key part of the planning process.

- **Monitoring cash flow:** A business should compare the predicted figures in the cash flow forecast with those that actually occur. By doing this it can find out where problems have occurred. It could then try to find out why differences have occurred.

Chapter review – Evans Garden Maintenance

Jill Evans set up her own garden maintenance business in 2010. She put in some of her own capital and persuaded a bank to lend her more. By February 2010 Jill had found several customers who promised her regular work. Figure 29.4 shows the predicted revenue for the first nine months of trading. The following financial information was also gathered:

- A bank loan of £3,000 would be needed in April.

- Jill would contribute £2,000 of her own savings as capital in April.

- A van for £2,000 would be purchased in April.

- Tools and equipment for £3,400 would be purchased in April.

- A laptop computer with specialist design software for £600 would be purchased in April.

- A business directory listing will cost £100 in May.

- General overheads would be £400 per month.

- Advertising will be £100 in alternate months starting in May.

- Jill would take out £800 per month starting in June.

- Loan repayments will be £200 per month from April.

(a) What is a 'cash flow forecast'? **(2 marks)**

(b) Draw up a nine-month cash flow forecast for Evans Garden Maintenance. (Use a spreadsheet if possible.) **(12 marks)**

(c) (i) Comment on the cash position of the business during the nine-month period. **(2 marks)**
(ii) What would you expect to happen to the cash position of the business in early 2011? **(4 marks)**

	APR	MAY	JUN	JUL	AUG	SEP	OCT	NOV	DEC
Predicted revenue (£)	2,000	2,100	2,000	2,500	2,500	2,000	1,000	500	0

Figure 29.4 *Predicted revenue for Evans Garden Maintenance (first nine months)*

Chapter 30: Costs

Getting started...

Businesses have to pay for the resources they use. These expenses might include wages, raw materials, components, energy and machinery. They are called **costs**. *However, there are different types of business costs. Some costs stay the same when a business produces more output. But others go up when more is produced. Look at the examples below.*

Agustina's Zapatos

Agustina Mendes runs a shoe shop in Buenos Aires, Argentina. Two of the main costs are rent of 2,500 pesos and interest of 1,500 pesos on a bank loan. These are paid monthly. Other large costs include stocks of shoes and other footwear and wages to sales assistants. These are employed to help out with busy weekend trade.

Costantini Design

Costantini Design produce a line of home furnishings, lighting and art. They use a variety of hardwoods, leathers and fine fabrics in production. The business manufactures its products in Buenos Aires and has a showroom in Los Angeles. The company employs 50 skilled craftsmen and the products are hand made. In 2009, the company invested in an exhibition to show some of their newest models in Milan, Italy.

If output in the above examples increases.

(a) Which of the costs described will increase?

(b) Which of the costs described will remain unchanged

Figure 30.1 *Home furnishings*

Why does production generate costs?

The production of goods and provision of services use up resources. For example, tyre production uses resources such as rubber, synthetic fabrics, steel bands, machinery, a factory, labour and energy. These resources represent some of the costs generated during tyre production. Other costs will also be incurred. In this example, the selling of tyres will incur marketing, distribution and administration costs. Also, if the business has borrowed any money there will be interest to pay on the loan. All these costs, and many others, can be classified. Two methods of classification of costs are outlined below.

Fixed costs

Costs can be classified according to how they behave when output changes. Some production costs remain the same whatever the level of output. These are called **fixed costs**. Examples of fixed costs include rent, business rates, advertising, insurance premiums, interest payments and research and development costs. These costs will not increase even if a firm produces more output. However, fixed costs will still have to be met if the firm produces nothing. Fixed costs are sometimes called *overheads*.

Fixed costs can be shown on a graph. Figure 30.2 shows the fixed cost for Millhouse Training. This business provides training courses for HGV drivers. The business incurs fixed costs of $40,000 pa. The graph shows that fixed costs stay the same at all levels of output. If the business provides 100 training places, fixed costs are $40,000. If the number of places rises to 150, fixed costs are still $40,000.

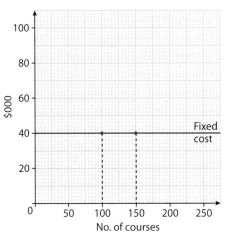

Figure 30.2 *Fixed costs for Millhouse Training*

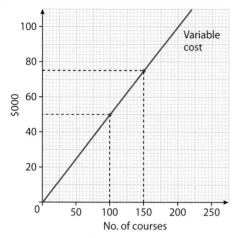

Figure 30.3 *Variable costs for Millhouse Training*

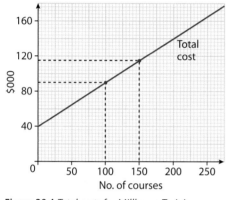

Figure 30.4 *Total costs for Millhouse Training*

Variable costs

Production costs that do vary with output are called **variable costs**. If a firm produces more output variable costs will increase. Similarly, if output levels are cut, variable costs will fall. Examples of variable costs include raw materials, packaging, fuel and labour. If a firm produces nothing variable costs will be zero.

Figure 30.3 shows variable costs for Millhouse Training. The business has variable costs of $500 per course. If 100 courses are provided, the variable costs will be $50,000 (100 × $500). If 50 extra courses are provided, variable costs rise to $75,000 (150 × $500). The graph shows that variable costs change whenever output changes.

Total costs

The cost to a firm of producing all output over a period is called **total cost**. Total cost (TC) can be calculated by adding fixed costs (FC) and variable costs (VC) together.

$$TC = FC + VC$$

If Millhouse Training provides places for 100 training courses, total costs will be:

TC	=	$40,000 + (100 × $500)
	=	$40,000 + $50,000
	=	$90,000

The total cost graph in Figure 30.4 shows that total cost increases from $90,000 to $115,000 when the number of courses provided rises from 100 to 150.

QUESTION 1

BatCraft Pty manufactures high quality cricket bats. The company, which is based in Canberra, Australia, employs six skilled craftsmen. The table in Figure 30.5 shows some cost information for the company.

Rent	$50,000 pa
Business rates	$5,000 pa
Other fixed costs	$25,000 pa
Wood	$30 per bat
Other raw materials	$10 per bat
Labour	$50 per bat
Other variable costs	$10 per bat

Figure 30.5 *Cost information for BatCraft Pty*

Figure 30.6 *A man playing cricket*

(a) Using examples from the case study state what is meant by a fixed cost.

In 2008, BatCraft produced 4,800 bats.

(b) Calculate the total cost of production.

In 2009, the rent increased to $60,000 and 6,000 bats were produced.

(c) What would happen to total costs?

Average costs

The **average cost** of production is the cost of producing a single unit of output. The formula for calculating average cost is given by:

$$\text{Average cost} = \frac{\text{Total cost}}{\text{Quantity produced}}$$

So, for example, the average cost of a training course provided by Millhouse Training, if 100 places were provided, would be:

$$AC = \frac{TC}{Q} = \frac{\$90,000}{100} = \$900$$

This means that each course provided, to trainee HGV drivers costs Millhouse Training $900.

Direct and indirect costs

The costs discussed above are classified according to how they behave when output changes. Another way of classifying costs is to distinguish between direct and indirect costs. **Direct costs** are costs which can be identified with a particular product or process. Examples of direct costs are raw materials, packaging and direct labour. **Indirect costs** or **overheads** result from the whole business. It is not possible to link these costs directly with particular products or processes. Examples are rent, insurance, the salaries of office staff and accountancy fees. Indirect costs are usually fixed costs and direct costs variable costs, although in theory both direct and indirect costs can be fixed or variable.

Total revenue and profit

Total revenue: The amount of money a firm receives from selling its output is called **total revenue**. Total revenue can be calculated by multiplying the price of each unit by the number of units sold:

$$\text{Total revenue} = \text{Price} \times \text{Quantity}$$

If Millhouse Training, in the earlier example, charged £1,500 for its HGV training courses, the total revenue from the sale of 100 courses is given by:

$$\text{Total revenue} = \$1,500 \times 100 = \$150,000$$

This means that Millhouse Training generated $150,000 of revenue from providing 100 places on its HGV driving course.

Profit: One of the main reasons why firms calculate their costs and revenue is to work out *profit* or *loss*. Profit is the difference between total revenue and total costs.

$$\text{Profit} = \text{Total revenue} - \text{Total costs}$$

The profit made by Millhouse Training from providing 100 places is given by:

Profit	=	£150,000 × 100 − (£40,000 + £50,000)
	=	£150,000 − £90,000
	=	£60,000

It is possible to calculate the profit for a firm at any level of output using this method.

Chapter 30: Costs

Key terms

Costs – expenses that must be met when setting up and running a business.

Direct cost – a cost which can be clearly identified with a particular unit of output.

Fixed costs – costs that do not vary with the level of output.

Indirect cost or overhead – a cost which cannot be identified with a particular unit of output. It is incurred by the whole organisation or department.

Total costs – fixed cost and variable cost added together.

Total revenue – the money generated from the sale of output. It is price multiplied by quantity.

Variable costs – costs which rise as output levels are increased.

QUESTION 2

Jenkins Ltd manufactures electronic control systems which open and shut swing gates. Its most popular product is the underground system which sells for $250. The systems are assembled in a factory using components supplied by firms nearby. In 2008, Jenkins sold 4,500 systems. Total fixed costs for the year were $160,000 and variable costs were $120 per system.

In 2008, Jenkins produced and sold 4,500 control systems.

(a) Calculate the total cost.

(b) Calculate the total revenue.

(c) Calculate the profit.

In 2009, fixed costs and the price charged remained the same. However, variable costs rose to $140 per system.

(d) Calculate the profit made in 2009 if 5,200 systems were sold.

Chapter review – Glenn's Fishing Trips

Glenn Alderman owns a fishing cruiser. In 2008, he decided to operate daily fishing trips at Lakes Entrance, Victoria. The venture went very well and during the peak season he was very busy. He charged $500 per day for a fishing trip and could take fishing parties of up to six people. He provided all tackle, which he hired from a tackle shop, bait, fishing lessons and a picnic hamper for the day. Figure 30.8 shows costs for January and February 2008.

Costs	January	February
Tackle hire	$560	$440
Insurance	$50	$50
Interest payment	$3,000	$3,000
Picnic hampers	$2,800	$2,200
Fuel	$1,400	$1,100
Advertising	$100	$100
Other fixed costs	$300	$300
Number of trips	**January**	**February**
	28	22

Figure 30.8 *Cost information for Glenn's Fishing Trips*

Figure 30.7 *A man on a fishing trip*

(a) What is the difference between direct costs and indirect costs? (Use examples from the case study.) **(2 marks)**

(b) **(i)** What is fixed cost per month? **(1 mark)**
　　(ii) What is the variable cost per trip in January? **(1 mark)**
　　(iii) Plot fixed cost and variable cost on a graph. (Use a range of output of 0 to 30 trips) **(4 marks)**

(c) Calculate Glenn's total costs in January. **(2 marks)**

(d) Calculate the profit made by Glenn in January. **(4 marks)**

(e) Calculate the average cost of a trip in January. **(2 marks)**

In January 2009, Glenn plans to raise the price of the trips to $600. Assume that all costs remain the same and that he manages to sell 28 trips again.

(f) Calculate the new level of profit. **(4 marks)**

Chapter 31: Break-even analysis

Getting started...

*In business it is helpful to know how much output needs to be sold to cover costs. If costs are not covered by revenue, the business will make a loss. If revenue is greater than costs, the business will make a profit. If costs are exactly the same as revenue, the business will **break even**. Look at the examples below.*

ANEK Lines

ANEK Lines is a Greek shipping company. It owns 11 vessels and provides passenger services across the Adriatic and Aegean Seas. In 2008, the company's total revenue was €278.9m. Its total costs before tax were €285.3m.

Chellappan Ltd

Chellappan Ltd assembles satellite dishes for a major television broadcaster in India. Its fixed costs were Rs20,000,000 in 2008. Variable costs were Rs2,000 per dish and in 2008, 100,000 dishes were made and sold. So its total variable costs were Rs20,000,000 (Rs2,000 × 10,000). The total revenue resulting from the sale of 10,000 satellite dishes was Rs40m.

(a) Show whether the firms in the above examples are making a profit, loss or breaking even.

Figure 31.1 *A passenger liner on the Adriatic*

The break-even point

A business will break even if its total costs (TC) and total revenue (TR) are exactly the same. This is called the break-even point. At this point the business does not make a profit or a loss. For example, if a business produces 40,000 units and sells them for $5 each, total revenue will be $200,000 ($5 × 40,000). If fixed costs are $100,000 and variable costs are $2.50 per unit, total costs will also be $200,000 ($100,000 + $2.50 × 40,000). Here the business is breaking even and 40,000 units is the break-even point.

Calculating the break-even point

To calculate the break-even point, the following information is needed:

● fixed cost

● variable cost per unit

● selling price per unit.

The following formula can be used to calculate the break-even point:

$$\text{Break-even point} = \frac{\text{Fixed cost}}{\text{Selling price} - \text{variable cost per unit}}$$

NB Selling price − variable costs is known as the *contribution*.

Ed Winchester Ltd has a contract with a local authority to install fire alarms in council houses. Ed charges $25 for each installation. Fixed costs are $20,000 pa and variable costs are $5 per installation. How many alarms have to be installed before the business breaks even?

$$\text{Break-even point} = \frac{\text{Fixed cost}}{\text{Selling price} - \text{variable cost per unit}}$$

$$= \frac{\$20,000}{\$25 - \$5}$$

$$= \frac{\$20,000}{\$20}$$

$$= 1,000 \text{ units}$$

So, Ed has to fit 1,000 fire alarms to break even.

Figure 31.2 *Ice cream*

QUESTION 1

Galle Ice Cream Ltd makes ice cream which is sold to retailers and caterers in Sri Lanka. Its standard ice cream product sells for Rs100 a kilo. The fixed costs in standard ice cream production are Rs100,000. Variable costs of production are Rs50 a kilo.

(a) How many kilos of ice cream must the business sell to break even?

(b) What is total cost and total revenue at the break-even point?

(c) What would happen to the break-even point if fixed costs were reduced to Rs80,000?

Break-even chart

The break-even point can be shown graphically. The **break-even chart** in Figure 31.3 shows total cost and total revenue for Ed Winchester's business in the above example. Output is measured on the horizontal axis and revenue, costs and profit are measured on the vertical axis. What does the break-even chart show?

- The break-even point is where total cost and total revenue intersect. In this example, the business breaks even when 1,000 fire alarms are fitted. At this point total cost and total revenue are both $25,000.

- At any level of output below the break-even point the business makes a loss.

- At any level of output above the break-even point the business makes a profit. For example, if Ed Winchester fits 2,000 fire alarms, the business will make a profit of $20,000. (Total costs are $30,000 and total revenue is $50,000).

- If Ed Winchester fits 2,000 alarms, the **margin of safety** is 1,000 units. This is the range of output over which the business can make a profit (the difference between current output and the break-even level of output).

- Some break-even charts show fixed cost. In this example, fixed cost would be shown by a horizontal line at $20,000.

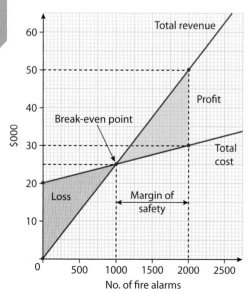

Figure 31.3 *Break-even chart for Ed Winchester*

QUESTION 2

The Grand Hotel, Singapore, has 600 rooms. The price charged (on average) by the hotel for a room is $100. Figure 31.4 shows a break-even chart for the hotel.

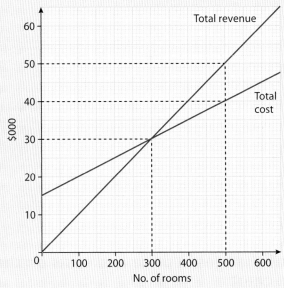

Figure 31.4 *Break-even chart for The Grand Hotel, Singapore*

(a) What is the value of fixed cost for the Grand Hotel?

(b) **(i)** How many rooms need to be occupied to break even?
 (ii) What is total revenue at the break-even point?
 (iii) What is total cost at the break-even point?

(c) If 500 rooms are occupied, what is the **(i)** amount of profit **(ii)** margin of safety?

Constructing a break-even chart

A break-even chart can be drawn by following the steps shown in the example below.

Nanjing Holdings assembles circuit boards. Fixed costs are $10,000, variable costs are $10 per circuit board and the assembled boards are sold for $20 each.

Step 1: It is useful to know the break-even point before constructing the chart. This helps to check that your chart is correct. Calculate the break-even point using the formula given earlier. In this example, the break-even point is 1,000 units ($10,000 ÷ $20 − $10).

Step 2: Since both total cost and total revenue are straight lines, two sets of co-ordinates are needed to construct the lines. It is necessary to choose two levels of output and work out the total cost and total revenue at each level.

● Choosing 0 as one level makes the calculations easier. If output is 0, TC will be $10,000 (remember that fixed costs are still incurred even when nothing is produced).

● When output is 0, TR will also be 0 (there are no sales if nothing is produced).

Output	TC	TR
0	$10,000	0
2,000	$30,000	$40,000

Figure 31.5 *TC and TR at two different levels of output for Nanjing Holdings*

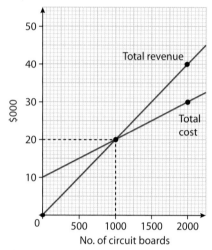

Figure 31.6 *Break-even chart for Nanjing Holdings*

- When choosing the second level of output choose a value which is double the break-even point. This means the break-even point will appear right in the middle of the chart. Therefore, the second level of output will be 2,000 (2 × 1000).

- When output is 2,000 TC = $10,000 + ($10 × 2,000) = $30,000.

- When output is 2,000 TR = $20 × 2,000 = $40,000.

- The values for TC and TR at each level of output are summarised in Figure 31.5.

Step 3: The values shown in Figure 31.5 represent two sets of co-ordinates which can be used to plot TC and TR for the break-even chart.

- Output is measured on the horizontal axis and goes up to 2,000.

- Costs, revenue and profit are measured on the vertical axis and go up to $40,000.

- TC can be drawn by plotting the co-ordinates (0, $20,000) and (2,000, $30,000) on the chart and joining them with a straight line.

- TR can be drawn by plotting the co-ordinates (0,0) and (2,000, $40,000).

- The chart is shown in Figure 31.6.

The effect of changes in price and costs on the break-even chart

The break-even chart can be used to show the effects on the break-even point when there are changes in costs and price.

- If price is higher, TR will be steeper and the break-even point will move to the left. This is shown in (A) in Figure 31.7.

- If price is lower, the TR will be flatter and the break-even point will move to the right.

- If FC is higher, TC will make a parallel shift up and the break-even point will shift to the right.

- If FC is lower, TC will make a parallel shift down and the break-even point will shift to the left.

- If VC are higher, TC will be steeper and the break-even point will shift to the right. This is shown in (B) in Figure 31.7.

- If VC are lower, TC will be flatter and the break-even point will shift to the left.

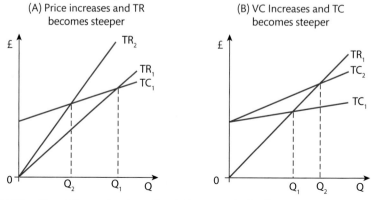

Figure 31.7 *The effect of changes in price and variable cost on the break-even point*

The limitations of a break-even chart

A break-even chart shows:

- how much output a business has to produce in order to break even;
- the costs, revenue and profit at different levels of output;
- the margin of safety.

However, the chart does have some limitations. Some examples are given below.

- The TC and TR are shown as straight lines. In practice they may not be straight lines. For example, a business may have to offer discounts on large orders, so total revenues fall at high outputs. In this case the total revenue line would rise and then fall. A business can lower costs by buying in bulk. So costs may fall at high outputs and total cost will be curved.

- It is assumed that all output is sold and no stocks are held. Many businesses hold stocks of finished goods to cope with changes in demand. There are also times when firms cannot sell what they produce and choose to stockpile their output to avoid laying off staff.

- The accuracy of the break-even chart depends on the quality and accuracy of the data used to construct total cost and total revenue. If the data is poor and inaccurate, the conclusions drawn on the basis of the data will be wrong.

Chapter review – Style Travel

Style Travel is owned by Mohammed Abass. He operates a limousine taxi service between hotels in Dubai and the airport. He charges $100 per trip. His main costs are fixed costs which include leasing the limousine, insurance and other fixed motor expenses. Total fixed costs for the year are $40,000. The main variable costs are fuel, labour and other running costs. Total variable costs per trip are $20. Mohammed plans to make 800 trips during the year.

(a) Construct a break-even chart for Style Travel. **(6 marks)**

(b) (i) What is the break-even point for Style Travel? **(1 mark)**
   (ii) What is the total cost and total revenue at the break-even point? **(2 marks)**

Mohammed plans to make 800 trips during the year.

(c) How much profit will be made? **(2 marks)**

(d) (i) Explain what is meant by the margin of safety. **(2 marks)**
   (ii) What is the margin of safety for Style Travel if 800 trips are made? **(1 mark)**

Figure 31.8 *A limousine at an airport*

(e) Describe what would happen to the break-even point for Style Travel if variable costs were to increase. **(2 marks)**

(f) Analyse the limitations of break-even analysis to Style Travel. **(4 marks)**

Chapter 32: The profit and loss account

Getting started...

Most business owners want to make a profit. It is the main reason why they start a business. At the end of the financial year businesses produce a profit and loss account. This shows all the income and the costs for a business and is used to calculate the profit. It might also be used to help make decisions such as how much should the business invest in the future. Look at the example below.

Profit and loss account for Golf Discount Store

The Golf Discount Store is run by Hank Donavan, a sole trader. He buys golf clubs, accessories and golf wear from suppliers and rents a shop in Jacksonville, Florida.

Figure 32.1 *Interior of a golf store*

Golf Discount Store		
Profit and loss account		
Year ended 31 December 2008		
	$	$
Sales		256,400
Cost of sales		137,100
Gross profit		**119,300**
Less expenses:		
Wages	24,100	
Rent	36,000	
Business rates	2,300	
Interest	600	
Motor expenses	3,900	
Other expenses	11,600	78,500
Net profit		**40,800**

Figure 32.2 *Profit and loss account for the Golf Discount Store for the year ended 31 December 2008*

(a) State the **(i)** turnover; **(ii)** total expenses; and **(iii)** profit made by the Golf Discount Store.

(b) How might Hank Donavan use the profit and loss account?

Measuring profit

Businesses usually calculate their **profit** at the end of the *financial year*. This is a twelve-month trading period and can vary. For example, it might be from 1 June 2008 to 31 May 2009. A business normally calculates its profit using two steps. First it calculates **gross profit**. This is the profit made before expenses or overheads are subtracted. It is found by calculating:

Gross profit = turnover − cost of sales

Then it calculates **net profit**. This is profit after expenses and is found by:

Net profit = gross profit − expenses

Sometimes a business receives other income such as interest. Net profit is then:

Gross profit + other income − expenses

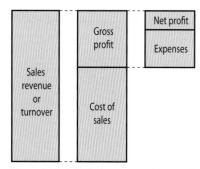

Figure 32.3 *Calculating gross and net profit*

Retained and distributed profit

Some of the net profit made by a business is used to pay taxes. Sole traders and business partners may pay *income tax* whereas limited companies may pay *corporation tax*. The profit after tax can be **distributed** or **retained**. Some of the profit is likely to be distributed to the owners of the business. For example, limited companies may return some of the profit to shareholders. They are paid a **dividend**. Any undistributed profit is retained by the business. This may be invested in the business. This means it may be used to help fund investment projects. It may also be kept as a reserve in case trading conditions become difficult in the future or to help fund expansion.

QUESTION 1

French Ltd produces packaging for the food industry. In 2009, its turnover was $12.56m. Its cost of sales was $7.6m and expenses were $2.56m.

(a) Calculate: **(i)** gross profit; **(ii)** net profit.

French Ltd distributes $0.8m to shareholders.

(b) **(i)** How much profit is retained?
(ii) What is likely to happen to the profit retained by the business?

The profit and loss account

The **profit and loss account** or the **income statement**, as it is now called, shows the income and expenses of a business during the financial year. It is used to calculate the gross profit and net profit. The layout of the account is important. Information must be presented in a standard way. For example it is divided into three sections: the **trading account**; the **profit and loss account**; the **profit and loss appropriation account**.

The trading account: This is the first section of the account and is used to calculate gross profit. The trading account for Xu Hong Ltd, a large cloth and fabric merchant, is shown in Figure 32.4. What does the trading account show?

- It shows the turnover of the business. In this case it is the money generated from the sale of cloth and fabric to retailers, i.e. $23.7m.

- The second figure is the **cost of sales**. This is the direct costs of a business. In this case it represents the cost of the fabric and cloth bought from suppliers. For a manufacturer it would be direct production costs such as direct labour and raw materials. In this case the cost if sales is $13.2m.

- Gross profit is calculated by subtracting cost of sales from turnover. In this case the gross profit is $10.5m. It is the profit made before expenses are deducted.

The profit and loss account: The second section is called the profit and loss account. It shows how net profit is calculated. The profit and loss account for Xu Hong Ltd is shown in Figure 32.5. What details does it contain?

- The account starts with gross profit. This was calculated in the trading account.

- The total expenses or overheads are $6m.

- Operating profit is the gross profit less total expenses. In this case it is $4.5m.

- Non-operating income includes any income which does not come from sales. It may be dividends or rent from the lease of business property. It must be shown separately in company accounts and in this case is $0.4m. This is added to operating profit.

	$ million
Sale turnover	23.7
Cost of sales	13.2
Gross profit	10.5

Figure 32.4 *Trading account for Xu Hong Ltd – 2008*

	$ million
Gross profit	10.5
Expenses	6.0
Operating profit	4.5
Non-operating income	0.4
	4.9
Interest paid	0.6
Net profit	4.3

Figure 32.5 *Profit and loss account for Xu Hong – 2008*

	$ million
Net profit	4.3
Taxation	0.9
Profit after taxation	3.4
Dividends	1.2
Retained profit for the period	2.2

Figure 32.6 *Profit and loss appropriation account for Xu Hong Ltd – 2008*

Key terms

Distributed profit – profit that is returned to the owners of a business.

Dividend – money paid to shareholders (owners of the business) when profit is distributed.

Gross profit – sales revenue less cost of sales.

Net profit – gross profit less expenses.

Profit – the money left over after all costs have been subtracted from revenue.

Profit and loss account or income statement – a financial document showing a firm's income and expenditure in a particular time period.

Profit and loss account – shows how net profit is calculated by subtracting expenses from gross profit.

Profit and loss appropriation account – shows how the profit after tax is distributed between owners and the business.

Retained profit – profit that is kept by the business and may be used in the future.

Trading account – shows how gross profit is calculated by subtracting cost of sales from turnover.

● Interest paid also has to be shown separately in company accounts. In 2008 Xu Hong Ltd paid $0.6m interest. This is subtracted from operating profit.

● Net profit is the profit before tax and is $4.3m for XU Hong Ltd.

The profit and loss appropriation account: This third section shows how the net profit is distributed. Figure 32.6 shows the profit and loss appropriation Account for Xu Hong Ltd.

● It starts with net profit. This was calculated in the profit and loss account.

● Taxation of $0.9m is deducted to get net profit after tax. This is $3.4m.

● It shows that $1.2m has been distributed to shareholders in dividends.

● A total $2.2m has been retained in the business.

In practice, the profit and loss account is not split into three sections. It is shown as one account like the one in Figure 32.7. There are also differences between the accounts of sole traders, like the one shown in Figure 32.2, and those of companies, like that of Xu Hong Ltd. A more detailed breakdown of expenses is usually given in sole trader accounts. Finally, accounts usually show the figures for the current year and the previous year. This allows comparisons to be made.

QUESTION 2

SoftHart plc produces software for computer games. It employs 230 staff and operates from Bermuda. Figure 32.7 shows an incomplete profit and loss account for 2009.

SoftHart plc Profit and loss account Year ending 31 December 2009		
Net profit	$m	$m
	2009	2008
Sales turnover	26.9	29.2
Cost of sales	17.4	?
Gross profit	9.5	11.1
Expenses	4.6	4.8
Operating profit	?	6.3
Interest paid	1.8	1.5
Net profit	3.3	4.7
Taxation	1.1	1.6
Profit after taxation	2.2	?
Dividends	0	1
Retained profit for the period	?	2.1

Figure 32.7 *Profit and loss account for SoftHart plc (incomplete)*

(a) Complete the profit and loss account for SoftHart plc by calculating the operating profit and retained profit for 2009 and the cost of sales and profit after tax for 2008.

(b) Comment on the performance of the business over the two years.

The difference between cash and profit

It is important to recognise that cash and profit are different. At the end of a trading year the value of profit will not be the same as the cash balance. Some of the reasons for this are outlined below.

● Some goods are sold on credit. So, at the end of the year, some customers will still owe money. Therefore, profit is greater than cash. Similarly, a business may receive cash at the beginning of the trading year from credit sales made in the previous year. This would increase the cash balance, but not affect profit.

● Sometimes owners might put more cash into the business. This will increase the cash balance, but have no effect on the profit made. The effect will be the same if a business borrows money from a bank.

● Purchases of fixed assets will reduce cash balances, but have no effect on the profit a company makes. This is because the purchase of assets is not included as a cost in the profit and loss account.

● The amount of cash at the end of the year will be different from profit because at the beginning of the year the cash balance is unlikely to be zero.

It is possible for a business to trade for several years without making a profit. Provided it has enough cash it can carry on trading. However, if a business runs out of cash it will collapse.

Chapter review – Spring Valley Farm Ltd

Spring Valley Farm Ltd is located in Kenya. It produces flowers and specialises in rose growing. Most of its output is exported to Europe. The farm is a Gold member of the Kenya Flower Council. This has an internationally respected code of practice. Membership helps to sell flowers in Europe. Some financial information is shown in Figure 32.9.

	$ 2009	$ 2008
Sales turnover	560,400	470,600
Dividends	20,000	10,000
Interest paid	20,000	20,000
Cost of sales	302,100	270,500
Distribution expenses	89,600	81,900
Administration expenses	24,100	21,300
Taxation	40,000	25,000

Figure 32.9 *Financial information for Spring Valley Farm Ltd (year ending 31 December 2009)*

(a) Using this case study as an example, state what a profit and loss account shows. **(2 marks)**

(b) Draw up a profit and loss account for Spring valley Farm Ltd. **(8 marks)**

(c) Comment on the performance of the business over the two years. **(4 marks)**

At the end of the financial year the cash balance for Spring Valley Farm Ltd was $136,700.

(d) Analyse two possible reasons why this cash balance is different from the profit made in 2009. **(6 marks)**

Figure 32.8 *A rose farm in Kenya*

Chapter 33: Balance sheets

Getting started...

Businesses keep a record of all the resources they own such as land, property, machinery, tools, stock and cash. They also keep a record of all the money they owe to banks, suppliers, the owners and other businesses. At the end of the financial year, a business produces a summary of these financial details called a balance sheet. Look at the example below.

Benazir Patel

In 2008, Benazir Patel set up an interior design business. She bought a car, a computer, some design software and rented a small office. She used $10,000 of her family's money and a five-year bank loan for $3,000 to start the business. By the end of the first trading year Benazir had made a profit of $16,200. She was owed $2,400 by customers, had $4,500 cash in the bank and owed $1,200 to suppliers. During the year she took $11,000 from the business for personal use. Figure 33.1 shows the balance sheet for Benazir Patel's business at the end of the first trading year.

(a) What is the value of all the assets owned by the business?

(b) How much money does the business owe to: **(i)** the owner; **(ii)** all other creditors.

(c) What do you notice about the value of assets and the total amount owed by the business?

Benazir Patel Balance sheet as at 31 August 2009		
	$	$
Fixed assets		
Car		9,000
Computer equipment		3,500
		12,500
Current assets		
Debtors	2,400	
Cash	4,500	
	6,900	
Current liabilities		
Trade creditors	1,200	
Working capital		5,700
Long-term liabilities		
5-year bank loan		(3,000)
Net assets		**15,200**
Capital		
Opening capital	10,000	
Add profit	16,200	
	26,200	
Less drawings	11,000	
Closing capital		**15,200**

Figure 33.1 *Balance sheet for Benazir Patel as at 31 August 2009*

What is a balance sheet?

In addition to a profit and loss account, most businesses produce a balance sheet at the end of the financial year. A balance sheet is like a photograph of a firm's financial position a particular point in time. It provides a summary of a firm's **assets, liabilities** and **capital**.

- **Assets** are the resources owned by a business. Examples include buildings, machinery, equipment, vehicles, stock and cash. Businesses use assets to make products or provide services.

- **Liabilities** are the debts of the business, i.e. what it owes to others. Liabilities are a *source of funds* for a business. They might be short term, such as an overdraft, or long term, such as a mortgage.

- **Capital** is the money put into the business by the owners. It is used to buy assets.

Key facts

In all balance sheets the value of assets (what a business uses or owns) will equal the value of liabilities and capital (what the business owes). This is because all resources purchased by a business have to be financed from either capital or liabilities. Therefore:

Assets = capital + liabilities

So, if a business has capital of $5m and liabilities of $2.6m, the value of assets must be $7.6m ($5m + $2.6m).

QUESTION 1

Anwa Gawli runs a garage and petrol station. The value of the assets is $145,600. Anwa has $105,600 of his own money invested in the business and a 25-year mortgage. Anwa sells petrol and motor accessories and carries out minor repairs in a workshop at the back of the petrol station.

(a) Using this case study as an example, explain the difference between assets and liabilities.

(b) Calculate the value of the mortgage for this business. (There are no other liabilities).

The structure of a balance sheet

The balance sheet for Li Shangbin, a refrigeration engineer, is shown in Figure 33.2. Li Shangbin is a sole trader and provides a refrigeration maintenance service for businesses in Hong Kong.

The presentation of balance sheets may vary between different businesses. For example, the balance sheets of limited companies are slightly different to those of sole traders. The details likely to be found in a balance sheet are outlined below.

Fixed assets: Details of a firm's **fixed assets** are given at the top of the balance sheet. Fixed assets are those which last for more than one year. They are the most productive resources of a business. Li Shangbin's business has two fixed assets – a van, and tools and equipment. The total value of these fixed assets at 31 December 2008 was $18,000.

Current assets: Current assets are assets that will be changed into cash within one year. They are *liquid* assets. The liquidity of an asset is how easily it can be changed into cash. Examples might include:

● **Stocks** of raw materials, semi-finished goods and finished goods. Li Shangbin's business holds stocks of spare parts for refrigerators. These are valued at $2,300.

● **Debtors –** customers that owe money to the firm. In this case Li Shangbin is owed $2,400.

● **Cash** 'in hand' or in the bank. The balance sheet in Figure 33.2 shows that Li Shangbin has $4,300 in cash.

Current liabilities: Current liabilities are business debts which must be repaid within 12 months. They might include:

● **Trade creditors,** which is money owed to suppliers. Li Shangbin's business owes $3,700. This money might be owed to suppliers of spare parts, utility providers or any other business supplying commercial services.

● **Leases and hire purchase,** which are other forms of borrowing.

● **Short-term loans and overdrafts,** which is money owed to banks repayable within 12 months.

Li Shangbin's business does not have any lease, hire purchase, short-term loans or overdrafts.

Li Shangbin Balance sheet as at 31 December 2008		
	$	$
Fixed assets		
Van		9,500
Tools and equipment		8,500
		18,000
Current assets		
Stocks of spare parts	2,300	
Debtors	2,400	
Cash	4,300	
	9,000	
Current liabilities		
Trade creditors	3,700	
Working capital		5,300
Long-term liabilities		
5-year bank loan		(5,000)
Net assets		18,300
Capital		
Opening capital	12,500	
Add profit	26,800	
	39,300	
Less drawings	21,000	
Closing capital		18,300

Figure 33.2 *Balance sheet for Li Shangbin at 31 December 2008*

Working capital or net current assets: Figure 33.2 shows that Li Shangbin's business has $5,300 of working capital. Working capital is also known as **net current assets**. It is calculated by subtracting current liabilities from current assets ($9,000 − $3,700). This is an important figure in the balance sheet. It shows the amount of liquid resources a business has available. Working capital is used to meet the running costs of a business. If a business is short of working capital it could have cash flow problems.

Long-term liabilities: Any money owed for more than one year is called a **long-term liability**. Examples might include:

● **A mortgage,** which is a long-term secured loan usually taken out to buy property. It is secured against the value of property so that if the borrower cannot repay the loan, the lender can repossess the property.

● **A long-term loan** is any loan taken out for more than one year. Li Shangbin's business has a 5-year loan for $5,000. Note that this is shown in brackets in the balance sheet. This means that it is subtracted when calculating net assets.

● **Long-term leases and hire purchase** if the money has been borrowed for more than a year.

Li Shangbin's business does not have any mortgages or long-term leases or hire purchase.

Net assets: **Net assets** is the total at the bottom of the first part of the balance sheet. It is the value of all assets less the value of all liabilities. It can be calculated by adding working capital to fixed assets and subtracting long-term liabilities. The value of net assets for Li Shangbin's business is $18,300.

Capital: The bottom of the balance sheet shows the capital of the business. Closing capital is found by adding profit to the opening capital and then subtracting drawings. **Drawings** is the money taken from the business for personal use. The opening capital is the closing balance from the previous year. In 2008, Li Shangbin made a profit of $26,800 and withdrew $21,000 for personal use. The closing capital is therefore $18,300. This is what the business owes Li Shangbin and is also equal to the net assets.

QUESTION 2

Tariq Khan runs a small construction company. He specialises in the construction of conservatories, property extensions and loft conversions. He employs six other people and has enjoyed a profitable run since setting up in business in 2002. Figure 33.3 shows an incomplete balance sheet for his business at 31 July 2009.

Tariq Khan Balance sheet as at 31 July 2009		
	$	$
Fixed assets		
Van		18,000
Tools and equipmentequipment		25,000
		43,000
Current assets		
Stocks of spare parts	?	
Debtors	30,000	
	33,400	
Current liabilities		
Lease	5,000	
Trade creditors	7,800	
Overdraft	?	
	20,400	
Working capital		13,000
Long-term liabilities		
Mortgage		(25,000)
Net assets		?
Capital		
Opening capital	23,000	
Add profit	53,200	
	76,200	
Less drawings	45,200	
Closing capital		31,000

Figure 33.3 *Balance for Tariq Khan as at 31 July 2009 (incomplete)*

(a) Calculate the value of **(i)** stocks; **(ii)** overdraft; **(iii)** net assets.

(b) Using this case study as an example, outline the difference between fixed assets and current assets.

Key terms

Assets – resources used or owned by the business in production.

Balance sheet – a summary at a point in time of business assets, liabilities and capital.

Capital – a source of funds provided by the owners of the business used to buy assets.

Current assets – assets likely to be changed into cash within a year.

Current liabilities – debts that have to be repaid within a year.

Drawings – the money taken from the business by the owner for personal use.

Fixed assets – assets with a life span of more than one year.

Liabilities – the debts of the business which provide a source of funds.

Long term liabilities – debts that are payable after 12 months.

Net assets – the total at the bottom of the first part of the balance sheet. It is the value of all assets less the value of all liabilities.

Net current assets – current assets minus current liabilities. Also known as working capital.

Mecasystems Ltd Balance sheet as at 31 May 2009		
	2009	**2008**
	$m	**$m**
Fixed assets		
Factory	34.65	36.44
Plant and equipment	9.12	7.34
	43.77	43.78
Current assets		
Stocks	4.56	4.33
Debtors	6.99	4.34
Cash	2.11	4.19
	13.66	12.86
Current liabilities		
Trade creditors	6.77	6.21
Taxation	2.50	3.00
	9.27	9.21
Net current assets	4.39	3.65
Long term liabilities		
Mortgage	(5.00)	(5.00)
Net assets	48.04	47.99
Capital and reserves		
Share capital	10.00	10.00
Retained profit	34.14	32.78
Other reserves	3.90	5.21
Capital employed	48.04	47.99

Figure 33.4 *Balance sheet for Mecasystems Ltd as at 31 May 2009*

Limited company balance sheets

The balance sheet for a limited company is set out slightly differently to that of a sole trader. An example is shown in Figure 33.5. Note that figures for two years are shown so that comparisons can be made.

How might the balance sheet be used?

Balance sheets show the financial position of a business at a given point in time and can be used to evaluate its performance and potential.

- It shows the value of all business assets, capital and liabilities.

- It shows the asset structure of a business. It can show how the money raised by the business has been spent on different types of asset.

- It shows the capital structure of a business. A business can raise funds from many different sources, such as shareholders' capital, retained profit and long term and short-term sources.

- Looking at the value of working capital can indicate whether a firm is able to pay its everyday expenses or is likely to have problems. It shows the money left over after all current liabilities have been paid that can be used to settle the day-to-day debts of the business.

- A balance sheet may provide a guide to a firm's value. Generally, the value of the business is represented by the value of net assets.

Chapter review – The Golden Inn Ltd

The Golden Inn is a small hotel located in Plettenberg Bay, South Africa. It employs eight staff and has a good reputation for high quality accommodation. In 2009, a $60,000 mortgage was taken out to build an indoor swimming pool. Some financial information for the hotel is shown in Figure 33.5.

	$000		$000
Property	440	Trade creditors	112
Fixtures and fittings	100	Taxation	12
Stocks	120	Share capital	100
Debtors	108	Retained profit	395
Cash	56	Other reserves	45
Mortgage	60		

Figure 33.5 *Financial information for The Golden Inn Ltd*

Figure 33.6 *An indoor swimming pool at a hotel*

(a) State two ways in which a balance sheet might be used. **(2 marks)**

(b) How is The Golden Inn funding its business activities? **(4 marks)**

(c) Prepare a balance sheet for The Golden Inn Ltd. **(10 marks)**

(d) What is the value of The Golden Inn Ltd? **(2 marks)**

(e) Do you think the business has enough working capital? **(2 marks)**

Chapter 34: The purpose of accounts

Getting started...

Accounts are produced by businesses because they provide useful information for shareholders and other stakeholders. However, different stakeholders may look at the accounts for different reasons. For example, a bank may look at accounts when deciding whether or not lend a business some money. Employees may look at accounts to see whether a business can afford a pay rise. Look at the examples below.

Zheng Peng

Zheng Peng has been farming for 41 years. He supplies restaurants and retailers with chicken meat. However, due to increasing competition profit has fallen in recent years. He has decided that if the farm does not make a profit of $25,000 in 2009, he will retire from farming. Figure 34.2 shows the Profit and Loss Account for his business in 2009.

The Birmingham Brick Company

The Birmingham Brick Company produces building materials for the construction industry. In 2009, the company began looking for a new supplier of calcium silicate, an important raw material. A suitable supplier was found but would not supply goods on credit until it had looked at the company's accounts. The new supplier was particularly interested in the amount of working capital the Birmingham Brick Company had.

(a) How will Zheng Peng use the profit and loss account in this case study?

(b) Which stakeholder is interested in the accounting information in Figure 34.3?

(c) What conclusion might the stakeholder in (b) draw from the information shown in Figure 34.3?

Figure 34.1 *A chicken farm*

Zheng Peng Profit and loss account year ending 30 June 2009		
	$	$
Sales		145,600
Cost of sales		102,000
Gross profit		43,600
Less expenses:		
Wages	10,000	
Business rates	700	
Interest	500	
Motor expenses	3,200	
Other expenses	9,500	
		23,900
Net profit		**19,700**

Figure 34.2 *Profit and loss account for Zheng Peng Year ended 30 June 2009*

	2006	2007	2008	2009 (£)
Current assets				
Stock	128,500	132,900	123,700	121,200
Debtors	78,500	86,400	78,500	65,800
Cash	12,800	13,900	4,800	300
Total	219,800	233,200	207,000	187,300
Current liabilities				
Trade creditors	132,100	134,300	143,100	165,400
Other creditors	22,100	14,300	25,200	27,600
Total	154,200	148,600	168,300	193,000

Figure 34.3 *Current assets and current liabilities for The Birmingham Brick Company*

Stakeholders

A wide range of stakeholders may be interested in the accounts of businesses.

● **Managers** need up-to-date financial information to run the business.

   ● **Control:** Managers need financial information such as budgets, details of current assets and creditors to help keep control of the money flowing in and out of the business. This becomes more important as the firm grows.

Did you know?

Managers might use cost information in profit and loss accounts to help identify targets for cost cutting.

- **Analysis and evaluation:** Managers will want to assess the performance of the company. They might make comparisons with competitors and with accounts from previous years.

- **Decision making:** Managers use financial information to help make business decisions. Financial information is numerical, which is very useful when making decisions.

- **Employees** might need financial information during wage negotiations. Information about profit and the prospects of the business could be used to decide whether it can afford to raise wages. They may also look at accounting information to see whether their jobs are secure.

- **Owners** of small businesses will obviously be interested in the performance and the financial position of the business. For example, a sole trader might look at the profit to see if targets have been met for the year.

- **Shareholders** in limited companies will also be interested in the performance of the business. They may look at the size of dividends. They may use ratio analysis to see how their investment is performing and make comparisons with other companies in which they could invest.

- **Bankers** need up-to-date financial information when deciding whether to lend money to a business. Banks will look at the accounts to see whether a business can repay the loan with interest. Banks often want to look at accounts from several years of trading.

- **Suppliers** Many businesses buy resources using trade credit. However, a supplier is likely to carry out a credit search before granting trade credit. Accounts can be used by suppliers to see whether new customers are creditworthy.

- **Investors and financial analysts** The accounts of public limited companies are published and help to inform shareholders about the progress and performance of the company. They are also used by potential investors and *financial analysts* to help make decisions when buying shares.

Did you know?

Some big shareholders, such as pension funds and insurance companies, employ financial analysts to manage the return from their investments. A lot of this money is invested in shares and analysts will use accounts to help them decide in which companies to invest.

QUESTION 1

Arnolds Insurance plc provides boat insurance in the US serving clients in Florida. The shareholders expect a 10 per cent return on capital employed. They use the accounts each year to check whether this target has been achieved. Figure 34.4 shows some financial information for Arnolds Insurance which has been extracted from the accounts.

	2006	2007	2008	2009
Sales turnover ($m)	45.66	47.85	49.41	47.11
Net profit ($m)	3.98	4.12	4.1	3.16
Return on capital employed	11.10%	11.40%	10.90%	8.30%

Figure 34.4 *Financial information for Arnolds Insurance plc*

(a) What do you think is the main reason why owners use accounts?

(b) Has the business reached the targets set by the shareholders in this case study?

Other users

- **Government:** Many governments gather business and financial information. This is made available to the public. Some of the data is taken from accounts. The government uses the information to monitor the progress of the economy and help evaluate the success of its economic policies. It might also be used by people when doing research.

- **Competitors:** Limited company accounts are available to the public. Therefore competitors can analyse them to make comparisons. Also, if a competitor is thinking about a takeover, it can use the information to help make a decision.

- **The media:** Newspapers, TV and radio often produce reports on business and commerce. There are specialists that focus on business information. For example, in the US and the UK *The Financial Times* is a business and financial newspaper.

- **Tax authorities:** The tax authorities may require details of income when working out how much tax businesses and their owners must pay. Accounts can be used to provide details of income. They may require access to business accounts when calculating VAT and excise duties owed by businesses.

- **Auditors:** Every year the accounts of limited companies have to be checked by an independent firm of accountants and registered auditors. The process of checking the accuracy of accounts is called **auditing**.

- **Registrar of Companies:** In many countries limited companies have to register with the Registrar of Companies. One of the conditions of registration is that they submit a copy of their final accounts every year. These accounts are available to the general public.

Key term

Auditing – an accounting procedure which checks thoroughly the accuracy of a company's accounts.

Chapter review – Goldenport Holdings

Goldenport Holdings provides shipping services. It transports containers and bulk loads of iron ore, coal and grain. Goldenport is committed to updating its fleet with the acquisition of newer ships. Some information from the accounts is shown in Figures 34.5 and 34.6.

(a) State two possible reasons why employees at Goldenport Holdings might be interested in the information shown. **(2 marks)**

One objective of Goldenport Holdings is growth.

(b) What evidence is there to suggest that this objective has been achieved? **(2 marks)**

(c) How might a manager of Goldenport Holdings use the information shown in this case? **(2 marks)**

(d) Outline why: **(i)** the media; **(ii)** competitors might wish to look at the accounts of Goldenport Holdings. **(4 marks)**

(e) Why do auditors need to see company accounts? **(2 marks)**

(f) Evaluate the performance of Goldenport Holdings between 2005 and 2008. **(8 marks)**

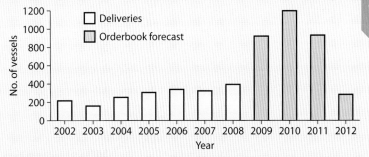

Figure 34.6 *Trading information for Goldenport Holdings*

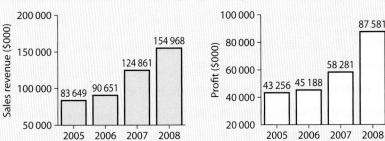

Figure 34.5 *Financial information for Goldenport Holdings*

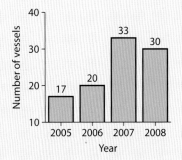

Chapter 35: Ratio analysis

Getting started...

The balance sheet can show the financial position of a business and the profit and loss account can show how well it has performed. For example, the profit and loss account shows how much profit a business has made and the balance sheet shows whether a business can pay its bills. Look at the example below.

LemCo Ltd

Bangkok-based LemCo Ltd makes soft drinks for the Thai market. At the end of 2008, a competitor entered the market, which had an impact on the performance of LemCo. LemCo Ltd announced that it would lay off 12 of its 32 staff in 2010.

LemCo Ltd Profit and loss account year ending 31 August 2009		
	$	$
	2009	2008
Sales turnover	890,600	1,231,500
Cost of sales	302,100	334,100
Gross profit	588,500	897,400
Distribution expenses	254,700	298,700
Administration expenses	276,400	325,600
Operating profit	57,400	273,100
Interest paid	59,800	34,000
Net profit	(2,400)	239,100
Taxation	0	80,500
Profit after taxation	(2,400)	158,600
Dividends	0	50,000
Retained profit for the period	(2,400)	108,600

Figure 35.1 *Profit and loss account for LemCo Ltd*

	2009	2008
Current assets		
Stocks	129,600	111,400
Debtors	412,400	445,200
Cash	12,000	128,900
	554,000	685,500
Current liabilities		
Creditors	539,700	446,200
Working capital	14,300	239,300

Figure 35.2 *An extract from the balance sheet for LemCo Ltd as at 31 August 2009*

LemCo Ltd has been badly affected by the arrival of new competition in the market for soft drinks.

(a) What evidence is there to support this view?

(b) How might the staff lay-offs improve financial performance at LemCo in 2010?

What is ratio analysis?

It is possible to look at a balance sheet and profit and loss account and draw some conclusions about the financial position of a business. However, a more precise way is to use **ratio analysis**. This involves taking key figures from the accounts and calculating financial ratios. There are different types of financial ratios.

● **Profitability ratios:** These measure the performance of the business and focus on profit, turnover and the amount invested in the business.

● **Liquidity ratios:** These measure how easily a business can pay its debts.

- **Gearing ratios:** These look at the capital structure of a business and compare the amount of share capital a business has in relation to its loan capital

- **Shareholders' ratios:** These measure the returns to shareholders on their investment in the business.

Gross profit margin

Figure 35.3 shows some financial information which has been taken from the accounts of Ecohomes plc, a supplier of environmentally friendly homes in Sweden. The information will be used in this unit to calculate a number of useful ratios.

The gross profit margin is also known as the **mark-up**. This shows the gross profit made on sales turnover. It is calculated using the formula:

$$\text{Gross profit margin} = \frac{\text{Gross profit}}{\text{Turnover}} \times 100$$

For Ecohomes in 2008 gross profit was £11,000,000 and turnover was $23,500,000.

$$\text{For 2008, gross profit margin} = \frac{\$11,000,000}{\$23,500,000} \times 100 = 46.8\%$$

$$\text{For 2007, gross profit margin} = \frac{\$8,300,00}{\$18,400,000} \times 100 = 45.1\%$$

Higher gross margins are better than lower ones. The gross profit margin for Ecohomes plc has improved slightly over the two years from 45.1% to 46.8%.

Net profit margin

The **net profit margin** helps to measure how well a business controls its overheads and cost of sales. If the difference between the gross margin and the net margin is small, this suggests that overheads are low. The net profit margin can be calculated by:

$$\text{Net profit margin} = \frac{\text{Net profit}}{\text{Turnover}} \times 100$$

For Ecohomes in 2008 net profit was $4,600,000 and turnover was $23,500,000.

$$\text{For 2008, net profit margin} = \frac{\$4,600,000}{\$23,500,000} \times 100 = 19.5\%$$

$$\text{For 2007, net profit margin} = \frac{\$3,200,000}{\$18,400,000} \times 100 = 17.4\%$$

The net profit margin for Ecohomes has improved over the two years. This suggests that the business kept control of overheads more effectively in 2008 than in 2007.

QUESTION 1

The Guangzhou Metal Company (GMC) makes metal components for the construction industry. In 2006 and 2007, the company received a flood orders to supply components to companies completing building work for the Beijing Olympics.

	2008	2007
	$000	$000
Turnover	23,500	18,400
Cost of sales	12,500	10,100
Gross profit	11,000	8,300
Net profit	4,600	3,200
Current assets	13,600	11,900
Stocks	4,900	5,000
Current liabilities	8,700	7,800
Capital employed	20,000	18,000

Figure 35.3 *Financial information from the accounts of Ecohomes plc*

Key fact

To increase the gross profit margin turnover must be increased or cost of sales reduced. The gross profit margin will be different for different industries. For example, firms which sell stock quickly, such as supermarkets, can operate with lower gross profit margins.

Key fact

Higher margins are better than lower ones. Net profit margins over 10 per cent would be regarded as good.

	2003	2004	2005	2006	2007
Sales turnover	12.4	13.8	14.9	19.8	24.1
Gross profit	4.9	5.6	6.1	9.8	12.3
Overheads	3.9	4.4	4.8	7.7	9.7
Net profit	1	1.2	1.3	2.1	2.6

Figure 35.4 *Guangzhou Metal Company Profit and Loss Account – 5-year summary*

Look at the sales figures for GMC between 2003 and 2007.

(a) How has the company performed?

(b) What impact has the flood of orders had on GMC?

(c) Calculate: **(i)** gross profit margin; and **(ii)** net profit margin.

(d) Discuss possible reasons for the changes in **(c)** between 2003 and 2007.

Current ratio

The **current ratio** is a liquidity ratio and focuses on current assets and current liabilities. It is calculated using the formula:

$$\text{Current ratio} = \frac{\text{Current assets}}{\text{Current liabilities}}$$

For Ecohomes current assets were £13,600,000 in 2008 and current liabilities were £8,700,000.

$$\text{For 2008, current ratio} = \frac{\$13,600,000}{\$8,700,000} = 1.56$$

$$\text{For 2007, current ratio} = \frac{\$11,900,000}{\$7,800,000} = 1.53$$

The current ratio for Ecohomes rose very slightly from 1.53 in 2007 to 1.56 in 2008.

Acid test ratio

The **acid test ratio** is a more severe test of liquidity. This is because stocks are not treated as liquid resources. Stocks are not guaranteed to be sold. Therefore, they are excluded from current assets when calculating this ratio.

$$\text{Acid test ratio} = \frac{\text{Current assets} - \text{stocks}}{\text{Current liabilities}}$$

$$\text{For 2008, acid test ratio} = \frac{\$13,600,000 - \$4,900,000}{\$8,700,000} = 1$$

$$\text{For 2007, acid test ratio} = \frac{\$11,900,000 - \$5,000,000}{\$7,800,000} = 0.88$$

Over the two years, the acid test ratio for Ecohomes has improved slightly from 0.88 in 2007 to 1 in 2008.

Key fact

It is suggested that a business will have enough liquid resources if the current ratio is between 1.5 and 2. If the ratio is below 1.5, it might be argued that a business does not have enough working capital. This might mean that a business is running short of liquid assets. Operating above 2 may suggest that too much money is tied up unproductively.

Key fact

If the acid test ratio is less than 1 it means that current assets less stocks do not cover current liabilities. This might be a problem. However, as with the current ratio, the acid test ratios of businesses in different industries tend to vary.

QUESTION 2

HR Owen operates vehicle franchises in the prestige car market. For example, it sells Rolls Royces, Maseratis, Ferraris and Lamborghinis. BPI (British Polythene Industries) manufactures over 300,000 tonnes of polythene products a year. Figure 35.5 shows current assets and current liabilities for the two companies.

	HR Owen		BPI	
	2008	**2007**	**2008**	**2007**
	£000	**£000**	**£000**	**£000**
Stocks	42,481	81,559	59,500	55,300
Other current assets	20,074	49,615	60,500	64,100
Total current assets	62,555	131,174	120,000	119,400
Current liabilities	53,757	136,531	68,300	75,500

Figure 35.5 *Current assets and current liabilities for HR Owen and BPI*

(a) Calculate the: **(i)** current ratios; **(ii)** acid test ratios for both companies in 2008 and 2007.

(b) Which is the more liquid of the two companies?

Return on capital employed (ROCE)

One of the most important profitability ratios is the **return on capital employed (ROCE)**. It compares the profit (return) made by the business with the amount of money invested (its capital). The advantage of this ratio is that it relates profit to the size of the business. ROCE can be calculated using the formula:

$$\text{ROCE} = \frac{\text{Net profit}}{\text{Long-term capital employed}} \times 100$$

Net profit for Ecohomes in 2008 was $4,600,000. Long-term capital employed was $20,000,000. Long-term capital employed is capital and reserves plus any long term loans.

$$\text{For 2008 ROCE} = \frac{\$4,600,000}{\$20,000,000} \times 100 = 23.0\%$$

$$\text{For 2007 ROCE} = \frac{\$3,200,000}{\$18,000,000} \times 100 = 17.7\%$$

The return on capital employed will vary between industries. Over the two years Ecohomes has seen its ROCE increase from 17.7 per cent to 23.0 per cent. These are good returns on capital if compared with the rate of interest at this time. Rates were around 3 or 4 per cent on bank deposits in 2008. However, it must be remembered that investing money in business is more risky compared with leaving it in a bank.

Key terms

Acid test ratio – similar to the current ratio but excludes stocks from current assets. Sometimes called the quick ratio.

Current ratio – assesses the firm's liquidity by dividing current liabilities into current assets.

Gross profit margin or **mark-up** – gross profit expressed as a percentage of turnover.

Net profit margin – net profit expressed as a percentage of turnover.

Ratio analysis – a numerical approach to investigating accounts by comparing two related figures.

Return on capital employed (ROCE) – the profit of a business as a percentage of the total amount of money used to generate it

Ratios and improving performance

Businesses are likely to use ratios to monitor their performance and achieve future objectives. One approach might be to set targets. For example, a business might have an objective to increase ROCE by 5 per cent over the next five years. It will know when it calculates the ROCE each year whether the business is on target to achieve that objective. Using ratios as targets is helpful because they are quantitative and can be used to set SMART objectives (see Chapter 2).

Chapter review – Muscat Shipping Co.

The Muscat Shipping Co. is owned by the Al-Dhabit family in Oman. Its main business is the transportation of oil. In 2008, the company was hit by the world recession and the owners injected $2m to help it survive. Some financial information for the company is shown in Figure 35.6.

	2007	2008	2009
Turnover	12.5	9.6	11.9
Net profit	1.13	0.34	1.17
Current assets	3.21	2.59	3.99
Current liabilities	2.16	2.55	2.43
Capital employed	10	12	12

Figure 35.6 *Extracts from the accounts of Muscat Shipping Co.*

Muscat Shipping Co. has been affected by the world recession.

(a) What evidence is there in Figure 35.6 to support this view? **(2 marks)**

The return on capital employed is a performance ratio.

(b) What does this mean? **(2 marks)**

(c) Calculate: **(i)** net profit margin; **(ii)** current ratio; **(iii)** ROCE; for Muscat Shipping Co. in each of the three years. **(9 marks)**

(d) Evaluate the performance of the business over the three-year period. **(7 marks)**

Chapter 36: Markets and the role of marketing

Getting started...

Most businesses operate in competitive markets. Customers will only buy products if they:

- *meet their needs*
- *are fairly priced*
- *are conveniently located*
- *are brought to their attention.*

Businesses are aware of this and understand that to be successful their products have to be marketed effectively. There are different ways of doing this. Look at the examples below.

Coca-Cola

There is a huge range of choice in the global market for soft drinks. However, Coca-Cola is the most recognised brand in the world. Coca-Cola uses a number of different marketing approaches to help maintain its position as market leader. For example:

- It has developed over 3,000 different brands such as Coca-Cola, Diet Coke, Coca-Cola Zero, Fanta, Dr Pepper, Sprite, Lilt, Powerade and Dasani.

- It spends hundreds of millions of dollars on advertising all over the world.

- It promotes its brand name by supporting sporting events. For example, Coca-Cola was one of the main sponsors of the 2008 Olympic Games in Beijing.

Nike

Some businesses use mobile phones to help sell their products. For example, Nike, the sports multinational, erected a large interactive billboard in Times Square, New York. Passers-by could use their mobile phones to text in their own design and receive a free pair of Nike ID trainers. After designing a trainer on screen, the user received a text message within seconds that had in it an image of the design. It then showed a link to the Nike ID site where the design could be bought. Nike gave away

3,000 pairs of shoes in this promotion. It was suggested that users were just as excited by seeing their design on the billboard as they were by the free trainers.

(a) Describe the approaches used in the above examples to help sell Coca-Cola and Nike products.

(b) Assess the importance of marketing to Coca-Cola and Nike.

What is a market?

Goods and services are sold in **markets**. A market exists when buyers and sellers communicate and exchange goods for money. Historically, markets were *places* where buyers and sellers would meet to exchange goods. Today it is possible to trade goods without buyers and sellers meeting up. For example, trading can be done over the telephone, using newspapers, through mail order or on the internet. Some examples of markets are given below.

- Consumer goods markets – where products such as food, cosmetics, furniture and magazines are sold.

- Markets for services – these are varied and could include services for individuals, such as banking, or business services, such as cleaning.

- The housing market – where people buy and sell properties.

- Commodity markets – where raw materials such as oil, copper, wheat and coffee are traded.

Market share

Businesses are often interested in their **market share.** This is the share of the total market that a particular business or product enjoys. The pie chart in Figure 36.1 shows the market shares for executive cars in the UK. The best selling model is the Mercedes-Benz. This is followed in second place by the BMW 7 series. Businesses often aim to increase their market share at the expense of rivals. If a firm can dominate the market it may be able to charge a higher price.

The formula below can be used to calculate the market share of a business or product.

$$\text{Market share} = \frac{\text{Total product or business sales}}{\text{Total sales in the whole market}} \times 100$$

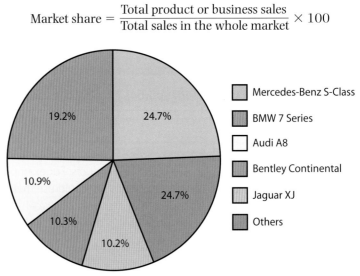

Figure 36.1 *Executive cars – 2009 market shares (UK)*

What is marketing?

Marketing involves a range of activities which help a business to sell its products. However, marketing is not just about selling, it involves:

- identifying the needs and wants of consumers

- designing products that meet these needs

- understanding the threats from competitors

- telling customers about products

- charging the right price

- persuading customers to buy products

- making products available in convenient locations.

Marketing can be defined as 'a management process involved in identifying, anticipating and satisfying consumer requirements profitably'.

Satisfying customer needs

Businesses have to satisfy customer needs and wants. To do this they have to identify what customers want. Businesses do this by carrying out *market research*. Market research is one of the most important marketing activities. It is the first step in satisfying customer needs. Market research is discussed in Chapter 43.

If possible, businesses need to anticipate customer needs. This means they try to predict what customers want in advance and respond to changes very quickly. Businesses operate in a changing competitive environment and have to keep up with the latest designs, trends, fashions and technology.

QUESTION 1

Catalina Gomez is the manageress of the Hotel El Prado, a four-star hotel in Mendoza, Argentina. She is always keen to improve the hotel service and aims to exceed the expectations of guests. Catalina uses a questionnaire left in the guest's room to gather feedback. If guests complete the questionnaire, they can collect a free gift when they check out. An extract from the questionnaire is shown in Figure 36.2.

HOTEL EL PRADO – MENDOZA

Please take a moment to rate our services.
Thank you for giving us the opportunity to serve you.

	Excellent	Good	Average	Below average	Poor N/A
Menu variety	○	○	○	○	○
Value for price paid	○	○	○	○	○
Quality of service	○	○	○	○	○
Quality of food	○	○	○	○	○
Quality of beverage	○	○	○	○	○

	Excellent	Good	Average	Below average	Poor N/A
Overall, how would you rate our staff's hospitality? (friendliness, courtesy, responsiveness)	○	○	○	○	○
Overall, how would you rate our hotel's public areas?	○	○	○	○	○
Overall, how would you rate the value for the price paid?	○	○	○	○	○
Overall, how would you rate the hotel's ability to provide a relaxing atmosphere ?	○	○	○	○	○

Comments

Figure 36.2 *An extract from a questionnaire used by Hotel El Prado*

(a) Describe how Hotel El Prado is attempting to identify customer needs.

(b) How might the hotel use the information it gathers?

Product and market orientation

In the past many businesses were **product orientated**. This meant that businesses were more concerned about the quality of their products. Their efforts concentrated on the design and manufacturing of the product itself. They then tried to persuade people to buy it. Some businesses today are still product orientated. For example, in the pharmaceuticals industry companies such as Pfizer and Bayer focus most of their attention on the development of a new drugs and medicines. They already know that a need exists.

In contrast, most firms today are **market orientated**. They are led by the market and their focus is on the customer. They do not make products until they know what people want. Market-orientated firms spend a lot of their time and resources on identifying, reviewing and analysing the needs of customers. As a result they attach a lot of importance to *market research*. This is discussed in Chapter 43.

The marketing mix

The activities which businesses use when marketing their products are known as the **marketing mix**. The marketing mix emphasises four particular elements, usually referred to as the 4Ps.

- **Product:** Businesses need to design high-quality products that meet customer needs and present them attractively.

- **Price:** Products must be priced so that customers think they are getting value for money. However, the price charged must also generate a profit for the business.

- **Promotion:** Customers must be given information about products and encouraged to buy them.

- **Place:** Products must be available in convenient locations at times when customers want to buy them.

The marketing mix is discussed in Chapter 38.

Marketing objectives

Although the general role of marketing is to help sell products, it is possible to identify specific marketing objectives. However, they may differ between organisations. Also, objectives will change according to a firm's marketing needs at the time. Examples of marketing objectives might be to:

- increase market share by 10 per cent

- increase weekly sales by $10,000

- rebrand an existing product – this usually means giving it new name and packaging

- increase the number of outlets by 50.

Marketing strategies

A **marketing strategy** is a set of plans that are drawn up so that a specific marketing objective can be achieved. For example, a business may decide to target a small segment in the market. Its strategy to achieve this objective might be to:

- adapt an existing product

- improve the packaging

- raise the price

- advertise in exclusive magazines

- distribute through exclusive outlets.

Notice that the strategy involves all aspects of the marketing mix.

Chapter review – Marketing in the car industry

Many car manufacturers use focus groups to find out what customers want and what they think of new products. This involves inviting a small group of customers to discuss products. In a recent focus group the following ideas emerged:

- **Low maintenance car:** Members of the focus group said that dealerships provide bad service and cars are too complicated for consumers to repair themselves. Therefore, why not design a car which requires limited maintenance that can also be done by owners?

- **Safe car for teenagers:** Members of the focus group said that teenagers are often at risk when driving which worries parents. Participants agreed that a sporty car should be designed that appeals to teenagers but also includes safety features. This would appeal to parents.

- **A more durable car:** Members of the focus group felt that cars were not built to last. Also, frequent design changes do not make any sense in a world of scarce resources and rising car prices. Thus, design and introduce a 5-year or a 10-year model. The money saved by firms on design, retooling etc. could be used to lower the prices.

Car manufacturers are one of the largest spenders on advertising. In 2007, $9.42bn was spent globally on advertising cars.

(a) Outline the role played by marketing in business? **(2 marks)**

(b) To what extent is the car industry product or market orientated? **(4 marks)**

Car manufacturers are one of the largest spenders on advertising. In 2007, $9.42bn was spent on advertising cars

(c) What might account for this high advertising spend? **(2 marks)**

The amount spent on television advertising by car manufacturers has fallen from $7bn to less than $6bn in four years.

(d) Outline two possible reasons for this change. **(4 marks)**

(e) Using this case as an example, explain what is meant by the marketing mix. **(4 marks)**

(f) Suggest a future marketing objective for the car manufacturer in this case study. (Hint: use the information gathered from the focus group.) **(4 marks)**

Chapter 37: Market segmentation

Getting started...

Many businesses aim their products at a particular part of the market. For example, Aston Martin, the sports car manufacturer, aims its products at the luxury end of the car market. Some businesses produce several products and target them at different customer groups in the same market. Look at the example below.

Etihad Airways

UAE-based Etihad Airways was set up in 2004. Like most other airlines it provides services for different customer groups. For example, a return flight from Abu Dhabi to Mumbai in September 2009 offered three different services:

- **Coral economy (Price = AED1,775)** This service offers spacious seats in comfortable cabins, the best entertainment and a warm welcome from in-flight hosts.

- **Pearl Business (Price = AED3,025)** This business class service offers a comfortable, 73-inch bed. Each self-contained seat is equipped with individual lighting and a reading lamp. There's also a built-in massage facility.

- **Diamond First (Price = AED5,495)** This is a luxury service. Each suite has its own wardrobe and mini bar, as well as 23-inch wide-screen LCD TV. Meals are served on an extra large wood-finished table.

(a) Describe the different groups of customers targeted by Etihad in this example.

(b) How might Etihad benefit from offering three different services?

Figure 37.1 *Interior of an aircraft*

What is meant by market segmentation?

Markets can be divided into different sections or **segments**. Each segment is made up of consumers that have similar needs. Businesses recognise this and target particular market segments with their products.

- Some businesses concentrate on producing one product for one particular segment. For example, Rolls Royce, which produces luxury cars, targets a very wealthy market segment in the car market.

- Some businesses produce a range of different products and target them at several different segments. In the above example, Etihad targets three different market segments with its different classes of airline service but in the same aircraft.

- Some businesses aim their products at nearly all consumers. For example, large food manufacturers such as Heinz are likely to target their brands at everyone.

However, by dividing markets into segments businesses can more easily supply products that meet customer's needs.

Methods of market segmentation

Geographic segmentation

Different customer groups are likely to have different needs depending on where they live. For example, groups living in very hot climates such as the Middle East will have different needs from groups living in temperate climates such as Germany. There might also be differences between groups living in different parts of the same country. For example, in India, different regions have slightly different tastes in cooking.

Demographic segmentation

It is common for businesses to divide markets according to the age, gender, income, social class, ethnicity or religion of the population.

- **Age:** Infants, teenagers, young adults and the over-65s are all likely to have different needs because of their age. Quite a lot of products are targeted to different consumer groups on the grounds of age. For example, clothes are produced in different sizes and styles for people in different age groups. Different types of holidays are likely to be sold to different age groups.

- **Gender:** Businesses are likely to target males and females with different products. For example, producers of clothes, cars, magazines, toiletries and drinks target different products to different genders.

- **Income:** Incomes in most countries vary considerably. As a result, businesses target products at certain income groups. For example, Rolex, the luxury watchmaker, targets its products at very high-income groups. In contrast, Lidl, the low-cost European supermarket chain, targets lower-income groups.

- **Social class:** Businesses pay a lot of attention to different **socio-economic groups**. Such groups are usually based on occupations. These can be used by businesses to target products. For example, sports cars might be targeted at young professionals.

- **Ethnicity:** Many countries in the world are becoming more cosmopolitan. This means that people from different ethnic groups are likely to live in the same country. This is important for businesses because different ethnic groups are likely to have different needs due to their different cultures.

- **Religion:** It is not uncommon for different religious groups to have different tastes. For example, Muslims do not eat pork or drink alcohol. In the US the market for Kosher food is thought to be worth $100bn a year.

Did you know?

In Canada, where there are over 200 different ethnic groups, Chinese consumers are likely to spend more on leather goods, furniture, appliances and electronic equipment.

QUESTION 1

The market for holidays contains many different segments. The companies described below all sell holidays.

- **Pontins:** Pontins offers low-cost holidays in a number of resorts around the UK such as Blackpool, Southport, Prestatyn Sands and Wall Park holiday centres. It provides self-catering and chalet accommodation and caters particularly for families.

- **Saga:** Sagatravelshop provides a wide range of holidays for the over-50s. These include touring, ocean cruising, resorts and river cruising.

Figure 37.2a *A British holiday resort*

Figure 37.2b *A Greek island resort*

● **Kuoni Travel Ltd:** Kuoni Travel is Britain's best known long-haul luxury holiday tour operator offering a wide range of tailor-made holiday types in over 65 countries.

● **DR Yachting:** DR Yachting provides sailing holidays in the Greek Islands for disabled people in their own-skippered yacht. The company has consulted with experts in special needs matters in order to outfit the boats for handicapped people. For example, accessing the yacht is easy. For boarding, a wide gangway, 90 cm, is provided in order to facilitate access.

There many different segments in the holiday market.

(a) Outline the main reason for this.

(b) Describe the market segments each of the above companies is targeting.

Other methods of segmentation

Some businesses group customers according to how they purchase products. Some customers are *repeat customers*. They are loyal and keep returning. A business might target such a group in a different way to other customers. For example, supermarkets offer regular customers loyalty cards which entitle them to discounts. Some customer groups use products or services at different times of the day. For example, commuters often use transport at 'peak' times. These might be targeted differently from those who travel 'off peak'. People travelling at 'peak' times are usually charged more.

Benefits of market segmentation

Generally a business is more able to meet the needs of different customer groups if the market is segmented. However, some specific advantages include the following:

- Businesses that produce different products for different market segments can increase revenue. In 'Getting started', Etihad charged first class passengers more than twice the rate paid by economy class passengers for the same flight. This helped to increase revenue from the flight.

- Customers may be more loyal to a business that provides products which are tailored specifically to them. For example, tailors on Savile Row in London make bespoke suits for wealthy customers. They often remain loyal because each suit is unique and made for one customer only.

- Businesses may avoid wasting promotional resources by targeting products at customers that do not want them.

- Some businesses can market a wider range of goods to different customer groups.

Mass and niche markets

Some businesses sell their products to *mass markets*. This is when a business sells the same products to all consumers and markets them in the same way. Fast-moving consumer goods such as crisps, breakfast cereals, McDonald's and Coca-Cola, are sold in mass markets. The number of customers in these markets is huge. This means that businesses can produce large quantities at a lower unit cost by exploiting economies of scale (see Chapter 44). This might result in higher sales and higher profits. However, there is often a lot of competition in mass markets and therefore businesses often spend a lot of money marketing these products.

A *niche market* is a small market segment – a segment which has sometimes gone 'untouched' by larger businesses. Niche marketing is the complete opposite of mass marketing. It involves selling to a small customer group, sometimes with specific needs. Small firms can often survive by supplying niche markets. They can often avoid competition. It is also a lot easier to focus on the needs of the customer in a niche market. Examples of niche markets might include graduation gifts, dog training, wedding planning and BBC Radio 3 (which mainly broadcasts classical music).

Key terms

Market segment – part of a whole market where a particular customer group has similar characteristics.

Socio-economic groups – division of people according to social class based on employment status.

QUESTION 2

Nomads is an online clothing retailer. It produces quality clothing from a variety of designs including Celtic, tie dye, ethnic and hippy. All of its products use Fair Trade materials and suppliers who both give and receive a fair rate of pay.

(a) Using this case study as an example, explain what is meant by a niche market.

(b) Outline two advantages of producing for a niche market.

Figure 37.3 *Clothing produced for a niche market*

Chapter review – Toyota

Toyota is the largest car manufacturer in the world. It currently produces 14 models in many different countries. In 2008, the company sold 8.97million vehicles. Four of Toyota's models are described below.

● **Prius $27,700:** The Toyota Prius has become the byword for eco-conscious driving. It is a hybrid car which means that it runs on both electricity and petrol. It is considered environmentally friendly because it does not use as much petrol as other similar cars. It has very low CO_2 emissions. Many car manufacturers are launching hybrids but Toyota was the first.

● **Hiace $24,500:** The Hiace is a commercial vehicle. It has a strong load capacity and a space-efficient cargo area. The Hiace is said to deliver functionality, driveability and comfort. Its powerful engine supports an impressive workload while maintaining good economy.

● **AYGO $13,500:** The AYGO is small, low-priced and described by Toyota as the ultimate city car. It is nimble, easy to handle and made for narrow gaps and tight parking. It is also very economical – achieving over 60 mpg.

● **Land Cruiser $48,900:** The Land Cruiser is described as a Sports Utility Vehicle (SUV). It can be driven 'off-road' and is said to offer premium levels of comfort. Toyota claims that the Land Cruiser has led the way in 4 × 4 technology for more than 50 years.

(a) Describe the market segment that Toyota is likely to target with the vehicles described here. **(4 marks)**

(b) Assess if these products are likely to be targeted at particular:
  (i) geographical areas
  (ii) income groups. **(4 marks)**

(c) Examine whether Toyota relies on mass marketing or niche marketing. **(4 marks)**

(d) Analyse the benefits to Toyota of market segmentation. **(8 marks)**

Chapter 38: The marketing mix

Getting started...

Businesses use marketing to help sell their products. However, marketing involves using a number of elements to encourage people to buy products. Look at the examples below.

Sony

After months of rumours and anticipation, Sony slashed the price of the PlayStation 3 by $100, hoping to boost sales ahead of Christmas. Sony said it would cut the price of the 80 GB PlayStation 3 to $299. Sony also cut the price of its existing 160 GB PlayStation 3 by $100 to $399. All price cuts apply globally. When the Sony PlayStation 3 was launched in 2006, it cost around $600.

LG (Egypt)

LG is a multinational based in South Korea employing around 177,000 people. It produces electronic goods and chemicals, and provides telecommunications services. An advert designed to look like a trailer for a new TV programme, using the TV model name as the series name, Scarlet, was used in Egypt to promote the company and a new range of high definition (HD) TVs.

Figure 38.1 *An LG television screen*

McDonald's (India)

McDonald's is a world-famous burger chain. In 1996, the first McDonald's was opened in Delhi, India. However, in order to appeal to Indian consumers, around 75 per cent of the menu items had to be 'Indianised'. Some of the products on the Indian menu include McVeggie, McAloo Tikki, Paneer Salsa Wrap and Veg McCurry.

(a) Describe the marketing methods used in the above examples to help sell the products.

What is meant by the marketing mix?

A good marketing strategy is one that meets customers' needs. This means that a business must:

- design and produce high quality *products*
- charge a *price* that is acceptable to consumers
- let consumers know about products through *promotion*
- make products available in the right *place* at the right time.

This is called the **marketing mix** and usually referred to as the four Ps. To achieve marketing objectives a business must find the right balance or mix between product, price, promotion and place.

Product

Products have to fulfil or exceed customer expectations. Products have certain features that businesses must get right.

- **Functional:** This means that products must perform the function for which they were bought. For example, a waterproof anorak must keep the rain out.

- **Appearance:** Products should look good. The shape, size and colour of products must be appealing to consumers. For some products, such as jewellery, fashion items and cars, this is vitally important.

- **Unique selling point (USP):** Products will be more successful if they have a USP. This means that the product has a particular characteristic that makes it different from those of its competitors.

- **Product life cycle:** Many products have a limited life. During that life, sales will rise and then fall. A business will need to modify products or create new ones when they decline.

  The importance of each of these features will vary according to the nature of the product. For example, a garage selling petrol does not have to consider the appearance of the product because it is never seen. The product is discussed in Chapter 42.

Price

Consumers want value for money. This means that the price charged is important. The price charged by a business depends on a number of factors. These include:

- the quality of the product

- the costs of production

- the prices charged by competitors

- how much customers are prepared to pay.

Businesses can choose from a number of *pricing strategies* when setting the price of products. These are discussed in Chapter 39.

Promotion

Businesses have to make sure that consumers know about their products. This means they have to provide consumers with information. This may include details about the nature and range of products, the prices charged and where products can be purchased. Businesses might also try to persuade people to buy their products. Businesses do this by promoting their products. Businesses can choose between a wide range of promotional methods. For example, a small chain store might place an advertisement in a local newspaper. Promotion is discussed in Chapter 40.

Place

Part of the marketing mix involves the distribution of products to customers. Products must be made available in convenient locations at times when consumers want to buy them. Businesses can use a number of different distribution channels. For example, some manufacturers choose to sell their products using retailers such as supermarkets or wholesalers. However, others try to sell their products directly to consumers using, for example, mail order. Distribution is discussed in Chapter 41.

Choosing the right mix

Businesses have to find the right balance between product, price, promotion and place. In some markets price is the most important element. For example, supermarkets often emphasise the prices they charge. Some supermarkets also display the prices charged by competitors for the same products. This is to show that their competitors are dearer. The marketing mix may be influenced by the following:

● **Nature of the product:** For example, firms selling technical products might emphasise the quality and reliability of their products rather than price or place.

● **Competition:** In highly competitive markets price is likely to be very important.

● **Marketing budget:** Firms with larger marketing budgets can spend more on promotion.

● **Competitors' mix:** Businesses often copy the marketing activities of competitors.

● **Technology:** For example, an increasing number of businesses are advertising and selling online.

● **Market research:** Some market research is designed to assess the effectiveness of a firm's marketing activities. If a survey suggests that consumers are responding well to a particular promotion, a business will make more use of that promotion.

Key term

Marketing mix – the elements of a firm's marketing that are designed to meet the needs of customers. Often called the 4Ps, they include product, price, promotion and place.

Chapter review – Ryanair

Ryanair is an Irish low-cost airline with main bases in Dublin and Stansted Airports. It is the third largest airline in Europe in terms of passenger numbers. Details of its marketing mix are shown in Figure 38.2.

Product
• Low-cost, no frills air travel to European destinations
• No free food or drink on board

Promotion
• Ryanair spends as little as possible on advertising
• Simple adverts are used to tell passengers that Ryanair has low fares

Price
• Ryanair has low fares – often the lowest in the market
• 70% of seats are sold at the lowest two fares

Place
• Ryanair does not use travel agents or pay agency commissions
• Bookings are made online – this saves it 15% in agency fees

Figure 38.2 *Ryanair's marketing mix*

(a) Using this case study as an example, outline what is meant by the marketing mix. **(4 marks)**

(b) Describe the product being sold by Ryanair. **(2 marks)**

Ryanair sells tickets online.

(c) Outline two advantages of this approach. **(4 marks)**

(d) Analyse two factors that are likely to affect the marketing mix chosen by a business. **(4 marks)**

(e) Assess which element of the marketing mix is the most important to Ryanair. **(6 marks)**

Chapter 39: Price

Getting started...

Setting the price of a product is a vital marketing decision. If the price is set too high customers may not buy the product. On the other hand, if it is too low this might suggest that the product is of a poor quality. The business might also struggle to make a profit. Businesses can use a number of methods to set their prices. Look at the examples below.

Dell Computers

When Dell Computers launched their personal computers the price was set lower than those of competitors. They were able to do this because their costs were lower. With a lower price Dell was able to penetrate the market effectively.

For example, when Dell penetrated the Chinese market in 2007, the price of PCs was set between 2,599 yuan to 3,999 yuan. The prices of competitors' PCs were around 5,000 yuan.

Sanjay Stores

Sanjay runs a general store in Mylapore, Chennai. He uses a very simple method to calculate the prices of all products sold in the shop. He adds 20 per cent to the cost of buying them in. So, for example, a product that cost him Rs100 from a supplier is sold for Rs120 {100 + (20% × 100)}.

(a) How are prices set in the above examples?

(b) Outline one possible advantage of using the pricing method in each case.

Figure 39.1 *A general store in India*

Supply and demand

In most markets the prices charged by a business reflect prevailing market conditions. This means that prices are heavily influenced by the forces of *supply* and *demand*. Demand is determined by *customers*. Demand is what customers are willing and able to buy at a given price. Increasing demand from customers will drive the price up. Falling demand forces firms to lower prices. If firms do not lower their prices, their sales will fall.

Supply is determined by *businesses*. Supply is the amount businesses are willing to offer for sale at a given price. If supply is increased because, for example, more businesses join the market then prices will be forced down. In contrast, if there are shortages in the market caused by a lack of supply, prices will be forced up.

What factors affect price?

Businesses have to take into account a number of factors when setting the price of products. Some of the important factors are summarised in Figure 39.2.

Did you know?

Rising demand from China for commodities such as copper and coal has driven their prices up. Also, in 2010, a fall in the global supply of commodities such as wheat (due to poor harvests) forced prices up.

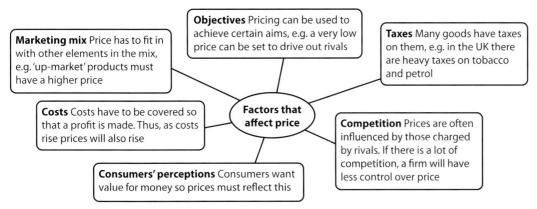

Figure 39.2 *Factors that affect the prices charged by a business*

Pricing strategies

Businesses can choose from a range of different *pricing strategies* when setting the prices. A pricing strategy is a set of plans designed to meet a specific marketing aim.

Cost-based pricing

Businesses have to set prices that generate a profit. One method which ensures that all costs are covered is **cost plus** or **cost-based pricing**. It is simple and involves adding a **mark-up** to total costs. For example, the cost to a manufacturer of making a bicycle is $60. The manufacturer adds a markup of 25 per cent to get the price. Therefore the price of the bicycle is $75 {$60 + (25% × $60)}. This method is common with retailers. However, one of the drawbacks of this method is that it ignores market conditions. For example, the $75 price set by the cycle manufacturer may be far too high in relation to the prices of other bicycles in the market. This might result in low sales.

Market-orientated pricing

One of the drawbacks with cost plus pricing is that it completely ignores conditions in the market. **Market-orientated pricing** involves setting the price of a product after looking at market conditions. There are several pricing strategies which adopt this approach.

- **Skimming or creaming:** Some businesses may launch a product into a market charging a high price for a limited time period. This is called **skimming** or **creaming**. The main objective is to generate high levels of revenue with a new product before competitors arrive on the scene.

  Pharmaceuticals companies also use this method. They sell new drugs for high prices when they are first launched. However, when patents run out competition emerges and prices fall. Charging a high price initially helps such companies recover high research and development costs.

- **Penetration pricing:** Sometimes a business will introduce a new product and charge a low price for a limited period. This is called **penetration pricing**. The aim of this strategy is to get the product established in the market. Businesses using this strategy hope that customers are attracted by the low price, and then carry on buying it when the price rises. A number of industries favour this strategy.

● **Psychological pricing:** One common pricing strategy is to set the price slightly below a round figure – charging $99.99 instead of $100. This is called *psychological pricing*. Consumers are 'tricked' into thinking that $99.99 is significantly cheaper than $100. Of course it is not but this psychological effect often works for businesses.

● **Loss leaders:** Some products are sold at a price lower than cost. These are called **loss leaders** and are popular with supermarkets. The objective of this strategy is to draw customers into a store where they will buy the loss leader. Once in the store it is hoped that customers buy other products. This will generate a profit overall.

● **Discounts and sales:** Businesses often cut prices for a short period. They have *sales* where goods are sold below the standard price. Some of these sales are seasonal.

QUESTION 1

SmithKline Beecham (now GlaxoSmithKline) introduced an anti-ulcer drug in 1978. The drug, called Tagamet, was priced at $10 per unit in the US. By 1990, the price had come down to less than $2 and by 1994 it had fallen to 60 cents. Tagamet lost its patent protection in the US in 1995. As a result, other producers launched their own versions of the drug onto the American market. Today, a unit of Tagamet can be purchased for 29 cents.

(a) Identify the pricing strategy used by SmithKline Beecham for Tagamet.

(b) Why did the price of Tagamet fall in 1994?

(c) Outline the main advantage to SmithKline Beecham of this pricing strategy.

Competition-based pricing

Some businesses take a very close look at what their rivals are charging when setting their prices. This approach is called **competition-based pricing** and is likely to be used by businesses operating in fiercely competitive markets. One approach is to charge the same price as competitors. The advantage of this strategy is that a price war is likely to be avoided. It is considered to be a safe pricing strategy. Another approach is for the market leader to set the price and all others follow. This is called *price leadership.*

Sometimes a business might lower its price to drive out competition. This is called **destroyer** or **predatory pricing.** In 2008, Amazon.com, the online book retailer, was accused of predatory pricing in France where it was selling books without charging for shipping.

QUESTION 2

Eduardo Urondo runs a busy coffee shop in the centre of Rosario, Argentina. However, in 2009 a multinational coffee chain opened a branch opposite Eduardo's shop. The thing that upset Eduardo the most was the pricing policy of the new rival. The prices charged by the multinational were half of what Eduardo was charging. Naturally, customers started to drift away. Eduardo said 'I know what will happen. Eventually I will be forced out of business. And then, when I'm gone, their prices will rise. I can't win. The multinational has huge resources and can afford to trade at a loss until I leave the market.'

(a) Describe the pricing strategy being used by the multinational.

(b) How can the new rival afford to trade at a loss?

Price elasticity of demand

The prices charged by businesses will also be affected by **price elasticity of demand**. Price elasticity of demand measures how responsive demand is to price changes. Most goods fall into one of two categories.

- **Goods with price elastic demand:** The demand for most products is **price elastic**. This means that a price change will result in a significant change in demand for the product. For example, if a business lowered price by 10 per cent, demand would rise by a greater proportion, say, 20 per cent. Goods which have price elastic demand tend to be non-essentials and products with lots of substitutes. Businesses which sell goods with price elastic demand can increase total revenue by lowering price. However, if they raise price demand and revenue will fall because customers can easily switch to other brands.

- **Goods with price inelastic demand:** For a minority of goods demand is **price inelastic**. This means that a price change will have little impact on the amount demanded. For example, if a business lowered the price by 10 per cent, demand might only increase by 3 per cent. Goods which have price inelastic demand tend to be essential goods or goods with very few substitutes. Tobacco and petrol are examples. If a business sells goods with price inelastic demand, revenue can be increased if prices are increased. However, a price cut will result in lower revenue because demand will not increase significantly after a price cut.

Key terms

Competition-based pricing – pricing strategies based on the prices charged by rivals.

Cost plus or cost-based pricing – adding a percentage (the mark-up) to the costs of producing a product to get the price.

Destroyer or predatory pricing – setting a low price until rivals have gone out of business.

Loss leader – a product sold below cost to draw in customers.

Market orientated pricing – pricing strategies based upon the conditions in the market.

Mark-up – the percentage added to costs which makes a profit for a business when setting the price.

Penetration pricing – setting a low price to start with in order to get established in the market. Price may be raised once established.

Price elasticity of demand – measures the responsiveness of demand to a change in price.

Price elastic demand – where a price change will result in a significant change in demand.

Price inelastic demand – where a price change will result in a much smaller change in demand.

Skimming or creaming – setting a high price initially and then lowering it later.

Chapter review – The Sharjah Tile Centre

The Sharjah Tile Centre is located in Industrial Area 2 in Sharjah, UAE. The business, which is owned by Faris Mubarak, has done very well

recently. Tile sales in the UAE market exceeded €393.2 million in 2008, representing a 29 per cent increase from the previous year. The outlet sells wall and floor tiles for a wide range of uses. To ensure that the business returns a profit Faris Mubarak uses cost plus pricing. He adds 50 per cent to the cost of tiles which he buys direct from manufacturers. The Sharjah

Figure 39.3 *An example of a product by the Sharjah Tile Centre*

Tile centre serves both home owners and trade customers.

(a) **(i)** Using this case study as an example, explain what is meant by cost plus pricing. **(2 marks)**

    (ii) Calculate the price Faris would charge for a pack of ceramic tiles costing him AED30. **(4 marks)**

    (iii) Outline one advantage and one disadvantage of cost plus pricing. **(4 marks)**

(b) Define competition-based pricing. **(2 marks)**

The products sold by The Sharjah Tile Centre have price elastic demand.

(c) Describe what this means. **(4 marks)**

Faris is considering a price cut for tiles.

(d) Assess the likely effect on demand and revenue. **(4 marks)**

Chapter 40: Promotion

Getting started...

Businesses have to make consumers aware of their products. They have to give them details about the features of the product, its price and where it can be purchased. However, many businesses go further than this. They use a variety of methods to encourage people to buy their products. Look at the examples below.

Supermarkets

One of the methods used by supermarkets to keep customers informed is to distribute leaflets to people's homes. These leaflets are generally used to promote the latest special offers available in the stores.

La Villa Des Orangers

La Villa Des Orangers is a luxury hotel located in Marrakech, Morocco. The hotel is an old palace built around a courtyard. The five-star property looks stunning and has its own website that is used to promote the Villa.

Figure 40.1 *A supermarket leaflet* **Figure 40.2** *Greenhouse Bonanza advertisement*

Greenhouse Bonanza

Greenhouse Bonanza sells a range of garden products such as greenhouses, greenhouse accessories, cold frames, fencing, bird tables, nest boxes and plant racks. One of the methods the business uses to promote its products is by placing adverts in magazines. The advert in Figure 40.2 appeared in a gardening magazine.

(a) Describe the methods used by these businesses to promote their products.

(b) Which of these businesses is most likely to use TV advertising?

(c) How is Greenhouse Bonanza targeting customers?

What is promotion?

Businesses have to communicate with their customers. They use two different methods of promotion to draw attention to their products.

- **Above-the-line promotion:** This approach is to advertise using the media. Advertising in newspapers and magazines, advertising on the television and the radio and banner adverts on websites are all examples.

- **Below-the-line promotion:** This is any other form of promotion that does not involve using the media. Examples might include press releases, point-of-sale displays, merchandising, coupons and direct mailing.

Section 4: Marketing

What are the aims of promotion?

Generally, businesses use promotion to obtain and retain customers. However, promotion is likely to be used to achieve some specific aims.

● Tell consumers about a new product.

● Remind customers about an existing product.

● Reach a widely dispersed target audience.

● Reassure customers about products.

● Show consumers that rival products are not as good.

● Improve or develop the image of the business.

Above-the-line promotion

Above-the-line promotion involves **advertising** in the media. Businesses pay television companies or newspapers, for example, to have their adverts broadcast or printed. Figure 40.3 shows the advantages and disadvantages of the main media.

Media	Advantages	Disadvantages
Television	Huge audiences can be reached The use of products can be demonstrated Creative adverts can have great impact Scope for targeting groups with digital TV	Very expensive Message may be short lived Some viewers avoid TV adverts Delay between seeing adverts and shopping
Newspapers and magazines	National and local coverage Reader can refer back Adverts can be linked to articles and features Scope for targeting with specialist magazines Relatively cheap	No movement or sound Individual adverts may be lost in a sea of adverts Rivals' products may be advertised as well
Cinema	Big impact with a big screen Can be used for local and national advertising Specific age groups can be targeted Sound and movement can be used	Limited audience Message may only be seen once Message is short-lived
Radio	Sound can be used Minority audiences allow targeting Cheap production Can target youngsters	Not visual May be ignored May lack impact Can be intrusive when listening
Posters and billboards	Can produce national campaigns Seen repeatedly Good for short sharp messages Large posters can have big impact	Posters can get damaged by vandals Only limited information can be shown Difficult to evaluate effectiveness
Internet	Can be updated regularly Can be targeted Hits and response can be measured Cheap and easy to set up	Some adverts such as pop-up adverts are irritating Possible technical problems

Figure 40.3 *The advantages and disadvantages of selected advertising media*

QUESTION 1

The amount of money spent on advertising is huge. Between 1997 and 2007 the amount spent on advertising rose from $187,529m to $279,612m in the USA. An analysis of the expenditure is shown in Figure 40.4.

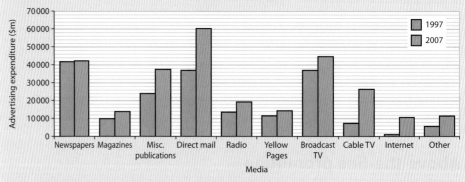

Figure 40.4 *US advertising by media 1997 and 2007 ($million)*

(a) What is meant by above-the-line promotion?

(b) Outline three key changes in advertising expenditure shown by Figure 40.4.

Informative and persuasive advertising

Some businesses use *informative advertising* when advertising their products. This means that the adverts are designed to increase consumer awareness of products. They may give clear information about the features of a product, for example. The classified advertisements in newspapers are examples of informative advertising. In contrast, *persuasive advertising* is designed to put pressure on consumers to buy a product. Persuasive advertisements often try to convince consumers to buy a particular brand rather than that of a competitor. A lot of television and cinema adverts are persuasive.

Below-the-line promotion

Below-the-line promotion is usually designed and produced by a business 'in-house'. It refers to any form of promotion that does not involve advertising. There is a huge range of promotions that might be used.

Sales promotions

These are incentives to encourage people to buy products. They are used to boost sales in the hope that if new customers are attracted they will continue to buy the product. Sales promotions include:

● **Free gifts:** Businesses might give free gifts to customers when they buy the product. Newspapers often give away DVDs and computer companies often give away free software, for example.

● **Coupons:** Money-off vouchers can be used by businesses to attract customers. They may be attached to products, appear in newspaper adverts, or pushed through letter boxes.

- **Loyalty cards:** Some businesses reward customers according to how much they spend. Points are collected and then exchanged for cash, vouchers or free goods. Loyalty cards are popular with supermarkets, credit card companies and stores.

- **Competitions:** People may be allowed free entry into a competition when they a buy a particular product. An attractive prize is offered to the winners.

- **BOGOF offers:** This stands for Buy One Get One Free. These are popular with many businesses such as supermarkets, transport services and restaurants.

- **Money off deals:** Businesses may offer customers discounts such as '30% off' or 'an extra 20% free'. These are similar to BOGOF deals and are used by a range of suppliers.

Public relations

Some businesses communicate with stakeholders using *public relations* (PR). The main purpose of PR is to increase sales by improving the image of the business. A number of approaches might be used by businesses to attract publicity.

- **Press release:** Some information about the business may be presented to the media. This might be used to write an article or feature in a television programme. For example, a business might announce that it is to create 2,000 new jobs. Such positive news would be of interest to the media and they might want more information.

- **Press conference:** This is where representatives confront the media and present information verbally. This allows for questioning and other feedback. The press might be invited to a new product launch for example.

- **Sponsorship:** Many companies attract publicity by linking their brands with sporting events. For example, DFL Building, Kingfisher Airlines, Vodafone and Pepsi were some of the companies making financial contributions to the Indian Premier League in return for publicity at the event. They were the *sponsors*. The sponsoring of television programmes is also becoming popular.

- **Donations:** Donations to charities and the local community might be used by businesses to improve their image. A large donation from a business is likely to be reported in the media unless it is made anonymously.

The main advantage of PR to businesses is that it is often a cheap method of promotion. Some businesses have been known to deliberately seek bad publicity by being controversial. This can raise the profile of a business very quickly, sometimes at no cost.

Merchandising and packaging

Some businesses may arrange the point of sale so that it is interesting and eye catching and likely to encourage sales. This is called **merchandising**. Some examples are outlined below.

- **Product layout:** The layout of products in a store is often planned very carefully indeed. This is to encourage shoppers to follow particular routes and look at certain products. Products which stores want you to buy are placed at prominent locations such as at the end of aisles and at eye level.

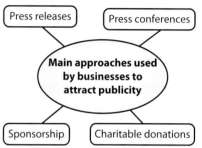

Figure 40.5 *The main approaches used by businesses to attract publicity*

- **Display material:** Posters, leaflets and other materials may be used to display certain products with the aim of persuading customers to buy. Lighting and other special effects might be used to improve the environment. Window displays are considered important to retailers. They are used to draw in customers.

- **Stock:** Businesses must keep shelves well stocked because empty shelves create a bad impression. Also, if items are out of stock customers may shop elsewhere.

Direct mailing

Direct mailing is where businesses send households leaflets or letters. The supermarket leaflet shown in 'Getting started' is an example. Sometimes personal letters are used. They may contain information about new products or details of price changes, for example. In some cases, email is being used to contact consumers rather than the postal system. The development of IT and use of customer databases has resulted in more use of personalised marketing.

Direct selling or personal selling

Direct selling or personal selling might involve a sales rep calling at households or businesses hoping to sell products. It could also be a telephone call from a call centre where an 'army' of sales staff is employed to sell over the telephone. One advantage of this approach is that the features of the product can be discussed. However, people are often irritated by this approach because the callers have not been invited.

Exhibitions and trade fairs

Some businesses attend trade fairs or exhibitions to promote their products. Businesses set up a stand and promote their products face-to-face. They may be attended by commercial buyers or consumers, or both. In the UK some popular exhibitions are the Motor Show, the Ideal Homes Exhibition and the Boat Show. The main advantages of this method are outlined briefly below.

- Products might be tested out on consumers before a full launch.

- Some exhibitions are overseas and can be used to break into foreign markets.

- Products can be physically demonstrated and questions can be answered.

- Exhibitions often attract the media.

- Customers can speak to business owners or senior personnel face to face.

QUESTION 2

Gifts India 2009 was India's largest trade fair for corporate and personal gifts. It claims to be the number one marketing vehicle for business in Indian and international markets. Around 20,000 visitors were expected to attend representing distributors, catalogue houses, gift buyers and many other commercial buyers. Exhibitors at the trade fair included gift wrappers, souvenirs, handicrafts, promotional toys and jewellery.

(a) What is meant by a trade fair? (Use this case study as an example.)

(b) Discuss three advantages to a Chinese toy manufacturer of attending Gifts India.

Choosing methods of promotion

Many businesses use a range of different promotional methods. However, the methods must be co-ordinated so that they support each other. Small businesses often have limited budgets so careful consideration is needed when choosing a method of promotion. What affects the choice of promotion method?

- **Cost:** Many businesses are forced to use cheaper promotions because advertising on television and in national newspapers is beyond their means and not always appropriate.

- **Market type:** Local businesses often rely on adverts in local newspapers and publications such as *Yellow Pages*. In contrast, businesses aiming their products at mass markets are more likely to use television and national newspapers or specialist magazines.

- **Product type:** Certain products are better suited to certain methods of promotion. For example, a car manufacturer is not likely to use sales promotions such as coupons, buy-one-get-one-free deals or loyalty cards. Indeed, their favoured method is television advertising. Similarly, supermarkets are unlikely to use personal selling.

- **Stage in the product life cycle:** It is common for promotional methods to change as a product gets older. For example, PR is often used at the beginning but when the product matures other methods will be used.

- **Competitors' promotions:** It is common for businesses to copy the method of promotion used by a rival. Once one business comes up with a successful promotion, others soon bring out their own versions.

- **Legal factors:** In many countries legislation designed to protect consumers can affect the method and style of promotion. For example, in the EU tobacco products cannot be advertised on television.

Chapter review – UEFA Champions League

The UEFA Champions League is one of the most famous football tournaments in the world. Every season Europe's top football clubs, such as Real Madrid, Barcelona, Inter Milan, Manchester United and Liverpool, take part. The tournament is sponsored by multinationals including Ford, Sony, UniCredit, Mastercard, Adidas and Heineken. Each sponsor is allocated four advertising boards around the edges of the pitch. They also get logo placement at pre- and post-match interviews and free tickets to each match. They also get priority on TV adverts during matches to give them maximum exposure.

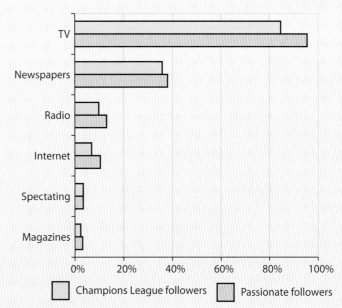
Figure 40.6 *Percentage of followers using each medium to follow the Champions League*

(a) 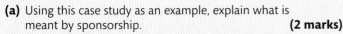Using this case study as an example, explain what is meant by sponsorship. **(2 marks)**

(b) Outline two advantages to the sponsors of their involvement in the UEFA Champions League. **(4 marks)**

(c) 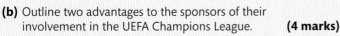Give two other methods of PR that businesses might use to promote their products. **(2 marks)**

(d) (i) What does the graph in Figure 40.6 show? **(2 marks)**
　(ii) Suggest how the graph in Figure 40.6 might be helpful to the sponsors of the UEFA Champions League? **(4 marks)**

(e) 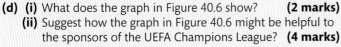Evaluate the factors that might influence the choice of promotion for a company like Ford. **(6 marks)**

Chapter 41: Place

Getting started...

One important activity in the marketing mix is making sure that products are in the right place at the right time. Consumers are more likely to buy products if they are available in convenient locations. Businesses can distribute their products using a number of methods. Look at the examples below.

Mars

Mars is a worldwide manufacturer of confectionery, pet food and other food products. It had sales of US$21 billion in 2008. The company is most famous for brands such as Mars Bar, Snickers, Skittles, Twix and Milky Way. Products such as these are sold in as many outlets as possible. They can be bought in newsagents, sweet shops, supermarkets, petrol stations, bars, cinemas, sports venues and vending machines.

Loot Online

Loot Online Ltd is an online retailer serving the residents of South Africa. It was set up in 2003 and has been growing ever since. At first Loot sold only books but added DVDs, games and music to the site in 2005. Loot's product range includes over 1½ million different books and thousands of CDs, DVDs and games.

(a) Outline the methods of distribution used in the above examples.

(b) State two advantages to Mars of selling goods through vending machines.

(c) Is Mars likely to use the internet to distribute confectionery?

What is place?

Place is one of the 4Ps in the marketing mix. It refers to the location where people can buy products. If businesses cannot get products in the right place at the right time they are not likely to be successful. If products are not available in convenient locations, consumers may not have the time to search for them. For example, if motorway service stations were located two or three miles from the motorway, they may struggle to survive. Also, food producers in many countries would have limited sales if they did not make groceries available in supermarkets.

Distribution channels

The route taken by a product from the producer to the customer is called a **distribution channel**. Businesses can choose from a number of different distribution channels. Some of the main ones used for consumer goods are shown in Figure 41.1. One approach is to sell goods directly to consumers but others involve using *intermediaries* such as retailers and wholesalers. These are businesses that provide links between producers and consumers. The diagram shows that some producers may use more than one channel of distribution.

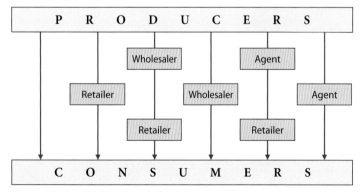

Figure 41.1 *Distribution channels for consumer goods*

Direct selling

Some producers market their products directly to consumers. **Direct selling** can take a number of forms. These are summarised in Figure 41.2.

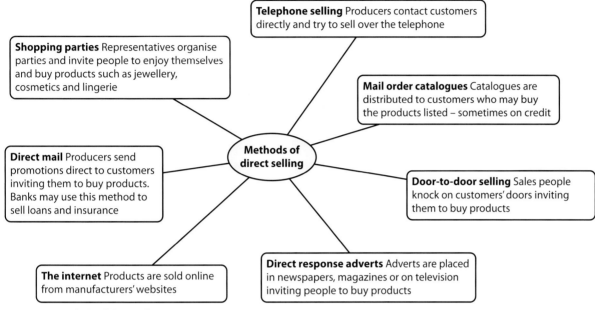

Figure 41.2 *Methods of direct selling*

QUESTION 1

Dove Chocolate Discoveries sells chocolate products direct to customers. The company, owned by Mars, sells at shopping parties organised by 'chocolatiers'. At the parties, guests learn about chocolate while sampling the products. According to the company's president, there is a growing interest in chocolate. People can learn where chocolate is grown, how it is harvested and other interesting facts. At the end of the party they may have a fun quiz to test what they have learned. Chocolate prizes are given to the winners.

Figure 41.3 *Chocolates*

'Chocolatiers' learn about the business from their kits. These contain a training manual and a DVD showing a sample party and the basics of hostess coaching. Dove provides further training and support through conference calls, as well as face-to-face meetings.

(a) What is meant by direct selling? (Use this case study as an example.)

(b) Outline two advantages to Dove Chocolate Discoveries of direct selling.

(c) Give four other methods of direct selling.

Retailing

Figure 41.1 shows that most distribution channels use **retailers**. These are businesses which buy goods from manufacturers or other suppliers and sell them straight to consumers. Figure 41.4 shows the different types of retailers involved in distribution.

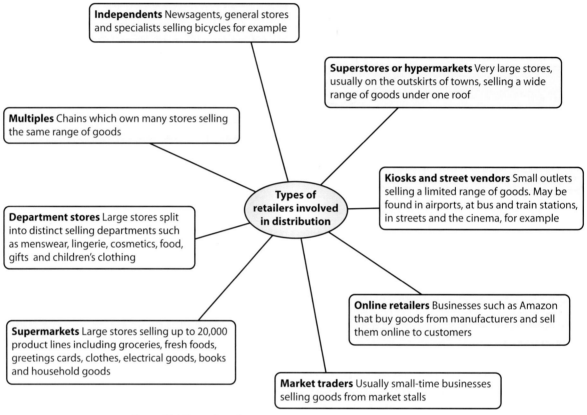

Independents Newsagents, general stores and specialists selling bicycles for example

Superstores or hypermarkets Very large stores, usually on the outskirts of towns, selling a wide range of goods under one roof

Multiples Chains which own many stores selling the same range of goods

Kiosks and street vendors Small outlets selling a limited range of goods. May be found in airports, at bus and train stations, in streets and the cinema, for example

Department stores Large stores split into distinct selling departments such as menswear, lingerie, cosmetics, food, gifts and children's clothing

Types of retailers involved in distribution

Online retailers Businesses such as Amazon that buy goods from manufacturers and sell them online to customers

Supermarkets Large stores selling up to 20,000 product lines including groceries, fresh foods, greetings cards, clothes, electrical goods, books and household goods

Market traders Usually small-time businesses selling goods from market stalls

Figure 41.4 *Types of retailers*

Wholesaling

Some producers use **wholesalers** to help distribute goods. Wholesalers usually buy from manufacturers and sell to retailers. Some wholesalers are called Cash and Carry stores. This is because customers can come to the store, buy goods, pay cash and take goods away with them. Wholesalers may break bulk, repack goods, redistribute smaller quantities, store goods and provide delivery services. A wholesaler stocks goods produced by many manufacturers. Therefore retailers get to select from a wide range of merchandise.

Agents or brokers

The role of **agents** or **brokers** is to link buyers and sellers. They are used in a variety of markets. For example, travel agents sell holidays and flights for holiday companies, airlines and tour operators. Estate agents sell properties on behalf of vendors. Agents are also used to sell insurance, life assurance and other financial products.

Key fact

Manufacturers may use agents when exporting. Agents can reduce the risk of selling overseas. This is because they have knowledge of the country and the market.

QUESTION 2

The use of online selling is growing rapidly all over the world. Shopping online is particularly favoured by those who:

- live in rural and isolated locations
- do not have the time to go shopping
- dislike going to shops
- have mobility problems.

Online shopping can be cheaper because business costs are lower. It can be done 24/7 and there is generally a lot of choice. People can also shop from different locations such as at work, at home or while travelling on a train. All they need is access to the internet. Figure 41.5 shows the pattern of online retail spending in the US between 2001 and 2008.

Category	Online retail spending ($bn)				
	2001	2005	2006	2007	2008 (proj)
Computer hardware and software	11.0	18.1	21.2	24.1	26.7
Consumer electronics	1.5	4.7	6.8	8.4	10.0
Books, music and videos	3.8	7.5	9.0	9.8	11.1
Tickets	1.8	4.6	5.5	6.3	6.8
Consumer health	0.4	2.6	3.4	4.2	5.3
Apparel, accessories, footwear and jewellry	4.7	14.0	19.1	23.2	27.1
Grocery and pet food	0.8	4.1	5.6	7.4	9.1
Toys and video games	1.0	2.9	4.1	5.2	5.9
Sporting goods	0.7	2.0	2.3	2.5	2.8
Flowers and speciality gifts	1.2	3.1	3.9	4.3	4.9
Home	1.8	10.0	15.0	18.8	22.7
Office products	0.6	3.2	4.1	4.7	5.1
Other	1.8	6.7	8.1	9.1	10.1
Total	**31.0**	**83.6**	**108.1**	**128.1**	**147.6**

Figure 41.5 *Online retail spending in the US 2001–07 and 2008 projections*

(a) Outline two advantages to producers of selling online.

(b) Calculate the percentage increase in total online spending between 2001 and 2008.

(c) Briefly account for the pattern in (b).

(d) Which products are the most popular with online shoppers?

Choosing appropriate distribution channels

The nature of the product

Different types of products may require different distribution channels. Some examples are given below.

- Most services are sold directly to consumers. It would not be appropriate for window cleaners, gardeners and hairdressers, for example, to use intermediaries.

- Fast moving consumer goods like breakfast cereals, confectionery, crisps and toilet paper cannot be sold directly by manufacturers to consumers. Wholesalers and retailers play an important role in the distribution of these goods because they break bulk.

- Businesses producing high-quality 'exclusive' products such as perfume and designer clothes will choose their outlets very carefully. The image of their products is important so they are not likely to use supermarkets, for example.

- Some products need explanation or demonstration.

Cost

Businesses will choose the cheapest distribution channels. They will also prefer direct channels. This is because each time an intermediary is used they will take a share of the profit. Large supermarkets will try to buy direct from manufacturers. This is because they can bulk buy and get lower prices. Independents are more likely to buy from wholesalers. They have to charge higher prices as a result. Many producers now sell direct to consumers from their websites. This helps to keep costs down.

Key terms

Agent or broker – an intermediary that brings together buyers and sellers.

Direct selling – where businesses sell their products directly to consumers.

Distribution channel – the route taken by a product from the producer to the customer.

Retailer – a business which buys goods from manufacturers and wholesalers and sells them in small quantities to consumers.

Wholesaler – a business which buys goods from manufacturers and sells them in smaller quantities to retailers.

Did you know?

Technical products or complex financial products might need to be sold by expert sales people. These products are likely to be sold by specialists.

Did you know?

Some products, such as heating systems, require expert installation to comply with health and safety legislation. Producers of such products might prefer to handle installation themselves and deal directly with customers. They can ensure safe installation more easily.

The market

Producers selling to mass markets are likely to use intermediaries. In contrast, businesses targeting smaller markets are more likely to target customers directly. For example, a building contractor in a small town will deal directly with customers. Producers selling in overseas markets are likely to use agents because the agents will know the market better. Businesses selling goods to other businesses are likely to use more direct channels.

Control

For some producers it is important to have complete control over distribution. For example, producers of exclusive products do not want to see them being sold in 'down market' outlets. This might damage their image.

Chapter review – Distribution channels

Banking services

Figure 41.6 *A bank*

Figure 41.7 *A power station*

Agricultural goods

Figure 41.8 *A farm*

Look at the images.

(a) Suggest suitable distribution channels for these businesses. **(6 marks)**

(b) Outline the main disadvantage to farmers of using an intermediary to help distribute produce. **(2 marks)**

(c) Discuss two reasons why banks are making increased use of online services. **(4 marks)**

(d) Why might a business selling overseas use an agent? **(4 marks)**

(e) Analyse two factors that a business is likely to take into account when choosing an appropriate distribution channel. **(4 marks)**

Chapter 42: Product

Getting started...

The goods or services sold by a business have to be designed, named and packaged. Products also have to be modified, improved and possibly replaced. This is because some products have a limited life cycle. Look at the example below.

Golf GTI

The Golf GTI is produced by Volkswagen, the German-based car maker. It was launched in 1975 and 1.7 million have been sold. The Mk 1 GTI was unveiled at the Frankfurt Motor Show. The powerful hatchback could hit 60 mph in 9 seconds. Designed with the emphasis on fun, it had a tartan trim and a golf ball gearshift. The model has been updated several times since then. For example, in 2009 the New Golf GTI won the 'Best Compact Family Car' and the 'Best Hot Hatch' awards at the Auto Express New Car Awards. The sharp handling, impressive refinement and excellent comfort make the latest Golf the best yet.

(a) What is the name of the product in the example?

(b) What is the length of the product's life cycle to date?

(c) Give one reason why Volkswagen brings out new models.

(d) Do you think the Golf GTI will ever be withdrawn from the market?

Goods and services

The goods and services produced by businesses are called *products*. These products can be split into different categories. For example, some businesses supply *consumer goods* such as clothes, food and entertainment. However, others supply *producer goods* such as machines. These are sold to other businesses. This is discussed in Chapter 1.

Product design

Ideas for new products may come from business owners, customers, competitors, staff, and *research and development*. Most products go through a design process which might involve a number of stages such as:

● producing a *design specification* (a precise description of what is needed)

● suggesting alternative solutions

● selecting a particular solution

● testing the product

● modifying the product and then launching it.

Market research data might be used to ensure that product designs meet the needs of customers. Some businesses use special *CAD (computer aided design)* programs to speed up the design process and improve the quality of designs. The Golf GTI, in 'Getting started' was designed by Volkswagen's chief designer Walter de'Silva.

Branding

Many businesses give their products a name. In 'Getting started' the Volkswagen car was called a Golf GTI. Names like these are called **brand names**. A brand might be the name of a product, a product group or the business itself. Some brand names are very well known and worth a great deal of money. For example, Coca-Cola is worth around $70 billion. Branding is used to:

● differentiate the product from others

● create customer loyalty

● help recognition

● develop an image

● raise prices when the brand and image becomes strong.

Brand	Brand Value 09 ($m)
Google	100,000
Microsoft	76,300
Coca-Cola	67,600
IBM	66,600
McDonald's	66,600
Apple	63,100
China Mobile	61,300
General Electric	59,800
Vodafone	53,700
Marlboro	49,500

Figure 42.1 *Top ten world brands*

QUESTION 1

Google is a search engine and recognised worldwide. In 2009, it was suggested that the Google brand was worth around $100 billion. In the last two years the value of shares, property, pensions and other assets have fallen due to the global recession. However, the value of many brand names has continued to rise. Figure 42.1 shows the top ten brands in the world.

(a) Using an example from this case study state what is meant by a brand name.

(b) Analyse three reasons why businesses use brand names.

Packaging

One aspect of the product is its packaging. Businesses should consider packaging carefully. This is because consumers often link the quality of packaging with the quality of the product itself. With some products such as perfume, confectionery and make-up, packaging is vital because it says so much about the product. It also helps people to recognise it when placed next to rival products. Figure 42.2 summarises the factors that may be considered when a business designs its packaging.

Protection Fragile or perishable goods need strong packaging to provide protection in storage and transit

Environment Materials used should be minimised and when possible packaging should be recyclable

Convenience It should be easy to handle, open and use

Factors that may influence the choice of packaging

Cost-effective The weight and shape of packaging should not be too bulky to keep production and distribution costs down

Design It should be appealing, reflect the nature and quality of the product and identify the brand

Information Labels etc. should comply with the law and give information about ingredients and safe usage

Figure 42.2 *Factors which may influence the choice of packaging*

QUESTION 2

(a) What is the main role of packaging for the products shown in the image?

Businesses might need to change their packaging when selling goods abroad.

(b) Suggest reasons for doing this.

Figure 42.3 *Confectionery products*

Product life cycle

Marketing may be more effective if businesses understand the **product life cycle**. This shows the level of sales at the different stages through which a product passes over time. Figure 42.4 shows that a product might pass through five stages over its life.

1. **Development:** During the development stage sales are zero. This is because the product is being researched, designed and tested. It is not yet on the market. This may be an anxious time for businesses because many products do not make it beyond this stage. Consequently, money invested in product development is lost. Development costs are also high and can damage the cash flow of a business.

2. **Introduction:** Businesses often introduce new products with an official *launch*. There may be a presentation or a party to give a new product a good promotion when it is launched. Costs will continue to be high. New production facilities may be needed and spending on promotion will be high. The price charged by a business when a product is first introduced will vary. Some may start with a high price (skimming). Others may start with a low price (penetration) to get established in the market.

3. **Growth:** If a product is successful, sales will start to grow. If the line on the product life cycle is very steep, this shows that sales are growing sharply. The business will now get increased revenue and begin to recover the costs of development. Costs are likely to fall and the product may start to make a profit. Towards the end of this stage sales may start to grow less quickly. This may be because competitors are starting to launch their own versions of the product.

4. **Maturity and saturation:** Eventually sales will start to level off. Development costs will have been recovered and the product will be making a profit. Cash flow will also be improving. As more businesses enter the market it will become saturated and some businesses will be forced out. The price is likely to fall and promotion methods may change. Some businesses will try to prolong the life of the product before it declines. They use **extension strategies** which are discussed below.

5. **Decline:** Sales of many products decline and they are eventually withdrawn. This is because consumer tastes change, new technology emerges or new products appear in the market. Where possible a business will replace declining products with a new ones. In the above example, the Golf was introduced to replace the Volkswagen Beetle, which was withdrawn from the European market (although the Beetle was reintroduced at a later date). Examples of products that are on the decline include typewriters, cheques and fax machines.

Did you know?

Sony's PlayStation 3 was $600 when launched in 2006. It is now just $299.

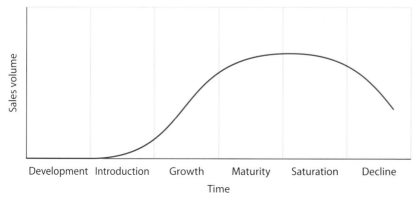

Figure 42.4 *The product life cycle*

Extension strategies

Extension strategies, which prolong the life of a product before it starts to decline, are popular with businesses. This is because the costs of product development are high and extension strategies help a product to generate more cash. Examples of extension strategies include:

● Finding new markets for the product – e.g. selling abroad.

● Finding new uses for a product – e.g. Ralph Lauren extending its Polo brand for clothes into towels and bedding.

● Modifying the product. In 'Getting started', Volkswagen did this several times with the Golf GTI.

● Develop the product range – e.g. a crisp manufacturer bringing out new flavours.

● Change the appearance or packaging – e.g. Coca-Cola selling coke in cans, glass bottles and different sized plastic bottles.

● Encourage more frequent use of the product – e.g. Kelloggs persuading people to eat cornflakes for supper as well as for breakfast.

The Boston Matrix

The **Boston Matrix** may be used to help analyse the products marketed by a business. The matrix enables a business to place their products into different categories according to their market share and position in the life cycle. There are four positions in the matrix where products might be placed. The matrix is shown in Figure 42.5.

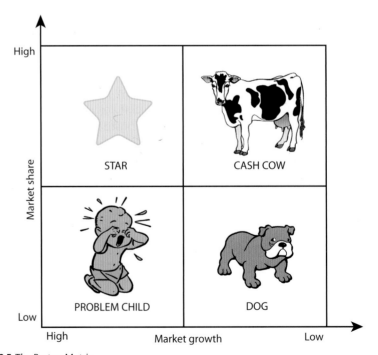

Figure 42.5 *The Boston Matrix*

The Boston Matrix describes products in four ways:

- **Stars** are valuable products for a business. They have a high market share but also the potential for growth. They are likely to be profitable.

- **Cash cows** are mature products. They have a high market share but the market is not likely to grow very much. Cash cows generate a steady flow of income for the business.

- **Problem child** products have a low market share but the market is growing. If the right marketing action is taken these products could do well. They have potential.

- **Dogs** are at the end of their life cycle. They have a low market share and the market is not likely to grow any more. Dogs are likely to be replaced with new products.

When managing its product range a business must try to make sure it has the 'right balance' of products. This means that it must avoid having too many dogs and try to increase the number of stars and cash cows. Some of the income from cash cows might be invested in new product development.

Chapter review – GlaxoSmithKline

GlaxoSmithKline (GSK) is a pharmaceuticals company. One of the features of this industry is the huge amount of money spent researching and developing new products. For example, in 2008, GSK spent around £3.7 billion on R & D (research and development). The discovery and development of a new product can take many years. This is because drugs have to go through long clinical trials to ensure that they are safe. However, companies can get patents. A patent is a special licence which allows businesses to market a product for up to 20 years without any competition. This means that once a new drug is launched sales grow quickly and can remain high until the patent runs out. A product life cycle for a pharmaceutical product might look like the one shown in Figure 42.6.

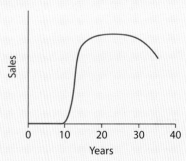

Figure 42.6 *Product life cycle for a pharmaceuticals product*

One of GSK's successful products is Requip. It is used to treat Parkinson's disease and was launched in 1997. After the initial growth stage sales remained steady for many years. However, a new use for Requip was found by targeting the drug at another illness, the 'restless legs syndrome' (RLS). After this the brand experienced strong growth. Sales of Requip grew from £120m in 2004 to £268m in 2007.

(a) Using this case study as an example, outline what is meant by a product life cycle. **(4 marks)**

The development stage is long for products in the pharmaceuticals industry.

(b) Outline the reason why. **(2 marks)**

The price of pharmaceutical products is likely to be high in the introductory and growth stages of the product life cycle.

(c) What is the main reason for this? **(2 marks)**

(d) Why do businesses use extension strategies? **(4 marks)**

(e) Evaluate the success of GSK's extension strategy in this case study. **(8 marks)**

Chapter 43: Market research

Getting started...

One of the most important marketing activities is gathering information. Businesses have to find out what customers need and want. This will help them to design products which people will buy. Information is also needed about the market. Businesses need to find out about their competitors, what sort of people buy the product and the size of the market. Look at the example below.

Eurostar

Eurostar provides a high-speed rail service through the Channel Tunnel linking London with mainland Europe. It employed a market research agency, Maritz Research, to carry out a survey. Maritz assessed the customer experience in the following key areas:

- the Eurostar Call Centre
- customer relations
- the Eurostar ticket offices
- the terminals
- on-board Eurostar
- the catering facilities
- customer relationship management
- frequent traveller service.

Figure 43.1 *A Eurostar train*

In order for Eurostar to respond quickly to problems, Maritz developed an online reporting tool. This allows Eurostar's managers to examine customer responses to the survey. Maritz also discussed the findings with managers in workshops. This helped Eurostar to identify customer problems quickly and make immediate improvements.

(a) What sort of information was gathered by Eurostar in this case?

(b) How did the information help Eurostar?

Eurostar employed a market research agency to gather information.

(c) State one possible advantage and one disadvantage of doing this.

The role of market research

Market research involves gathering, presenting and analysing information about the marketing and consumption of goods and services. Businesses spend money on market research because it helps to reduce the risk of failure. Products that are well researched are more likely to be successful. However, there are some specific uses of market research. Some examples are shown in Figure 43.2.

Primary research

Business use **primary** or **field research** to gather information that does not already exist. It involves collecting new information from new sources. Primary data is usually gathered by asking questions or observing people's behaviour. The main advantage of primary research is that it is original and the information gathered can be tailored to the needs of the business. However, primary research is often time consuming and expensive. Some businesses, like Eurostar in 'Getting started', employ a *market research agency* to carry out research. Agencies are experts in gathering, presenting and analysing information. However, they may be too expensive for many businesses.

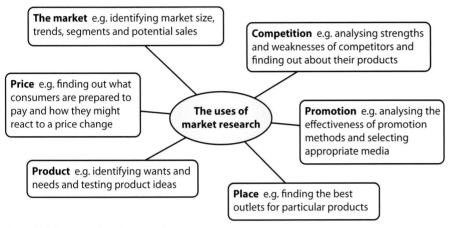

Figure 43.2 *The uses of market research*

QUESTION 1

In 2008, Wang Zhi opened the Cathay Garden, a new Chinese takeaway in Dubai. Before he started trading he gathered information about the market for Chinese takeaway food in the city. He spent a lot of time finding out about competitors. He found out about the:

● number and location of Chinese takeaways in Dubai

● menus and prices charged

● opening times

● advertising and promotions used

● additional services offered, such as delivery

● speed of service

● types of customers who bought Chinese takeaways.

The information gathered by Wang Zhi was very helpful. For example, he found that one of the main criticisms of current takeaways was the slow speed of service. When Wang Zhi opened the Cathay Garden his speed of service was a unique selling point.

Wang Zhi used primary research when gathering information about the Chinese takeaway market in Dubai.

(a) What does this mean?

(b) Analyse how this research might benefit his new business.

Figure 43.3 *A chef preparing Chinese food*

Methods of primary research

Some of the main methods of gathering primary data are discussed briefly below.

Questionnaires: A questionnaire is a list of written questions. They are very common in market research and are used to record the views and opinions of *respondents*. A good questionnaire will:

- Have a balance of *open* and *closed* questions. Closed questions allow respondents a limited range of responses. An example would be 'How many times have you flown with Emirates this year?' The answers to closed questions are easier to analyse and represent numerically. Open questions let people say whatever they want. They do not have to choose from a list of responses. Open questions are best used if there is a large number of possible responses. An example would be 'How would you improve the quality of the service provided by Emirates?'

- Contain clear and simple questions. Questions must be clear avoiding the use of jargon, poor grammar and bad spelling.

- Not contain leading questions. Leading questions are those which 'suggest' a certain answer. They should be avoided because otherwise the results will be bias.

- Be concise. If questionnaires are too long people will not give up their time to answer them.

Questionnaires can be used in different situations.

- **Postal surveys:** Questionnaires are sent out to people and they are asked to complete them in their own time. They may be more convenient for people but the vast majority of questionnaires are never returned. This means that resources are wasted.

- **Telephone interviews:** The main advantage of interviewing people over the telephone is that it is cheaper. A wide geographical area can be covered. However, some people do not like being telephoned by businesses.

- **Personal interviews:** These are often carried out in the street and the interviewer fills in the answers. The advantage is that questions can be explained if a respondent is confused. It may be possible to collect more detailed information. However, many people do not like being approached in the street.

- **Online surveys:** As access to computers increases around the world, so does the use of online surveys. These are similar to postal surveys except respondents may be directed to a questionnaire, after receiving an email confirming an online transaction, for example.

Focus groups or consumer panels: If a business wants very detailed information from customers it might use *focus groups* or *consumer panels*. A focus group is where a number of customers are invited to attend a discussion led by market researchers. The group must be representative of the whole population and be prepared to answer detailed questions. This is a relatively cost-effective method of collecting information but the group may be small.

Did you know?

Online surveys may be more sophisticated because they can use a wider range of images. They are cheaper to administer and can be made available to respondents 24/7. However, many people still ignore them.

Consumer panels are similar to focus groups except that groups of customers are asked for feedback over a period. This approach allows businesses to see how consumers react to changes in their products.

Observation: This is where market researchers 'watch' the behaviour of customers. This approach might be used in retail outlets. Observers might record the amount of time customers spend looking at particular products and displays in the store. However, because there is no feedback using this method a lot of questions may go unanswered.

Test marketing: This involves selling a new product in a restricted geographical area to test it before a national launch. After a set period feedback is gathered from customers. The feedback is used to make modifications to the product before the final launch. This reduces the risk of failure.

QUESTION 2

Some businesses use online surveys to gather data. This involves providing a link to a questionnaire on a company web site and inviting people to complete it. An online questionnaire can be completed quickly and responses can often be analysed immediately. Survey costs are lower because there is no printing and postage. Online surveys can be interactive and may be fun to complete. They can also be accessed 24/7 and be completed when it is convenient. However, there are problems. The sample used may not be representative. This is because online surveys are only presented to internet users. The views of others will be neglected even though they may be a potential customer.

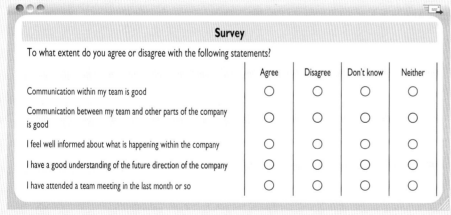

Figure 43.4 *An online survey*

(a) Analyse two advantages and two disadvantages of online surveys.

(b) Discuss whether an online survey would benefit a company selling to:
 (i) customers in isolated areas; **(ii)** less developed countries such as Bangladesh, Sudan and Vanuatu.

Secondary research

Businesses use **secondary** or **desk research** to collect information that already exists. It has been collected by someone else and may be available for other users. The information collected may be *internal*, which means that it already exists inside the business. It may also be *external*, which means it exists outside the business. Figure 43.5 shows some different sources of secondary data.

Secondary research is quick and easier to gather. For example, internal data may be immediately available on intranets. Also, a lot of external data is available online. However, the main problem with desk research is that the data collected might not be exactly what the business needs. It may also be out of date and therefore not accurate.

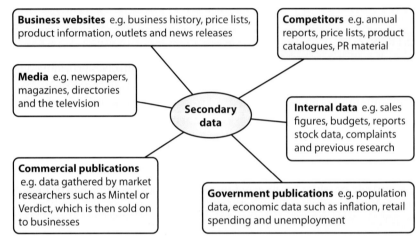

Figure 43.5 *Sources of secondary or desk research and the type of information*

Sampling

Ideally, information could be gathered from every single person in a market. However, this would take too long and cost too much money. To overcome this problem businesses use a **sample** of people. A sample is a much smaller group. However, their behaviour and views must be *representative* of all the people in the market.

There are different ways of choosing samples. The most common approach is to choose a *random sample* where every single person in a population has the same chance of being chosen. 'Picking names out of a hat' would generate a random sample. Samples may also be subdivided according to age, gender or income for example. This will help to get representation across different groups and is called a *stratified sample*.

Limitations of market research

Although carrying out market research can reduce the risk of products failing in the market, it is not entirely dependable.

● Market research data may be biased. For example, if the sample used by a business is not representative, any conclusions drawn on the basis of the sample will be inaccurate.

- Human behaviour is unpredictable. Although people may indicate their intentions in a questionnaire, what they do in reality might be quite different. People might change their minds or may misunderstand the question. They might also give answers that they think the interviewers wanted to hear.

- Poor research technique. If questionnaires are poorly designed or interviewers have not been trained, the quality of the research carried out might be poor.

Chapter review – Manzini Safari Tours

Manzini Safari Tours supervises trips around the Mlilane Wildlife Sanctuary in Swaziland. Animals found in the park include zebra, giraffe, antelope, crocodile, hippo and a variety of birdlife. Walking, cycling and horse riding is allowed in the reserve and there are many vehicle and walking trails. However, visitors to the park have fallen from 21,400 in 2004 to 9,400 in 2009. A survey was carried out by Manzini Safari Tours using telephone interviews. One thousand telephone numbers were chosen at random from a list of potential customers provided by a research agency.

1. Have you ever been on a Manzini Safari Tour?
   YES 7% NO 93%
2. Have you ever been on any other safari tour?
   YES 61% NO 39%
3. Would you go on a Manzini Safari Tour if it was cheaper?
   YES 44% NO 56%
4. Have you seen any adverts for the Manzini Safari Tours?
   YES 7% NO 93%
5. Would a holiday in Swaziland appeal to you?
   YES 46% NO 54%

Figure 43.7 *Answers to five questions from the survey*

'The tours appear too strictly supervised.'

'There aren't any tigers in the park.'

'I've never heard of Swaziland.'

'It's too expensive – it would cost me and my family over £300 to go for the day.'

Figure 43.8 *Comments made by some of the people surveyed*

Figure 43.6 *A game reserve*

Figure 43.7 shows answers to five key questions from the survey and Figure 43.8 shows a selection of comments made by the people interviewed.

(a) Why is the research carried out by Manzini Safari Tours primary research? **(2 marks)**

(b) Analyse one advantage and one disadvantage of using telephone surveys. **(4 marks)**

(c) What is the difference between open questions and closed questions in a survey? **(4 marks)**

(d) Consider the limitations that might exist in the survey carried out by Manzini Safari Tours. **(4 marks)**

(e) Analyse the data for Manzini Safari Tours and suggest reasons why the number of visitors have fallen in recent years. **(6 marks)**

Chapter 44: Economies and diseconomies of scale

Getting started...

*Setting up a business and surviving is very challenging. However, once a business is established the owners often want it to grow. They want to increase the **scale** of the business. This means that they want to increase its size. One of the benefits of increasing the scale of operations is that certain costs start to fall. Look at the examples below.*

CaterGroup

CaterGroup is a large catering company based near Sydney, Australia. It supplies sandwiches to supermarkets and sells about one million sandwiches a week. CaterGroup employs 210 workers and buys ingredients direct from farmers and manufacturers. For example, it buys tomatoes from a local farm for $1.50 a kilo and cheese for $5.00 a kilo. It buys thousands of loaves of bread from a Sydney baker for $1.10 each. It sells sandwiches at an average price of $1.40 per packet. CaterGroup pays 7.5 per cent interest on a $1,000,000 loan.

The Snack Box

The Snack Box sells sandwiches and other snacks from a kiosk by Sydney Harbour. It serves office workers, shoppers and some tourists. The Snack Box is run by two sisters and they sell about 900 sandwiches a week. They buy their ingredients from supermarkets and wholesalers. For example, the business buys about 20 loaves of bread per day at a cost of $1.80 each. Tomatoes cost $2.50 a kilo and cheese is $7 a kilo. Most of their sandwiches sell for $2.00 a round. The business has a $5,000 loan which was taken out to help set up the business. An interest rate of 8.9 per cent is paid on the loan.

(a) (i) Which of the two businesses is the largest?
(ii) Which business has the lowest costs?

(b) Which firm is likely to be the most efficient?

(c) How might CaterGroup benefit from its cost advantage?

Figure 44.1 *A sandwich bar*

Economies of scale

Big firms can usually produce goods more cheaply than small firms. The size of a firm has an important affect on the *average costs* (see Chapter 30) of production. As a firm increases its size, average costs start to fall. This is due to **economies of scale** and is shown in Figure 44.2. When the business is producing 20,000 units of output, the average cost is $25. If it raises output to 40,000 units, average costs fall to $15. The firm could carry on expanding and lower its average costs until it is large enough to produce 70,000 units. At this level of output average costs are minimised at $10 per unit. It is the ideal size because average costs are at an absolute minimum. If the firm grows beyond 70,000 units, average costs will start to rise. For example, if the firm increases its size and produces 90,000 units, average costs will now rise to $12.50 per unit. This is due to **diseconomies of scale** which arise because of inefficiency.

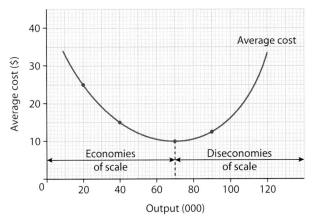

Figure 44.2 *Economies and diseconomies of scale*

Internal economies of scale

Internal economies of scale are the cost benefits that an individual firm can enjoy when it grows. The reasons why costs fall are summarised in Figure 44.3.

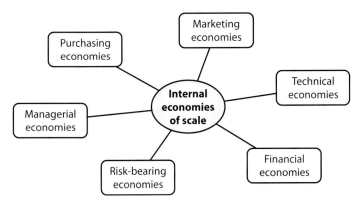

Figure 44.3 *Sources of internal economies of scale*

- **Purchasing economies:** Big firms that buy lots of resources get cheaper rates. Suppliers offer discounts to firms that buy raw materials and components in bulk. This is similar to consumers buying multi-packs in supermarkets. They are better value for money. Bulk buying is a purchasing economy. In the example above, CaterGroup was able to buy bread for $1.10 a loaf. However, The Snack Box was having to pay $1.80 because it was buying smaller quantities. In fact all their purchases were cheaper than those that Snack Box had to pay for the same products.

- **Marketing economies:** A number of marketing economies exist. For example, it may be cost effective for a large firm to run its own delivery vehicles. For a large firm, with lots of deliveries to make, this would be cheaper than paying a distributor. Marketing economies can occur because some marketing costs, such as producing a television advert, are fixed. These costs can be spread over more units of output for a larger firm. Therefore the average cost of the advert is smaller for a large firm.

- **Technical economies:** Technical economies arise because larger plants are often more efficient than smaller ones. There can be more specialisation and more investment in machinery. One example of a technical economy is the way a big firm will make better use of an essential resource than a smaller firm. For example, a small engineering company may buy some CAD (computer aided design) software for $1,000. It is needed by the business but is only used for one day a week. A much larger engineering company may buy the same software but use it every day of the week. Clearly, the larger company is making better use of the software and therefore its average cost will fall.

- **Financial economies:** Large firms can get cheaper money. They also have a wider variety of sources to choose from. For example, a large limited company can raise money by selling shares. This option is not available to a sole trader. Large firms can put pressure on banks when negotiating the price of loans. Banks are often happier lending large amounts to large companies at lower interest rates. In 'Getting Started', CaterGroup was paying 7.5 per cent to borrow $1,000,000. In contrast, The Snack Box was paying 8.9 per cent to borrow just $5,000.

- **Managerial economies:** As firms expand they can afford specialist managers. A small business may employ a general manager responsible for finance, human resources, marketing and production. The manager may find this role demanding and may be weak in some fields. A large firm can employ specialists. As a result, efficiency is likely to improve and average costs fall.

- **Risk bearing economies:** Larger firms are more likely to have wider product ranges and sell into a wider variety of markets. This reduces the risk in business. For example, many supermarkets have extended their product ranges to include household goods, consumer durables, books, a cafe, financial services, garden furniture, pharmaceuticals and clothes.

QUESTION 1

In 2008, the world's biggest printing plant was opened by News International, publisher of *The Times, Sunday Times* and the *Sun*. The plant contains 12 modern printing presses which cover an area the size of 23 football pitches. The presses are quieter and much faster than those they replaced. The plant can print 70,000 papers an hour compared to 30,000 at the previous plant. Also, the new presses require fewer staff – 200 instead of 600. This could give the newspaper industry a new lease of life in the digital media world.

Figure 44.4 *Newspaper production*

(a) What is likely to happen to average costs at News International as a result of the new plant opening?

(b) What is meant by technical economies of scale? (Use the example in the case study to illustrate your answer.)

External economies of scale

Sometimes all firms in an industry can enjoy falling average costs as the whole industry grows. This is called **external economies of scale.** External economies are more likely to arise if an industry is concentrated in a particular region.

- **Skilled labour:** If an industry is concentrated in an area, there may be a build up of labour with the skills and work experience required by that industry. As a result, training costs will be lower when workers are recruited. It is also likely that local schools and colleges will provide vocational courses which are required by the local industry.

- **Infrastructure:** If a particular industry dominates a region the roads, railways, ports, buildings and other facilities will be shaped to suit that industry's needs. For example, a specialised industrial estate may be developed to help a local IT industry.

- **Ancillary and commercial services:** An established industry in a region will encourage suppliers in that industry to set up close by. Specialist marketing, cleaning, banking, waste disposal, distribution, maintenance and components suppliers are likely to be attracted to the area. All firms in the industry will benefit from their services, like the car industry in the Midlands, England, for example.

- **Co-operation:** When firms in the same industry are located close to each other they are likely to co-operate with each other so that they can all gain. For example, they might join forces to share the cost and benefits of a research and development centre, as high-tech businesses do in the Silicon Valley, USA.

QUESTION 2

Silicon Valley is the southern part of the San Francisco Bay Area in the US. Originally it was home to a large number of silicon chip manufacturers. However, it gained a reputation as the major US high-tech businesses centre. Despite the development of other high-tech economic centres in the US, Silicon Valley is still the leading high-tech hub. This is because of the large number of computer experts, engineers and venture capitalists, who have their businesses there.

Figure 44.5 *A silicon chip*

Even in the 1970s there were many semiconductor companies in the area. There were also computer firms using their devices and programming and service companies serving both. Industrial space was plentiful and housing was inexpensive. The growth of Silicon Valley was also aided by the development of the venture capital industry, which specialised in providing funds for high-tech companies.

(a) What is meant by external economies of scale?

(b) Discuss examples of external economies that are evident in this case study.

Diseconomies of scale

Figure 44.2 shows that if a firm continues to expand average costs eventually rise. This is because the firm suffers from diseconomies of scale. Average costs start to rise because aspects of production become inefficient. Why might this happen?

- **Bureaucracy:** If a business becomes too bureaucratic, it means that too many resources are used in administration. Too much time may be spent filling in forms or writing reports. Also, decision making may be too slow and communication channels too long. If resources are wasted in administration, average costs will start to rise.

- **Labour relations:** If a firm becomes too big, relations between workers and managers may deteriorate. There may be a lack of understanding for workers and they may become demotivated. As a result, conflicts may arise and resources may be wasted resolving them.

- **Control and co-ordination:** A very large business may be difficult to control and co-ordinate. Thousands of employees, billions of pounds and dozens of plants all over the world can make running a large organisation demanding. There may be a need for more supervision which will raise costs.

Section 5: Production

Key terms

Diseconomies of scale – rising average costs when a firm becomes too big.

Economies of scale – falling average costs due to expansion.

External economies of scale – the cost benefits that all firms in the industry can enjoy when the industry expands.

Internal economies of scale – the cost benefits that an individual firm can enjoy when it expands.

Scale – the size of a business.

Chapter review – Sensations

Sensations is a Canadian clothes chain. It sells high-quality clothes, shoes and fashion accessories. It has an excellent reputation for good customer service and operates 96 shops in Canada and 52 in the US. In 2002, Sensations employed a specialist marketing manager. The new manager raised the profile of the Sensations brand right across Canada. As a result, the company grew quickly and became very profitable. Sensations buys most of its clothes and shoes from China.

Figure 44.6 *The interior of a clothes store*

In 2006, Sensations bought a clothes chain in the Middle East. It was thought that the company could further exploit economies of scale and make even more profit. However, there were some problems. Communications became difficult due to language and cultural difficulties. There was also a lack of employee understanding. Many of the staff did not seem to care whether the company succeeded or not. Some of the store managers also complained that the company was becoming too bureaucratic.

(a) Define the term 'scale' in business. **(2 marks)**

(b) Examine the affect that economies and diseconomies of scale are likely to have on Sensations' average cost. **(4 marks)**

(c) Why is employing a specialist marketing manager an economy of scale? **(4 marks)**

(d) Discuss whether Sensations has benefited from purchasing economies of scale. **(4 marks)**

(e) To what extent is Sensations experiencing diseconomies of scale? **(6 marks)**

Chapter 45: Methods of production

Getting started...

Businesses can use different production methods when making products. For example, the method used by a jeweller is different from that used by a computer manufacturer. There may also be differences in the same industry. For example, some furniture is mass produced in large factories while smaller producers make furniture by hand. Look at the production methods used in the examples below.

Kellogg's

Kellogg's is a multinational producer of breakfast cereals and convenience foods, such as cookies, crackers, cereal bars and frozen waffles. It is based in Michigan, US, but has factories all over the world. Kellogg's produces millions of units of output to serve huge global markets. Its production methods are capital intensive and many of its brands are produced on automated production lines which run continuously.

Mehreen Carpets

Mehreen Carpets makes hand-knotted oriental carpets and is based in Pakistan. It has its own looms and manufacturing facilities. It is able meet the needs of a wide range of customer designs. The business also produces high-quality rose wood handicrafts and furniture. All products are crafted by skilled workers and can be made to specific customer orders. Mehreen's factory is located in Chiniot, a town that is famous for its rich history in craftsmanship and skill.

(a) Compare the two production methods used in the above examples.

(b) Outline two reasons why the two businesses use different production methods.

Figure 45.1 *Bowl of cereal*

Figure 45.2 *An oriental carpet*

Job production

Job production is where a business produces one product from start to finish before moving on to the next. Each item produced is likely to be different. Job production is used when orders are small, such as 'one-offs'. Examples might include the construction of an office block, the making of a wedding dress, the drawing up of a person's will or the design of a television advert. The advantages and disadvantages of job production are summarised in Figure 45.3.

Advantages	Disadvantages
Quality is high because workers are skilled	High labour costs as a result of skilled workers
Workers are well motivated because work is varied	Production may be slow – long lead times
Products can be custom made	A wide range of specialist tools may be needed
Production is easy to organise	Generally an expensive method of production

Figure 45.3 *The advantages and disadvantages of job production*

QUESTION 1

Henry Ndzima is a chartered accountant and runs a small business from an office in Mbabane, Swaziland. He produces final accounts for sole traders, partnerships and small companies. He has around 110 business clients and employs a secretary and a young trainee accountant. In addition to preparing accounts he offers other services such as:

- completing tax returns
- taxation planning
- advice on the financial management of businesses and investment
- auditing.

(a) Using this case study as an example, explain what is meant by job production.

(b) Consider why job production might improve motivation.

Batch production

Job production is suitable when demand is relatively low. However, when demand grows and orders for multiple units are placed a business might switch to **batch production**. This is where a business makes a number (a batch) of products to the same design or specification and then changes production to another product with different specifications. When products are made in batches production is usually divided into a number of operations or *processes*. Figure 45.4 gives an example of batch production. An engineering company uses batch production to make the metal structure for an armrest in an aircraft seat. Armrests are made from 1.5 mm aluminium sheet. The operations needed on each unit in a batch of 2,000 are summarised below.

Operation	Description
Laser cutting	The correct profile is cut from the metal sheet
Part marking	The armrest is marked with a number for identification
Punching	Holes are punched in the armrest to make it lighter
Folding	The armrest is folded into the correct shape
Assembly	Components and fasteners are put together
Plating	The armrest is coated in zinc plating
Packaging	The armrests are packed into cases for transit

Figure 45.4 *Operations involved in the production of an armrest for an aircraft seat*

Many products are made using batch production, particularly in engineering, the clothes industry and food processing. For example, in a canning plant, a firm may can several different batches of soup, each batch being a different recipe. Products can be produced in large or small batches depending on the level of demand. Larger production runs tend to lower the *unit* or *average cost* of production. The advantages and disadvantages of batch production are shown in Figure 45.5.

Advantages	Disadvantages
Workers are likely to specialise in one process	More complex machinery may be needed
Unit costs are lower because output is higher	Careful planning and co-ordination is needed
Production is flexible because different orders can be met	Less motivation because workers specialise
More use of machinery is made	If batches are small costs will still be high
	Money may be tied up in work-in-progress

Figure 45.5 *Advantages and disadvantages of batch production*

QUESTION 2

Yalta Apparel makes work clothes, leisurewear and promotional clothing for European customers. In 2006, the company moved to a new factory in Colombo, Sri Lanka. The company has an excellent reputation in the industry. This is because it:

● provides a wide choice of quality clothing at low prices

● provides excellent customer service

● is flexible and can meet orders quickly.

Like most companies in the clothes industry, Yalta Apparel uses batch production. The company can meet a wide range of different orders due the flexibility of their machinery and multi-skilled workforce.

(a) Using this case study as an example, explain what is meant by batch production.

(b) Why is batch production common in the clothes industry?

(c) Discuss how Yalta Apparel has overcome some of the typical problems associated with batch production.

Flow production

Flow production may be used when a business can sell huge quantities of output into a mass market. Flow production results in lower unit costs. It is organised so that different operations can be carried out, one after the other, in a continuous sequence. Products move from one operation to the next, often on a conveyer belt.

What are the main features of flow production?

● Large quantities are produced.

● A standardised product is produced.

● A semi-skilled workforce, specialising in one operation only is employed.

● Large amounts of machinery and equipment are used.

Flow production is used in the manufacture of products as varied as newspapers, food and cement. *Repetitive flow production* is the manufacture of large numbers of the same product, such as plastic toy parts or metal cans. *Process production* is a form of flow production which is used in the oil or chemical industry. Materials pass through a plant where a series of processes are carried out in order to change the product. An example might be the refining of crude oil into petrol. The advantages and disadvantages of flow production are summarised in Figure 45.6.

Advantages	Disadvantages
Very low unit costs because of economies of scale	Products may be standardised
Output can be produced very quickly	Huge set-up costs before production can begin
Modern technology can allow some flexibility	Worker motivation can be very low – repetitive tasks
Production speed can vary according to demand	Breaks in production can be very expensive

Figure 45.6 *Advantages and disadvantages of flow production*

Key terms

Batch production – a method which involves completing one operation at a time on all units before performing the next.

Flow production – large-scale production of a standard product, where each operation on a unit is performed continuously one after the other, usually on a production line.

Job production – a method of production which involves employing all factors to complete one unit of output at a time.

Process production – a form of flow production where materials pass through a plant where a series of processes are carried out in order to change the product.

Choosing an appropriate method of production

Businesses have to decide on the most appropriate method of production for their product. The method chosen might depend on a number of factors.

● **The nature of the product:** Products often require a specific method of production. For example, in the construction industry, projects such as bridges, roads, office blocks and schools must be produced using job production. Farming involves batch production. A plot of land undergoes several processes before it 'produces' a crop.

● **The size of the market:** Fast moving consumer goods like soap, confectionery and canned drinks are normally produced using flow production because the market is so big. When the market is small, flow production techniques are not cost effective so batch or job production will be used.

● **The stage of development a business has reached:** When firms are first set up, they often produce small levels of output and employ job or batch production methods. As they expand and sell more they may switch to flow production.

● **Technology:** As technology advances, new materials and machinery become available. When technology changes, firms often use new production methods. For example, the development of computers and robotics has changed the way in which cars are made.

Chapter review – Saudi Aramco

Oil refining involves processing crude oil into several different products. It often starts with a fractional distillation column. Crude oil is heated and the different products are pulled out at different temperatures. For example, lubricating oil, used for motor oil, grease and other lubricants, boils at a temperature between 572 to 700 degrees. After this chemical processes are used to remove impurities. A system of pipes is used to link all the different processes so that refining continues unstopped.

Saudi Aramco is the largest oil corporation in the world and is involved in all stages of oil production. It manages over 100 oil and gas fields in Saudi Arabia. In 2006 its revenue was US$199.8bn.

Figure 45.7 *An oil refinery*

(a) Using this case study as an example, outline what is meant by flow production. **(2 marks)**

(b) What method of production would be used to build a new oil refinery for Saudi Aramco? **(2 marks)**

(c) Discuss how businesses choose an appropriate method of production. **(6 marks)**

(d) Evaluate the advantages and disadvantages to Saudi Aramco of flow production. **(10 marks)**

Chapter 46: Productivity

Getting started...

The performance of businesses will improve if productivity increases. Productivity is the amount of output that can be produced with a given quantity of resources. Firms can increase productivity by making better use of their resources. As a result, they become more efficient, their costs fall and profit rises. Look at the examples below.

AMZ Tyres

AMZ Tyres is a tyre manufacturer in Malaysia. The company employs 50 staff and in 2007 produced 450,000 tyres in the company's factory in Shah Alam, Selangor. In 2008, the firm retrained the entire workforce. The training was designed to improve worker flexibility. As a result, in 2008, tyre production rose to 520,000.

PepsiCo

In 2008, PepsiCo, installed a new $2.35 million heat and power system in its bottling plant in New York. To cut its electric consumption Pepsi installed four natural gas power generators. These produce 80 per cent of the power needed to run the filling, packaging and processing machines. The

Figure 46.1 *Tyres*

generators also give off heat which is converted into steam. This is used to warm bottles and clean machines. It has reduced Pepsi's boiler use by 70 per cent and is four times more efficient than the previous system.

(a) AMZ Tyres raised output by 70,000 tyres between 2007 and 2008. How did AMZ achieve this improvement?

(b) What measures were taken to improve productivity at PepsiCo?

(c) How might the two businesses benefit from the improvements in productivity?

Productivity

Businesses will want to use their resources as efficiently as possible. Output can be increased if **productivity** is raised. Productivity is the amount of output that can be produced with a given quantity of resources. It is common to measure the productivity of specific resources. For example, a business may measure labour productivity. This is output per worker. It can be calculated by:

$$\text{Labour productivity} = \frac{\text{Total output}}{\text{No. of workers}}$$

An example involving the calculation of labour productivity is shown in Figure 46.2.

A factory producing racing cycles employed 20 workers in 2008. During the year a total of 12,000 cycles were produced. In 2009, four more workers were employed and total production rose to 15,000. What has happened to labour productivity over the two years?

$$\text{2008 Labour productivity} = \frac{12{,}000}{20} = 600 \text{ cycles per worker}$$

$$\text{2009 Labour productivity} = \frac{15{,}000}{24} = 625 \text{ cycles per worker}$$

Over the two years labour productivity has increased at the cycle factory from 600 cycles per worker to 625 cycles per worker.

Figure 46.2 *Calculating labour productivity*

A business could also measure the productivity of its capital by calculating how much each unit of capital produces. This is called capital productivity. It can be calculated by:

$$\text{Capital productivity} = \frac{\text{Total output}}{\text{Capital employed}}$$

Factory	Output	No. of employees
India	28,500	150
Germany	54,000	270
China	79,050	310
Brazil	46,000	200

Figure 46.3 *Output and number of employees at four Huber factories (2009)*

QUESTION 1

In 2009, Huber, a German-based container manufacturer, decided that it must cut capacity due to a fall in demand. The directors said it would shut one of the four factories operated by the company. They plan to close the factory with the lowest labour productivity. Figure 46.3 shows the output and number of people employed in each of the four factories.

(a) Calculate the labour productivity in each of the four factories.

(b) Which factory is Huber likely to close down?

Increasing labour productivity

Businesses will try to increase productivity because they will lower costs and make more profit. Productivity may be increased by firms in a number of ways. One approach is to increase labour productivity. How can labour productivity be improved?

- **Education and training:** The government can help improve the quality of labour by investing in the education system. Providing more equipment for schools and improving the quality of teaching might help. Firms can also improve the productivity of their workers by providing training. Most workers receive some training when starting a new job. Further training may be provided if there are changes in the way people are expected to work.

- **Improve the motivation of workers:** If people are motivated at work they will be more productive. One approach might be to use financial incentives. A number of different schemes exist, such as piece rates, performance-related pay and profit sharing. These are explained in Chapter 23. Some workers are not motivated by money but may respond to non-financial incentives such as job rotation or team working.

- **Improve working practices:** The way labour is organised and managed can affect productivity. Working practices are the methods and systems that are used in the workplace. For example, it may be possible to change the factory layout by repositioning work stations or reorganising the flow of production. Such changes can improve labour productivity because workers may not have to move around as much, for example.

- **Increasing labour flexibility:** Labour can be more flexible if workers are trained to do different jobs and can switch at short notice. For example, some supermarkets train most of their workers to operate checkouts. Then, during a busy period, workers can be switched from other jobs to the checkout to prevent long queues. Some firms use flexitime, where workers can choose their hours of work (within limits). For example, a call centre could be kept open from 7.00 am to 8.00 pm if individual workers choose to work at different times of the day. Shift work can be used to keep factories running for 24 hours. For example, many factories operate three shifts in a day – 08.00 to 16.00, 16.00 to 24.00 and 24.00 to 08.00.

Increasing capital productivity

Capital productivity usually increases when new technology is introduced. This is because new technology is more efficient. Productivity is also likely to increase if production becomes more capital intensive. The impact of technology on business is discussed in detail in Chapter 48.

Other methods of improving productivity

Downsizing

Some firms have tried to improve efficiency by downsizing. This involves reducing capacity, i.e. laying off workers and closing unprofitable divisions. The advantages of downsizing may be:

- cost savings and increased profit
- a leaner, more competitive operation
- profitable businesses not subsidising unprofitable ones.

Work study

Work study involves looking at a particular job very carefully and working out the most efficient way it can be done. A work study may be carried out by a specialist engineer. The engineer identifies all the tasks in a job, analyses them and finds the best way to do the job. Once the best way has been established workers will adopt the new approach and efficiency will improve.

Relocation

Businesses often relocate their operations to improve efficiency. By relocating, firms can take advantage of cheaper resources such as lower rent, lower wages or lower transport costs.

Outsourcing

It may be possible to improve efficiency by outsourcing specific business activities. This means that work currently done by a business is given to specialists that can do the same work at a lower cost. For example, a manufacturer may decide to outsource its distribution operation. This might be done by a transport company more efficiently and at a cheaper rate.

Lean production

A modern approach to improving productivity in a business involves reducing the amount of resources used. This is called *lean production* and is discussed in detail in the next chapter.

Did you know?

A number of multinationals have located call centres in India to take advantage of cheap skilled labour. Also, a number of firms have located factories in China for similar reasons.

Did you know?

In the car industry the making of most components is now outsourced. The big car makers are often just giant assemblers.

Key terms

Downsizing – the process of reducing capacity, usually by laying off staff.

Outsourcing – the contracting out of work to other businesses that might otherwise have been performed within the organisation.

Productivity – the amount of output produced in relation to the resources used.

Work study – a process which identifies the best possible way to carry out a task by looking closely at the way a job is done.

QUESTION 2

Airbus is a European aircraft manufacturer. A number of countries contribute to production. In 2007, Airbus announced 1,600 job cuts in the UK. This was part of a general downsizing operation involving 10,000 staff cuts. It also involved the closure of three plants in France and Germany and plans for outsourcing. Some production is likely to go to China where costs are lower. Louis Gallois was appointed to stabilise the company following production delays and the impact of a falling dollar.

Most of the 1,600 UK job losses happened in Bristol, which makes parts for wings, fuel systems and landing gear. Three other sites, one in France and two in Germany were either sold or closed. Mr Gallois, who has a reputation for bold and decisive moves, said: 'We have no choice ... we have to reduce our costs.'

(a) What is meant by downsizing? (Use this case study as an example.)

(b) Why has Airbus decided to downsize its operations?

Airbus plans to outsource some production to China.

(c) What does outsourcing production mean?

Chapter review – Glen Morgan Mail Order (GMMO)

New Zealand-based GMMO sells a variety of electrical goods such as kettles, irons, blenders, microwave ovens, TVs, music systems and computers. It advertises heavily on TV and relies on low prices to generate sales. In 2008, the company directors decided to improve efficiency and develop online selling. Two key changes were made.

- **Improved labour flexibility:** GMMO introduced some new flexible working practices. For example, staff could choose 60 per cent of the hours they worked in return for being on call at certain times. One problem that GMMO had was a surge in demand immediately after an advert was shown on TV. This often meant that staff were overworked and mistakes were made with order picking and dispatch. Staff would also be trained to do a variety of different jobs so that they could be moved around when necessary.

- **Introduced new technology:** A sophisticated IT system was installed which could deal with both telephone orders and online orders and process them automatically. This included:

  - a voice recognition system which took telephone orders

  - an order reading facility which could read orders printed on a standard form available online.

As a result of this new technology staffing in the order processing department was cut from 120 to 32.The table in Figure 46.4 shows a comparison of performance indicators before and after the changes.

	2006	2009
Lead time*	10 days	3 days
Order picking errors	7,445	2,187
Absenteeism	10.10%	6.90%
Customer complaints	1,343	312
Sales revenue	$34 million	$47 million
Wage bill	$5.3 million	$4.1 million

Figure 46.4 *Key performance indicators at GMMO 2006 and 2009*

* The time between receiving an order and making the delivery.

(a) Describe the measures that GMMO has taken to become more flexible. **(4 marks)**

(b) What evidence is there to suggest that worker motivation has improved? **(2 marks)**

As a result of the new technology introduced at GMMO, staffing in the order processing department was cut from 120 to 32.

(c) Analyse the likely impact on labour productivity of this cut. **(4 marks)**

GMMO has used a number of measures to improve productivity in its organisation.

(d) Evaluate the success of these measures. **(10 marks)**

Chapter 47: Lean production

Getting started...

In recent years a number of Japanese production techniques have been introduced by businesses to improve productivity. This has helped businesses to reduce the amount of resources used up in production. It has also improved the quality of products. Look at the example below.

Thara Engineering

Thara Engineering is an Indian company and makes fasteners, studs, bolts and cap nuts. It has two plants and employs 34 people. To improve performance Thara introduced some Japanese production methods.

- It standardised some procedures and changed the factory layout. This led to a 17 per cent gain in production space.
- Thara recognised that improvements required staff involvement. Therefore more training was organised.
- Thara improved cleaning practices and stock storage and handling.

As a result of these measures, turnover increased by 50 per cent and production set-up time was reduced by 74 per cent. Also, machine down time was cut by 73 per cent, delivery targets were increased by 21 per cent and product rejection fell by 50 per cent. Investment in staff training also improved staff motivation.

(a) How important was staff involvement at Thara when trying to make improvements?

(b) Outline the benefits to Thara from introducing Japanese production methods.

What is lean production?

Lean production is an approach to production developed by Toyota, the Japanese car manufacturer. Its aim is to use fewer resources in production. Lean producers use less of everything. This includes factory space, materials, stocks, suppliers, labour, capital and time. As a result, lean production:

- raises productivity
- reduces costs and cuts **lead times**
- reduces the number of defective products
- improves reliability and speeds up product design.

Lean production involves using a range of practices designed to reduce waste and to improve productivity and quality. Some of these are discussed in this chapter.

Kaizen

There is a strong link between lean production and **Kaizen**. Kaizen is a Japanese word which means *continuous improvement*. There is a belief in Japan that everything can be improved. Even at work the Japanese believe it is possible to make small improvements continuously. This means that the workers are always coming up with ideas to improve quality, reduce waste or increase efficiency. The improvements may be very small but over a long period of time they have a huge impact. In Japan workers come up with ideas naturally. It is part of their culture. However, when Kaizen is adopted in other countries workers have to be trained.

The elimination of waste in business is an important part of Kaizen. This is why Kaizen has a strong link with lean production. Examples of waste may be:

● time wasted while staff wait around before starting tasks, such as waiting for materials to arrive

● time wasted when workers move unnecessarily in the workplace, such as walking to a central point in the factory to get tools

● the irregular use of a machine, such as one that is only used once a month.

Firms that adopt Kaizen train workers to continually search for waste and suggest how it might be eliminated.

Just-in-time production

If a business holds stocks, money is tied up and therefore wasted. For example, if a business has $1 million of stocks in a warehouse, that $1 million cannot be used for anything else. The money is unproductive. To overcome this problem many businesses have adopted **just-in-time** (JIT) production.

● This means that a business does not hold any stocks at all. Suppliers have to deliver resources straight to the production line at regular intervals. This might be several times a day.

● JIT also means that goods are not produced unless they have been ordered. This avoids the need to hold stocks of finished goods. The advantages and disadvantages of JIT are shown in Figure 47.1

Advantages	Disadvantages
Cash flow is improved	Higher ordering and administration costs
No waste, obsolete or damaged stock	Huge reliance on suppliers' reliability
Space is released	Advantages of bulk-buying may be lost
No stock holding costs	Hard to cope with fluctuations in demand
Stronger links with suppliers	Vulnerable to a break in supply
Fewer suppliers	

Figure 47.1 *Advantages and disadvantages of JIT*

QUESTION 1

Harley Davidson, the famous motorcycle manufacturer, nearly collapsed in 1985. To survive it had to improve efficiency. Therefore the company introduced lean production. One method used was JIT manufacturing. Previously, Harley had used a complex, computerised stock control system. This involved keeping stock levels high so the assembly line would not be halted if problems arose. This was inefficient because it assumed that problems would occur. It was like sweeping dirt under the carpet. After JIT was introduced there were some impressive improvements at Harley Davidson:

● Stock turnover up from 5 to 20 and stock levels down 75 per cent.

● Percentage of motorcycles coming off the line completed up from 76 per cent to 99 per cent.

● Scrap and rework reduced by 68 per cent.

● Productivity up by 50 per cent and space requirements down by 25 per cent.

Figure 47.2 *A Harley Davidson motorcycle*

(a) Harley Davidson introduced just-in-time manufacturing (JIT) in its business. What is meant by JIT?

(b) Discuss the benefits to Harley Davidson of JIT manufacturing.

Cell production

Flow production involves mass producing a standard product on a production line. In contrast, **cell production** involves dividing the workplace into 'cells'. Each cell produces a 'product family'. This is a group of products which use similar production methods. For example, a metal product might need cutting, punching, folding, welding and dispatch. This could all be carried out in one cell. Inside a cell, machines are grouped together and a team of workers sees the production from start to finish. The cell may also be responsible for tasks such as designing, planning, maintenance and problem solving.

Workers

Most lean production techniques rely heavily on the workforce. Workers are expected to play a more positive and decisive role in the business.

Team working

This involves dividing the workforce into small groups. Each team will focus on a particular area of production and team members will have the same common aims. Both the business and workers might benefit from teamwork.

● Workers should develop a 'team spirit'. This may improve motivation and productivity.

● Flexibility might improve. For example, team members might be more willing to cover for an absent colleague.

● Teams might plan their own work schedules, share out tasks and solve their own problems. This should lead to quicker decision making and more ideas.

● Communication and labour relations might also improve.

Key facts

There are several advantages of cell production.
• Floor space is released because cells use less space than a production line.
• Product flexibility is improved and lead times are cut.
• Movement of resources and handling time is reduced.
• Team working is encouraged.
• There may be a safer working environment and more efficient maintenance.

Key terms

Cell production – involves producing a 'family of products' in a small self-contained unit (a cell) within a factory.

Just-in-time manufacturing – a production technique which is highly responsive to customer orders and uses very little stock holding.

Kaizen – a Japanese term which means continuous improvement.

Lead time – the time between receiving an order and making a delivery.

Lean production – an approach to production aimed at reducing the quantity of resources used.

Multi-skilling – where workers are trained in more than one skill which enables them to do a range of jobs.

However, there may be conflict between team members and managers may resent the responsibility delegated to teams.

Multi-skilling

If workers are trained in a variety of skills they are said to be **multi-skilled**. Multi-skilled workers are more useful to a business because they provide more flexibility. For example, workers can cover for absent colleagues in different work areas more easily. Workers might also be better motivated if they are allowed to do a range of different jobs. It might help to make their work more interesting.

Suggestion schemes

Suggestion schemes encourage workers to suggest ideas for improving production or reducing costs. A simple scheme involves workers writing their ideas down and putting them into a suggestion box. If a worker's idea is adopted he/she will be rewarded – with cash or a prize perhaps. Suggestion schemes are often a feature of Kaizen.

Chapter review – Delhi Metal Products

Delhi Metal Products is an Indian company which employs over 200 staff. It produces metal components for domestic appliances and exports 25 per cent of its output. The company wanted to become a lean producer and improve performance. To achieve this it took several measures.

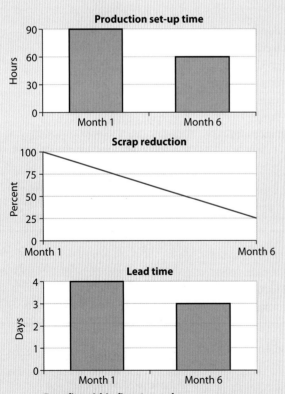

Benefits within first 6 months:
- 25% lead time reduction
- 45% production space increase
- 75% scrap reduction
- 60% machine down-time reduction
- 42% response time reduction

Figure 47.3 *Improvements made at Delhi Metal Products*

- Introduced Kaizen.

- Training was organised which focused on the standardisation of procedures and processes in the factory. As a result about 50 per cent of the production processes were standardised.

- Workers were trained in additional skills which increased labour flexibility. This meant that 57 per cent of the workforce became multi-skilled.

- Foremen were told to set aside at least half an hour every week as Kaizen time – time to do nothing but think about improvement in the factory. Factories are advised not to hold meetings during this 30-minute period, and foremen should not even answer the telephone.

Delhi Metal Products wanted to become a 'lean producer'.

(a) What does this mean? **(2 marks)**

Delhi Metal Products has introduced multi-skilling.

(b) How can this improve flexibility? **(4 marks)**

(c) Outline the benefits to Delhi Metal Products of suggestion schemes. **(2 marks)**

It is suggested that Delhi Metal Products is committed to Kaizen.

(d) (i) What evidence is there in the case study to support this view? **(2 marks)**
 (ii) How will Kaizen improve performance? **(4 marks)**

(e) Evaluate the performance of Delhi Metal Products since becoming a 'lean producer'. **(6 marks)**

Chapter 48: Technology and business

Getting started...

Many businesses introduce new technology to help improve productivity. New technology also results in new products which provide new market opportunities for businesses. It also helps to make work a lot easier for many people. Look at the example below.

Vidéotron

Vidéotron offers cable television, Internet access, cable telephony and wireless telephone services to customers in Quebec, Canada. Recently, the company introduced an automated system to deal with administration when handling service calls. This involved giving 1,200 field technicians BlackBerry® smart phones with a special application. The introduction of the system had the following benefits.

- **Savings of $1.6 million over three years:** The new system was about 40 per cent less expensive than giving each technician a laptop. When combined with staff reduction costs and improved efficiency, Vidéotron believes it will save approximately $1.6m over three years.

- **Reduces the need for dispatchers:** Switching from a paper- and phone-based system to the BlackBerry application reduced staff costs by 40 per cent and phone calls by 35 per cent.

- **More effective and happier technicians:** Technicians are enjoying the advantages of the BlackBerry solution because it helps them work faster and reduces customer waiting time.

(a) What impact did the automated administration system have on Vidéotron's costs?

(b) How might Vidéotron's labour requirement have been affected by the new system?

New technology in the primary sector

Advances in technology gather pace all the time. All business sectors have enjoyed the benefits of new technology. In the primary sector the use of tractors, mechanical harvesters, grain-drying machines and automatic feeding systems have helped to raise productivity in agriculture. This has reduced the need to employ large numbers of workers. Chemicals and pesticides have also helped to increase crop yields and biological research has developed plants which are disease-resistant. In the mining industry new cutting machinery has raised productivity and improved the health and safety of workers.

New technology in the secondary sector

Production has become more *capital-intensive* in many industries. This means that more machinery is used in production instead of other resources such as labour. New technology is flexible, sophisticated and highly efficient. Some examples of new technologies in the secondary sector are outlined below.

- **Computer Aided Design (CAD):** Before products are manufactured they have to be designed. The whole design process has been improved by the introduction of CAD. This allows a business to produce accurate drawings, which can be viewed in 3D and altered cheaply and quickly. Designs can be accurately measured and tested on computer for faults, such as unsuitable dimensions or components. In many cases, CAD also removes the need to build models and prototypes because they can be replicated by 3D computer generated images. CAD can also identify the best or 'optimal' design solutions because it can analyse a range of alternatives.

Did you know?

CAD has a wide range of applications but is common in the design of vehicles, plastic containers, furniture and clothing.

Did you know?

Robots are used by car manufacturers such as Volkswagen to paint car bodies. The robots each has its own set of paint cans and can spray paint cars different colours according to customer orders. Using the robot means that customers demanding less popular colours can be satisfied without having to clean out the pipes of the main painting operations.

Did you know?

CAM is used by Lego in the manufacture of plastic bricks and other Lego components and by McCain foods to make pizzas.

- **Computer Numerically Controlled machines (CNCs):** CNC machines can be programmed by computer to carry tasks such as cutting, milling, drilling, welding, sewing and printing. They can produce both uniform and irregular shapes and cut quickly and accurately. They can also carry out repetitive tasks without human error. This reduces waste and the need for rework. Some CNC machines use probes and *co-ordinate measuring machines* (CMMs).These can make simple or complex measurements and check batches or components. They can measure a number of variables such as dimensions, weight and temperature.

- **Robots:** Robots feature largely in assembly and on production lines. They have a mechanical arm which moves according to instructions given by a computer. Robots are used in welding, assembly and in the movement of components on a production line. They are employed to carry out repetitive work which is boring and de-motivating for humans. They are accurate, consistent and can operate 24/7.

- **Computer Aided Manufacturing (CAM):** If computers are used in both design and production the two processes can be linked. If this approach is used the whole of production can become automated. This is called Computer Aided Manufacturing (CAM). CAM may also refer to the use of a computer to assist in all production operations including planning, management, transportation and storage. CAM speeds up production and minimises waste. This is because CAM only uses the exact amount of raw material needed and less energy.

- **Computer Integrated Manufacturing (CIM):** This involves using computers for the entire production process. In a CIM system, functional areas such as design, planning, purchasing, cost accounting, stock control and distribution are linked through the computer with factory floor functions such as materials management, providing direct control and monitoring of all processes. People are only used for supervising, monitoring and maintenance work.

QUESTION 1

Japan and the United States lead the world in the development of robots. Robots in manufacturing can be divided into three categories:

- **material handling robots** are usually employed in the transport of goods, parts or cargo from one place to another, most often within the same factory or plant. Automated warehouses are an example of this.

- **processing operations robots** generally perform a specific task such as spot welding or spray painting. These robots are fitted with a specialised tool to perform the programmed task.

- **assembly line robots** usually perform a single task on assembly lines such as fitting a cap on a bottle. Inspection robots are used to check a finished part or product for defects. They may use a range of tools, such as lenses and scanners.

All manufacturing robots perform repetitive and often dangerous work involving heavy machinery, industrial pollutants, poisonous chemicals or other hazardous materials. On the down side some staff may lose their jobs, robots can be expensive to introduce and products may have to be standardised.

(a) What is the difference between material handling robots and processing operations robots?

(b) How can robots improve productivity in a business?

New technology in the tertiary sector

In the past, the provision of services has been mainly labour-intensive. This is because supplying services often requires direct and personal contact with customers. However, new technologies are being rapidly adapted for use in the tertiary sector. Some examples are outlined below.

● In **financial services** such as banking many transactions can be carried out online. Automatic teller machines (ATMs) can be used to withdraw cash 24/7 and money can be transferred from one account to another electronically. The development of Electronic Funds Transfer at Point of Sale (EFTPOS) means that plastic cards and other electronic methods reduce the need for cash. When making a purchase, the customer gives a plastic card to the cashier who inserts it into an on-site EFTPOS machine. When the customer confirms the purchase, either by signature or security PIN, the machine contacts the store's bank electronically about the transaction. A message is also sent to the customer's bank. Unless there is reason for the EFTPOS transaction not to be completed, the funds will then be transferred between the two accounts.

● In **marketing** the use of information technology (IT) has made market research easier. The gathering, processing and presentation of market research data is cheaper using IT. Data can also be gathered online. This is more convenient for consumers and therefore more data is likely to be gathered. In advertising, TV adverts use the latest film technology and special effects to make adverts more sensational and entertaining. The internet is used to promote products. Many businesses have their own web sites where information about products is posted and updated regularly.

● In **retailing** there have been a number of technological developments. Electronic Point of Sale (EPOS) is a well established example. EPOS refers to technologies which record the sale of goods or services to the customer at the point where they are purchased. In stores, goods are likely to be scanned into a machine by cashiers. Information from bar codes on packaging is recorded and used to generate a range of information such as till receipts, stock details and customers' purchases. EPOS saves time and reduces queues at the checkout. It also improves stock control and automatically orders new stock. The data gathered from customers about their purchases might be used for marketing purposes.

● In the **leisure industry** technology allows people to travel without a ticket. For example, flights can be booked using the internet or the telephone and a credit card. A boarding pass can be picked up at the airport using a passport. Bookings for hotels, holidays or the theatre can be also made online, which reduces administration costs.

● The use of IT has helped to reduce **administration and communication** costs in business. For example, many routine tasks can be carried out quickly by computer. These may include customer invoicing or billing. Huge amounts of data can be gathered, processed, manipulated, stored and retrieved using computer databases. A wide range of different information can be sent electronically anywhere in the world instantly.

Figure 48.1a *An ATM*

Figure 48.1b *A bar code scanner*

QUESTION 2

Quividi, a French software company, has developed a device which analyses the faces of passers-by who look at outdoor advertising. The software measures the attention that different consumers (men, women, older, teenagers) are paying to outdoor media. The hidden camera:

- counts the number of viewers

- records how long viewers look at an image

- shows the age and gender of viewers

- provides information about the links between viewership and content. For example, it can tell what sort of people look at an image showing an attractive landscape.

(a) How might businesses benefit from the technology illustrated in this case study?

(b) Analyse two advantages of gathering market research data online.

The costs and benefits of new technology

The table in Figure 48.2 provides a summary of the main benefits and costs of new technology in business.

Benefits	Costs
New products provide more choice	High set-up and purchase costs
Higher productivity and lower costs	Breakdowns can be expensive
Less waste of resources	Job losses may cause conflict and distress
Improved health and safety	Existing staff may need to be retrained
Tasks are easier for workers	
Improved communications	

Figure 48.2 *Costs and benefits of new technology in business*

What is e-commerce?

Another recent and important development in technology is **e-commerce**. This involves the use of electronic systems to buy and sell products. Most e-commerce takes place online. There are two main types.

- **Business to consumers (B2C):** This is the selling of goods and services by businesses to consumers. Some e-commerce is done entirely electronically. For example, an individual can make a payment, download some music and listen to it on their laptop, ipod or iphone. However, a great deal of e-commerce still involves trading in physical goods such as clothes and consumer durables. This is called **e-tailing** and involves ordering goods online and taking delivery at home. Most large retailers now have online services. Dell Computers and Amazon are examples of businesses that rely heavily on e-tailing. Some other examples of B2C e-commerce include:
  - tickets for air, rail and coach travel
  - tickets for sports fixtures, cinema, theatre and attractions such as Alton Towers
  - holidays, weekend breaks and hotel rooms
  - music for MP3 players
  - a wide range of goods on eBay, the auction site.

- **Business to business (B2B):** This involves businesses selling to other businesses online. In some cases the services sold to consumers are also available to businesses. Examples include travel tickets, accommodation, financial services and physical goods such as furniture. Businesses can also use specialist software to purchase resources. The software helps to find the cheapest supplier and carries out all the paperwork.

Benefits of e-commerce

Some consumers really like e-commerce. For example, those who:

- live in rural and isolated locations
- do not have the time to go shopping
- dislike going to shops
- have mobility problems.

Online shopping can be cheaper because business costs are lower. It can be done 24/7 and there is generally a huge amount of choice. People can also shop from different locations such as at work, at home or travelling on a train. All they need is access to the internet – via a laptop or a mobile phone. (See also Chapter 41.)

Benefits of e-commerce to businesses

- Businesses involved in e-tailing do not have to meet the costs of operating stores (although some do both). With lower costs they can reduce prices and attract more customers.

- The cost of processing transactions is lower (mainly because they are paperless).

Key terms

Computer aided design (CAD) – the use of computers to design products.

Computer aided manufacturing (CAM) – where computers link and control the design and production of goods in manufacturing.

Computer integrated manufacturing (CIM) – the use of computers to control the entire production process.

Computer numerically controlled machines (CNCs) – machines which carry out the instructions fed by computers.

E-commerce – the trading of goods and services electronically.

E-tailing – ordering goods online and taking delivery at home.

- Documents such as purchase orders and invoices can be generated and exchanged online.

- Payments can be made and received online.

- B2C businesses can offer goods to a much wider market. Many now offer their products internationally.

- Businesses can serve their customers 24/7. Online trading can be done when the shops are closed.

- Businesses have more choice when locating their operations. This is because they do not have to be close to their customers. This means cheaper locations can be chosen.

Chapter review – Online selling

Online sales in Britain reached £7.7bn in the 10 weeks leading up to Christmas 2006, marking a 54 per cent rise compared to last year. IMRG, the e-tailing body, reports that online sales exceeded all expectations, with sales of close to a billion pounds a week during the first three weeks of December. British consumers spent more than £3bn online in November, and £3.6bn in December. IMRG managing director Jo Tucker says the strong online sales resulted in annual online sales of £30.2bn.

Figure 48.3 *A bouquet of flowers*

'Consumers just could not get enough of internet shopping at Christmas; web sites struggled to cope with the soaring traffic levels, stocks sold out early, and delivery companies were at full stretch dispatching the 200 million parcels ordered,' she said.

'Sales demand outstripped supply capacity by a significant margin, otherwise sales would have been higher still.' Online sales were strong across all sectors, with gifts such as flowers and pre-wrapped items up 142 per cent, clothing and accessories rising 64 per cent and electrical sales up 50 per cent.

(a) What is meant by e-tailing? **(2 marks)**

It is suggested in the case study that online selling is growing rapidly.

(b) (i) What evidence is there in this case study to support this view? **(2 marks)**
(ii) Analyse two benefits to consumers of online selling. **(4 marks)**

Some online traders may use EPOS.

(c) (i) What is meant by EPOS? **(2 marks)**
(ii) Outline two benefits of using EPOS to businesses. **(2 marks)**

(d) Evaluate the costs and benefits of new technology in business. **(8 marks)**

Chapter 49: Quality

Getting started...

Businesses must produce good quality products. This means products have to be well designed, perform the function for which they were intended, look good and be safe to use. Businesses that fail to produce quality products are likely to lose out to competitors. For most businesses quality really matters. Look at the example below.

Quality at Casio

Casio is a Japanese multinational. It employs over 11,000 people and makes watches, cameras, calculators, musical instruments and other mobile technologies. Casio aims to impress customers. It creates products that are reliable, durable, safe and serviceable. Casio also considers the environment and complies with legislation in its designs. In 1996, Casio started its 'Delight Our Customers' programme. This was to ensure that employees became familiar with Casio's philosophy about products and services. The key aspects of Casio's quality policies are outlined below.

- Casio aims to create a good corporate image by offering products and services that please and impress customers.

- Casio responds to customers' feedback with sincerity and speed. Customer comments are reflected in its products and services.

- Casio uses a numerical approach to monitoring quality. Data is analysed and then used to make continuous improvements.

(a) How important do you think quality is to Casio?

(b) What was the purpose of Casio's 'Delight Our Customers' programme?

(c) State two possible advantages to Casio of producing good quality products.

Figure 49.1 *Quality as viewed by Casio*

What is quality?

When consumers are shopping they may consider **quality** when choosing products. Quality could be described as those features of a product or service that allow it to satisfy customers' wants. For example, a family buying a new car may consider some of the following features:

- physical appearance – they may want a certain style and colour

- reliability and durability – will it last for 10 years?

- special features – does it have a satellite navigation system?

- suitability – can it seat six people comfortably?

- repairs – how much does it cost to maintain the car?

- customer service – how prompt is delivery?

Traditional quality control

Traditionally, production departments were responsible for ensuring quality. Their objectives might have been to make sure that products:

● satisfy consumers' needs

● operate in the way they should

● can be produced cost effectively

● can be repaired easily

● conform to safety standards set down by legislation and independent bodies.

Quality control in the past often involved *quality controllers* or *quality inspectors* checking other people's work and the product itself after production had taken place. By today's standards this is not quality control. This is a method of finding a poor quality product before it is sold.

Quality assurance

Today inspection is carried out during the production process. This means that poor quality products can be prevented before production is complete. Such a preventive approach has been used by Japanese businesses and is known as **total quality management (TQM)**. It involves all employees being responsible for ensuring quality at all stages in the production process. Today many firms use TQM.

Quality assurance is a commitment by a business to maintain quality throughout the organisation. The aim is to stop problems before they occur rather than finding them after they occur. Quality assurance also takes into account customers' views in the production process.

QUESTION 1

VisitScotland.com is a business which provides a bookings and information service for visitors to Scotland. One of its roles is to assess the standard of accommodation and places to eat in Scotland. VisitScotland.com uses a five-star grading scheme to assess quality. The scheme is quick and clear and helps to reassure visitors. VisitScotland.com's quality assurance schemes also assess visitor attractions such as castles and museums, tours and leisure centres. The schemes look at the standard of the welcome, hospitality, cleanliness, accommodation, comfort and service they provide and are based on the grades below.

Acceptable	–	* (1 star)
Good	–	** (2 stars)
Very good	–	*** (3 stars)
Excellent	–	**** (4 stars)
Exceptional	–	***** (5 stars)

Figure 49.2 *A Scottish hotel*

(a) How does VisitScotland.com assess quality?

(b) Outline two benefits of the system to visitors.

Total quality management (TQM)

Total quality management is designed to prevent errors, such as poor quality products, from ever happening. What are the features of TQM?

- **Quality chains:** Every worker in a business is like a link in a chain and every worker is both a customer and a supplier. This is because a worker on a production line will only receive (as a customer) and pass on (as a supplier) semi-finished work if it has reached specified quality standards. This avoids faulty products ever being made. The chain also includes customers and suppliers outside the business.

- **Everyone is involved:** Every department, activity and worker is organised to take into account quality at all times. TQM must start from the top with the chairperson and spread throughout the business to every employee.

- **Quality audits:** Statistical data is used to monitor quality standards. These checks or audits aim to reduce variability, which is the cause of most quality problems. Variations in products, delivery times, materials and worker performance often occur. Such variations can be detected easily if statistical data is used.

- **Teamwork:** TQM stresses that teamwork is the most effective way of solving problems. This is because teams have more skills, knowledge and experience than a single person.

- **Customer focused:** Firms using TQM are committed to their customers. They respond to changes in people's needs and expectations.

- **Zero defects:** Many quality systems have a zero defect policy. This aims to ensure that every product that is manufactured is free from defects.

Advantages	Disadvantages
The focus is on customer needs	High training and implementation costs
Quality is improved in all aspects of business	Will only work if everyone is committed
Waste and inefficiencies are removed	May be bureaucratic (lots of documents)
Helps develop ways of measuring performance	The focus is on processes not the product
Improves communication and problem solving	

Figure 49.3 *Advantages and disadvantages of TQM*

The importance of quality control

Quality is more important than ever. Consumers are more aware. They get information through the media and the internet. As a result they have higher expectations than ever before.

- Increased competition has forced firms to improve quality. Consumers do not need to buy products from businesses that fail to deliver quality.

- Government legislation designed to protect consumers has forced firms to improve quality. For example, the production of food products has to be carried out in a hygienic environment and comply with health and safety legislation.

- Faulty products are costly for a business. Machinery that breaks down or constantly needs to be repaired will also be expensive. Late delivery and productivity that results from poor quality in production can harm a business's reputation.

Quality matters to a business because sales will be higher if they can deliver quality products. Poor quality is likely to result in lost customers. The case study in Question 2 shows what can happen if quality is poor.

QUESTION 2

Boots is a member of Alliance Boots, an international pharmacy-led health and beauty group. In September 2009, the following notice appeared in the press.

PRODUCT RECALL

Boots 100% Pure Cotton Buds (80 in a pack)

Item code: 42-90-550

Batch numbers: 01092103 and 01092093

As part of our ongoing quality-monitoring programme we've discovered a problem with the above product. We've found that the material used to make the cotton buds is contaminated. This could lead to an infection, especially if used in the eyes, nose or mouth. The safety and well-being of all our customers is very important to us. Therefore, we're asking that if your cotton buds are from the above batch numbers, that you stop using the buds immediately. Return them to your nearest Boots store where you'll receive an alternative or refund. We're sorry for any inconvenience this may cause you.

Figure 49.5 *Product recall notice*

(a) What is meant by a product recall? (Use this case study as an example)

(b) Why is quality so important for products like the one in this case study?

(c) How might Boots be affected by this product recall?

Quality standards

Businesses can earn a reputation for quality by following a *code of practice* or gaining quality awards. Recognition for quality in business may be awarded by a number of organisations. One important example is the *The British Standards Institution* (BSI). This is an independent organisation that sets quality standards in industry. One internationally recognised standard is the ISO 9000. Firms that achieve and maintain a certain standard can carry the BSI *kitemark*. The kitemark tells the customer that BSI quality standards are consistently achieved by the business. The benefits to a business of ISO 9000 certification are summarised in Figure 49.6.

Key terms

Quality – features of a product that allow it to satisfy customers' needs.

Quality control – making sure that the quality of a product meets specified quality standards.

Quality assurance – a method of working for businesses that takes into account customers' wants when standardising quality. It often involves guaranteeing that quality standards are met.

Total quality management (TQM) – a managerial approach which focuses on quality and aims to improve the effectiveness, flexibility, and competitiveness of the business.

The benefits to businesses of ISO 9000 certification

- Examines and improves systems, methods and procedures to lower costs

- Motivates staff and encourages them to get things right first time

- Defines key roles, responsibilities and authorities in a business

- Ensures orders are consistently delivered on time

- Highlights product or design problems and develops improvements

- Records and investigates all quality failure and customer complaints

- Shows customers that they are taking measures to improve quality

- Helps to identify staff training needs

Figure 49.6 *The benefits to businesses of ISO 9000 certification*

Chapter review – Bangalore Business Software (BBS Ltd)

BBS Ltd produces data management software for businesses. One of its products DataCare, helps businesses to manage large customer databases. BBS Ltd is committed to quality assurance and has been awarded ISO 9001, the internationally recognised standard for the quality management of businesses. Some of the basic requirements of certification include:

- a set of procedures that cover all key processes in the business

- monitoring processes to ensure they are producing quality products

- keeping records

- checking for defects, with corrective action where necessary

- regularly reviewing the quality system itself

- ensuring continual improvement.

Regular monitoring ensures that these standards are upheld and that BBS Ltd remains worthy of its title as an accredited ISO 9001 provider.

(a) How does BBS Ltd ensure quality in its business? **(2 marks)**

(b) What role does the BSI play in BBS Ltd quality assurance? **(4 marks)**

(c) Why does quality matter to businesses such as BBS Ltd? **(4 marks)**

BBS Ltd has been awarded the ISO 9001 certificate.

(d) Analyse two benefits from winning this award. **(4 marks)**

BBS Ltd is considering the introduction of TQM.

(e) Discuss the possible advantages of this to the company. **(6 marks)**

Index

Page numbers in italics refer to Key fact or Key terms boxes.